The First

American Frontier

The First American Frontier

Advisory Editor: Dale Van Every

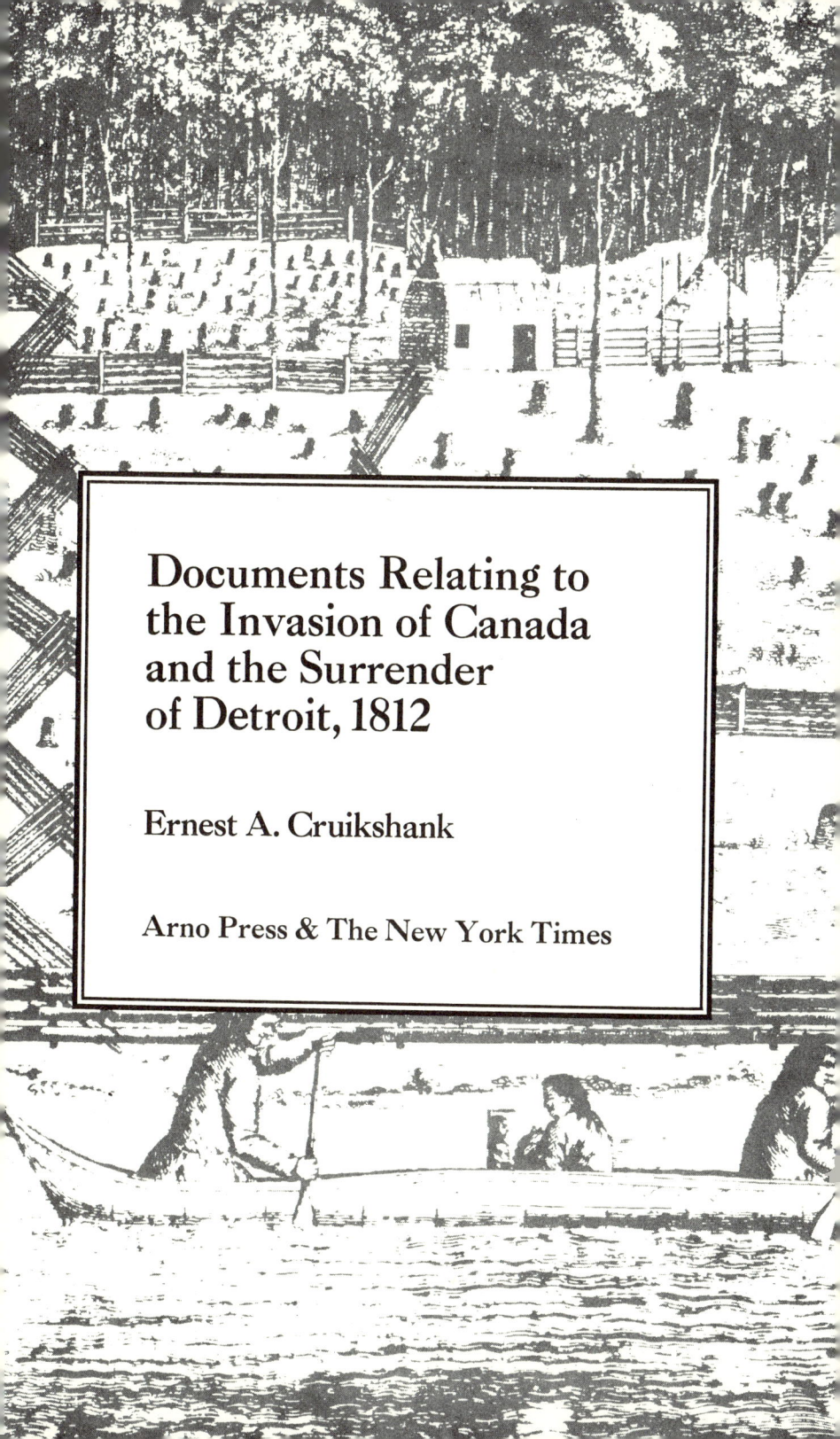

Documents Relating to the Invasion of Canada and the Surrender of Detroit, 1812

Ernest A. Cruikshank

Arno Press & The New York Times

Reprint Edition 1971 by Arno Press Inc.

Reprinted from a copy in
The Wesleyan University Library

LC # 70-146386
ISBN 0-405-02837-7

The First American Frontier
ISBN for complete set: 0-405-02820-2

See last pages of this volume for titles.

Manufactured in the United States of America

Publications of the Canadian Archives—No. 7.

DOCUMENTS

RELATING TO

THE INVASION OF CANADA

AND THE

SURRENDER OF DETROIT

1812

SELECTED AND EDITED BY

E. A. CRUIKSHANK, Lieut.-Colonel.

Published by authority of the Honourable the Secretary of State, under the direction of the Archivist.

OTTAWA
GOVERNMENT PRINTING BUREAU
1912

TABLE OF CONTENTS

	PAGE.
Preface	VII
Governor Hull to the Secretary of War, 15 June, 1811	1
John Armstrong to the Secretary of War, 2 January, 1812	3
Colonel M. Elliott to Major-General Brock, 11 January, 1812	4
Colonel M. Elliott to Major-General Brock, 12 January, 1812	6
Captain A. Gray to Sir George Prevost, 13 January, 1812	8
Memoranda on the defensive strength and equipment of the North West Company, 13 January, 1812	11
Memoranda of General Brock on plans for the defence of Canada	12
Captain A. Gray to Sir George Prevost, 29 January, 1812	14
Memorandum on loyalty of inhabitants of the Michilimackinac country	15
General Brock to Sir George Prevost, 6 February, 1812	16
General Brock to Sir George Prevost, 25 February, 1812	16
Captain J. B. Glegg to Mr. Robert Dickson, 27 February, 1812	17
General Hull to the Secretary of War, 6 March, 1812	19
General Hull to the Secretary of War, 3 May, 1812	23
Lieut.-Colonel T. B. St. George to General Brock, 7 May, 1812	23
General Brock to Sir George Prevost, 15 May, 1812	24
Sir George Prevost to the Earl of Liverpool, 18 May, 1812	26
General Brock to the Earl of Liverpool, with 3 enclosures, 25 May, 1812	27
Adjutant-General A. Y. Nicoll to Captain Nathan Heald, 19 June, 1812	30
Extracts (3) from the "National Intelligencer" of Washington, June and July, 1812	30
Robert Dickson to Captain Glegg, 18 June, 1812	31
Colonel Wm. Claus to General Brock, 16 June, 1812	32
Indian Speech in reply to message of Colonel Elliott, S.I.A., 8 June	33
The Secretary of War to General Hull, 18 June, 1812	35
General Hull to the Secretary of War, 24 June, 1812	36
The Secretary of War to General Hull, 24 June, 1812	37
Colonel E. Baynes to Captain C. Roberts, 25 June, 1812	37
General Hull to the Secretary of War, 26 June, 1812	38
Extract from Return of Brigade commanded by General Hull, 27 June	39
The Secretary of War to Major-General Dearborn, 26 June, 1812	40
General Hull to Colonel St. George, 6 July, 1812	40
Colonel St. George to General Hull, 6 July, 1812	41
Governor Harrison, of Indiana, to the Secretary of War, 7 July, 1812	42
General Hull to the Secretary of War, 7 July, 1812	43
Colonel St. George to General Brock, 8 July, 1812	44
Captain M. C. Dixon to Lt.-Colonel R. H. Bruyeres, R.E., 8 July, 1812	48
The Secretary of War to Governor Harrison, 9 July, 1812	49
General Hull to the Secretary of War, 9 July, 1812	50
General Hull to the Secretary of War, 10 July, 1812	50
Colonel St. George to General Brock, 10 July, 1812	51
Captain Roberts to Robert Dickson, 10 July, 1812	52
General Hull to Governor Meigs, of Ohio, 11 July, 1812	52
General Hull to the Secretary of War, 19 July, 1812	53

	PAGE.
Captain Roberts to General Brock, 12 July, 1812	53
Captain N. Heald to Lieut. Porter Hanks, 12 July, 1812	54
Captain N. Heald to Lieut. Porter Hanks, 13 July, 1812	55
Robert Dickson to General Brock, 13 July, 1812	56
General Hull to the Secretary of War, 13 July, 1812	57
Proclamation of General Hull to the inhabitants of Canada, 13 July, 1812	58
General Hull to the Secretary of War, 15 July, 1812	60
Colonel St. George to General Brock, 15 July, 1812	61
Colonel M. Elliott to Colonel Wm. Claus, 15 July, 1812	62
Articles of Capitulation of Michilimackinac, 17 July, 1812	63
Supplement to Articles of Capitulation of Michilimackinac, 17 July, 1812	64
Captain Roberts to Colonel Baynes, 17 July, 1812	65
Captain Roberts to General Brock, 17 July, 1812	66
John Askin, jr., to Colonel Claus, 18 July, 1812	67
Lieut. Porter Hanks to General Hull, 4 August, 1812	67
General Hull to Colonel St. George, 16 July, 1812	69
Colonel St. George to General Hull, 16 July, 1812	70
Lieut.-Colonel Cass to General Hull, 17 July, 1812	71
General Hull to the Six Nations Indians, 18 July, 1812	72
Mr. Mackenzie, Ft. William, to D. Mackintosh, Sandwich, 19 July, 1812	72
General Brock to Sir George Prevost, 20 July, 1812	73
Extracts (5) from American newspapers, August, 1812	75
General Hull to the Secretary of War, 21 July, 1812	78
Captain Wm. Wells to Governor Harrison, 22 July 1812	78
General Hull to the Secretary of War, 22 July, 1812	80
Proclamation of General Brock to the inhabitants of Canada, 22 July	81
Militia General Orders, Ft. George, 22 July, 1812	84
Captain Daniel Springer to General Brock, 23 July, 1812	85
Deposition of Anna Bicroft, 23 July, 1812	87
Deposition of Wm. Hamilton Merritt, 23 July, 1812	87
Arch. McMillan to Andrew Westbrook, 28 August, 1812	88
Deposition of Charles Nichols, 29 August, 1812	89
Colonel Procter to General Brock, 26 July, 1812	89
General Brock to Sir George Prevost, 26 July, 1812	90
Colonel Thos. Talbot to General Brock, 27 July, 1812	93
Lieut.-Colonel Bostwick to Major P. L. Chambers, 27 July, 1812	94
Hon. James Baby to Captain Glegg, 27 July, 1812	95
Sir George Prevost to General Brock, 27 July, 1812	97
Colonel Talbot to Colonel Jos. Ryerson, 28 July, 1812	98
General Brock to Sir George Prevost, 28 July, 1812	99
Captain Roberts to Major Glegg, 29 July, 1812	100
General Hull to Governor Scott, of Kentucky, 29 July, 1812	103
General Brock to Sir George Prevost, 29 July, 1812	103
Garrison Order, York, 29 July, 1812	104
Extracts (3) from the "Federal Republican", Georgetown, D.C., August-September, 1812	105
General Brock to Colonel Baynes, 29 July, 1812	106
Colonel Procter to General Brock, 30 July, 1812	108
Sir George Prevost to the Earl of Liverpool, 30 July, 1812	109

	PAGE.
Sir George Prevost to the Earl of Liverpool, 30 July, 1812	110
District General Orders, Ft. George, 31 July, 1812	112
Sir George Prevost to General Brock, 31 July, 1812	113
Major Chamber to Lieut.-Colonel C. Myers, 31 July, 1812	114
General Hull to the Secretary of War, 4 August, 1812	115
General Orders, Detroit, 4 August, 1812	117
Lieut.-Colonel J. Anderson to General Hull, 4 August, 1812	117
General Brock to Colonel Baynes, 4 August, 1812	118
General Brock to Sir George Prevost, 4 August, 1812	120
Captain Glegg to Colonel Baynes, 5 August, 1812	122
Governor Harrison to the Secretary of War, 6 August, 1812	123
General Orders, Quebec, 6 August, 1812	123
Wm. Stanton to Lieut.-Colonel J. Macdonell, A.D.C., 7 August, 1812	124
General Orders, Sandwich, 7 August, 1812	125
General Hull to the Secretary of War, 7 August, 1812	125
General Hull to the Secretary of War, 8 August, 1812	126
Major-General Dearborn, Greenbush, N.Y., to the Secretary of War, 9 August, 1812	127
Major-General Dearborn, Greenbush, N.Y., to General Hull, 9 August	129
Colonel Macdonell to Duncan Cameron, 10 August, 1812	130
Governor Harrison to the Secretary of War, 10 August, 1812	131
Colonel Procter to General Brock, 11 August, 1812	135
District General Orders, Lake Erie, 11 August, 1812	137
Lieut.-Colonel Cass to Governor Meigs, 12 August, 1812	137
District General Orders, Point aux Pins, 12 August, 1812	138
General Hull to the Secretary of War, 13 August, 1812	139
District General Orders, Amherstburg, 14 August, 1812	141
Sir George Prevost to the Earl of Liverpool, 14 August, 1812	143
General Brock to General Hull, 15 August, 1812	144
General Hull to General Brock, 15 August, 1812	144
District General Orders, Amherstburg, 15 August, 1812	145
Articles of Capitulation of Detroit, 16 August, 1812	146
Prize Pay List, Surrender of Detroit	147
General Order, Detroit, 16 August, 1812	148
Captain Roberts to (unaddressed), 16 August, 1812	150
Return of Prisoners of War, Detroit, 16 August, 1812	153
Return of Ordnance & Ordnance Stores, Detroit, 16 August, 1812	154
Proclamation of General Brock following the surrender of Detroit, 16 August, 1812	155
General Brock to Sir George Prevost, 16 August, 1812	156
General Brock to Sir George Prevost, 17 August, 1812	156
Sir George Prevost to Earl Bathurst, 17 August, 1812	160
Governor Harrison to the Secretary of War, 18 August, 1812	164
Colonel Procter to Chief Justice Woodward, 20 August, 1812	165
Chief Justice Woodward to Colonel Procter, 20 August, 1812	166
John Hays to Governor Edwards, of Illinois Territory, 20 August, 1812	170
Captain Wm. Elliott to Colonel Procter, 22 August, 1812	172
Lieut. Edward Dewar, D.A.Q.M.G., to Colonel Procter, 23 August, 1812	173
Colonel Procter to Major-General Brock, 24 August, 1812	174

	PAGE.
Major Chambers to Colonel Procter, 24 August, 1812	175
Return of Arms & Stores found at the River Raisin, 20 August, 1812	176
Return of Provisions found at the Miami Rapids, 21 August, 1812	177
Sir George Prevost to the Earl of Bathurst, 24 August, 1812	177
Colonel Procter to General Brock, 26 August, 1812	180
Sir George Prevost to the Earl of Bathurst, 26 August, 1812	181
General Hull to the Secretary of War, 26 August, 1812	184
General Brock to the Earl of Liverpool (with 5 enclosures), 29 August, 1812	190
Colonel Procter to General Brock, 29 August, 1812	201
Governor Harrison to the Secretary of War, 28 August, 1812	202
Governor Harrison to the Secretary of War, 29 August, 1812	204
Colonel Myers to General Brock, 30 August, 1812	205
Major-General R. H. Sheaffe to Captain Roberts, 1 September, 1812	207
Major-General R. H. Sheaffe to Colonel Procter, 1 September, 1812	208
J. Willcocks to Colonel J. Macdonell, 1 September, 1812	209
General Hull to Sir George Prevost, 8 September, 1812	212
A. W. Cochran, Quebec, to his mother, 13 September, 1812	213
Observations of Toussaint Pothier on Michilimackinac, 8 Sept., 1812	214
Colonel Cass to the Secretary of War, 10 September, 1812	218
A. W. Cochran to his father, 10 October, 1812	223
The Duke of York to Sir George Prevost, 7 October, 1812	224
Captain Heald to the Secretary of War, 23 October, 1812	225
Captain Glegg to Colonel Baynes, 11 November, 1812	227
Statement of Robert Dickson re expense for assistance of Indians, 3 December, 1812	230
Return of Prizes made by British vessels on Lake Erie	232
Memorial of Lieutenant Joseph Lambeth, 2 June, 1814	233
Memorial of John Askin, storekeeper, St. Joseph's, 15 October, 1816	233
Memorial of Pawquakoman, Ottawa chief, 6 November, 1826	234
Journal (extract) of Charles Askin, July-August, 1812	235

PREFACE.

The invasion of Upper Canada by a small American army commanded by Brigadier General William Hull and the surrender of this force at Detroit is one of the most interesting and instructive episodes of the War of 1812. This initial disaster to the arms of the United States unquestionably exerted a material influence on all subsequent operations on that part of the Canadian frontier.

The letters and documents now for the first time brought together have been transcribed from a variety of sources, but chiefly from the military correspondence preserved in the Dominion Archives. A considerable number of them have never been printed before. The original text has been carefully followed, wherever possible. No available document of historical significance has been omitted, and it is believed that every phase of the campaign is adequately covered.

E. A. CRUIKSHANK.

Calgary, 2nd October, 1911.

GOVERNOR WILLIAM HULL [1] TO THE HON. WM. EUSTIS, SECRETARY OF WAR.[2] (EXTRACT.)

(Memoirs of the Campaign of the North Western Army, by General Hull; Boston, 1824; p. 19.)

Detroit, 15th June, 1811.

From the present state of our foreign relations, particularly with England, I am induced to believe, there is little prospect of a continuance of peace. In the event of war with England, this part of the United States, (meaning the Michigan Territory) will be peculiarly situated. The British land forces at Amherstburg and St. Joseph's, are about equal to those of the United States, at this place and Michilimackinack. The population of Upper Canada is more than twenty to one as compared to this territory. That province contains about one hundred thousand inhabitants, while our population does not amount to five thousand. A wilderness of near two hundred miles separates this settlement from any of the states. Besides, the Indiana Territory and states of Ohio and Kentucky are thinly inhabited, have extensive frontiers, and their force will

---

[1] William Hull was born in Derby, Connecticut, June 24, 1753. He graduated with honours from Yale at the age of nineteen, studied law and was admitted to practice. He allied himself with the revolutionary party and obtained a commission from Congress in their military force, rising eventually to the rank of colonel. He commanded the rearguard in the retreat from Fort Edward, and distinguished himself by gallant conduct in the actions of Bemis's Heights and Stillwater. In January, 1781, he conducted a detachment which surprised De Lancey's corps of loyalists at Morrisania for which he received the thanks of Congress. He was held in high esteem by Washington as a brave and capable officer, and in 1784 was sent by him to Quebec to request the evacuation of the western posts. After the conclusion of peace he held a judicial office in Massachusetts; and served for eight years as a senator in the legislature of that state. In 1793 he was selected by President Washington as a special commissioner to proceed to Upper Canada and request the assistance of Lieutenant-Governor Simcoe in negotiating terms of peace with the western Indians. In 1805 he was appointed first governor of the territory of Michigan, and was commissioned a brigadier-general in the army of the United States April 8, 1812. He died at Newton, Massachusetts, in November, 1825.

[2] William Eustis, born at Cambridge, Mass., June 10, 1753. He graduated at Harvard College in 1772, and became a physician and surgeon, serving as such in the Continental army through the revolution. He sat in Congress as a representative from Massachusetts from 1801 until 1805. In 1809 he was appointed Secretary of War by President Madison. He resigned this office in the autumn of 1812, and was appointed minister to Holland in 1814. In 1820 he was again elected to Congress and served until 1823, when he was elected governor of Massachusetts. He died in 1825 while still holding the latter office.

17804—1

be necessary for their own defence. With respect to the Indians, their situation and habits are such, that little dependence can be placed on them. At present they appear friendly, and was I to calculate on the professions of their chiefs, I should be satisfied that they would not become hostile. Their first passion, however, is war. The policy of the British government is to consider them as allies, and in the event of war, to invite them to join their standard. The policy of the American government has been to advise them, in the event of war, to remain quiet at their villages, and take no part in quarrels, in which they have no interest. Many of their old Sachems and Chiefs would advise this line of conduct. Their authority, however, over the warriors would not restrain them. They would not listen to their advice. An Indian is hardly considered as a man, until he has been engaged in war, and can show trophies. This first, and most ardent of their passions, will be excited by presents, most gratifying to their pride and vanity. Unless strong measures are taken to prevent it, we may consider beyond all doubt, they will be influenced to follow the advice of their British Father. This then appears to be the plain state of the case; the British have a regular force, equal to ours. The province of Upper Canada has on its rolls, a militia of twenty to one against us. In addition to this, there can be little doubt, but a large proportion of the savages will join them; What then will be the situation of this part of the country? Separated from the states by an extensive wilderness, which will be filled with savages, to prevent any succour, our water communications entirely obstructed by the British armed vessels on Lake Erie, we shall have no other resource for defence, but the small garrisons, and feeble population of the territory. Under these circumstances, it is easy to foresee what will be the fate of this country.

It is a principle in nature, that the lesser force must give way to the greater. Since my acquaintance with the situation of this country, I have been of the opinion that the government did not sufficiently estimate its value and importance. After the revolution, and after it was ceded to us by treaty, the blood and treasure of our country, were expended in a savage war to obtain it. The post at this place, is the key of the northern country. By holding it the Indians are kept in check, and peace has been preserved with them to the present time. If we were once deprived of it, the northern Indians would have no where to look, but to the British government in Upper Canada.

They would then be entirely influenced by their councils. It would be easy for them, aided by the councils of the British agents, to commit depredations on the scattered frontier settlements of Ohio, Kentucky, Indiana, &c. They would be collected from the most distant parts of their villages, where the British factors have an intercourse with them, and would become numerous. Under these circumstances, if there is a prospect of war with England, what measures are most expedient? In my mind, there can be no doubt. *Prepare a naval force on Lake Erie superiour to the British, and sufficient to preserve your communication.*

JOHN ARMSTRONG[1] TO THE SECRETARY OF WAR.

(Notices of the War of 1812, by John Armstrong; New York, 1840; Vol. I, p. 237.)

Red Hook, January 2d. 1812.

Dear Eustis—

. . . .

For western defence employ western men, accustomed to the rifle and the forest, and not unacquainted with the usages and stratagems of Indian warfare. To their customary arms add a pistol and a sabre; and to ensure celerity of movement, mount them on horseback. Give them a competent leader and a good position, within striking distance of Indian villages or British settlements. Why not at Detroit, where you have a strong fortress and a detachment of artillerists? Recollect, however, that this position, far from being good, would be positively bad unless your naval means have an ascendancy on Lake Erie; because Buffalo, Erie, Cleaveland, and the two Sanduskys must be its base or source of supply. The maximum of this corps may be six battalions.

. . . .

---

[1] John Armstrong (1758-1833), born in Pennsylvania; served in the revolution on the staff of Generals Mercer and Gates, acting as adjutant-general to the latter officer; wrote the Newburg Addresses; became Secretary of State for Pennsylvania; married a sister of Chancellor Livingston of New York, and removed to that state; United States senator, 1800-04; minister to France, 1804-11; brigadier-general in the United States army, 1812; Secretary of War, 1813; resigned in September, 1814; author of 'Notices of the War of 1812,' 2 vols., 1840.

COLONEL MATTHEW ELLIOTT [1] TO MAJOR-GENERAL BROCK. [2]

(Canadian Archives, C 728, p. 61.)

Amherstburg 11th January 1812.

Sir,

The day before yesterday I was honored by your letter of the 24th ulto. and now proceed to answer some points on which you want information, deferring the other parts until I have procured further information, and procured a Plan of Detroit, which I expect to do before I set off for York, which will be in the course of a few days.

From a Gentleman of veracity and a keen observer, who was at Detroit last October, and saw the Fort and Guns I am informed, that they have Twenty 24 Pounders, many of which were mounted—besides four Twelves—one 10 Inch—Two 8

---

[1] Matthew Elliott was born in Maryland in 1739; and became a trader among the Indians of Ohio at an early age. When the revolutionary agitation began he was a resident of Fort Pitt (Pittsburg), and fled to Detroit, abandoning considerable property. He was appointed an interpreter in the Indian Department by Lieut.-Governor Hamilton, and subsequently promoted to the rank of captain. In 1780 he accompanied Captain Henry Bird of the 8th Regiment in his raid into Kentucky; and afterwards commanded the western Indians in the actions at the Blue Licks and Sandusky, in which the frontiersmen of Kentucky and Pennsylvania were defeated with severe loss; was thanked in despatches for his services. He was appointed assistant agent for the western Indians in 1790, and promoted to be deputy superintendent in 1795. He was summarily dismissed from the latter office in 1798 in consequence of a quarrel with Captain Hector Maclean of the Royal Canadian Volunteers, the commandant at Amherstburg, but was reinstated in 1808 (when war seemed imminent with the United States) at the urgent recommendation of Lieut.-Governor Gore, who stated in his letter on the subject to Sir James Craig, that "throughout this country (Upper Canada) it is the general sentiment that he is the only man capable of calling forth the energies of the Indians." He commanded the 1st Regiment of Essex militia from the time of its organization until his death, with the rank of colonel; and represented that county in the Legislative Assembly of Upper Canada from 1801 until 1812. He was awarded a gold medal for his services at Detroit; and was present at the actions at Frenchtown, Miami, Sandusky, Moraviantown and Buffalo. He died on service at Burlington Heights May 7, 1814, literally worn out by his exertions.

[2] Isaac Brock was born in the island of Guernsey on October 6, 1769, being the eighth son of John Brock. He was commissioned as ensign in the 8th (King's) Regiment of Foot, March 2, 1785, and was promoted to be lieutenant and captain in 1790. He exchanged into the 49th June 15, 1791, and was promoted to be major June 26, 1793, and lieutenant-colonel October 27, 1797. He was wounded in the action at Egmont-op-Zee in Holland in 1799; and served in the expedition against Copenhagen in 1801. He was promoted to be colonel in 1805 and succeeded to the command of the troops in Canada in 1806 on the departure of Major-General Bowes, being promoted to the rank of major-general June 4, 1811. He was appointed president of the Executive Council and administrator of the civil government of Upper Canada, September 30, 1811. He was awarded a gold medal for his services at Detroit; and on October 10, 1812, was appointed an Extra Knight of the Order of the Bath. He was killed in the action at Queenston, October 13, 1812.

Inch Howitzers—Four 4½ Inch Royals—Six Mortars of different Calibers, and two Travelling Forges for heating Shot: and for the Militia, Four Field 6 Pounders, with field equipage complete.

Another very intelligent Gentleman, has given me the following list of Vessels and their Tonnages.

Brig. *Adams*—14 Guns—about the size of the Old *Camden*, on the Stocks 4 miles up the River Rouge, repairing—

Schooner *Amelia* —70 Tons—at Prisque Isle or Black Rock.

do. *Selina* 80. " at Detroit Wharfe

do— *Nancy*— 90 " Black Rock or Prisque Isle—

Sloop—*Contractor*—60 Tons—Black Rock or Prisque Isle.

With five or six small craft, names unknown—

British Merchant Vessels.

Nancy, about 100 Tons.—Owners, N. W. Company, laying at Mackintosh's wharf opposite Detroit—

Caledonia—70. " —do— do—.

Eleanor —50 " —do—R^d. Pattinson

Thames —80— " In bad repair, Owners Innes and McGregor

The two last at Sandwich Wharfe—

The *Dover,* about 20 Tons—in the River Thames

I can add nothing more to my opinion respecting the attack upon Detroit, to what I submitted to Colonel Claus[1] in my letter in your possession—That Fort once taken, we would have nothing to dread, and we could open communication with the Indians.

I find, by authority I cannot doubt, that Detroit is garrisoned by 50 Infantry and the same number of Artillery—

---

[1] William Claus, born at Williamsburg, New York, September 7, 1765; he was a son of Colonel Daniel Claus and a grandson of Sir William Johnson. Towards the end of the revolutionary contest he was appointed a lieutenant in the British Indian Department. He was commissioned a lieutenant in the 60th Regiment (Royal Americans) October 31, 1787, and was promoted to be captain February 5, 1795. On the death of Colonel John Butler in 1796, he succeeded him as superintendent of the Six Nations, and on the death of Alexander McKee was appointed senior deputy superintendent-general of the Indian Department in Canada. He was appointed colonel of the 1st Regiment of Lincoln militia in 1812; and a member of the Executive Council for Upper Canada in 1818. He died at Niagara, November 11, 1826.

The three essentials you call my attention to, I beg leave to assure Your Honor, have guided my conduct since I have had the Superintendence of the Post.

As I shall be at York in the course of a short time, permit me to defer saying more at present on the different subjects which your letter embraces.

COLONEL MATTHEW ELLIOTT TO MAJOR-GENERAL BROCK.

Copy.
(Canadian Archives, C 728, p. 62.)

Amherstburg 12th January 1812

Sir

I have the honor to inform you, that just as I had finished writing you yesterday, a Kikapoo Chief who was in the action[1] on the Wabache arrived here, and reports that without having sent any previous message, Governor Hárrison[2] advanced from his Fort against the Indians with intention of surrounding the Village on all sides, that none might escape if they proved refractory.—

He completely surrounded it on the Land side, and attempted it by the River, but the Indians boldly order him to desist, or it would not go well with him—He then asked where he could Camp, and was told, "wherever he pleased except around their Village—" All this time the Officers and Cavalry had their swords ready drawn and the Infantry were drawn up ready to fire upon them.

He however retreated about a Quarter of a mile over a little rising ground and Camped by a small Rivulet; but before he retreated the Indians took a Negro and threatened to put him to death if he did not inform them of the Governors intention. The Negro told them that he intended to deceive them, and

---

[1] This was the action of Tippecance, fought on the morning of November 7, 1811.

[2] William Henry Harrison was born in Virginia, February 9, 1773. He served as aide-de-camp to General Wayne during his campaign against the Indians in 1794. On the organization of the Northwestern Territory he was apvointed Secretary; and in 1799 was elected the first delegate in Congress to represent it. When the territory of Indiana was created he was appointed governor. In 1812 he was appointed major-general of the Kentucky militia, and subsequently a brigadier-general in the army of the United States. He retired in 1814. He afterwards sat in the Ohio Legislature, and as a representative in Congress from that state. In 1824 he was elected a member of the Senate of the United States; and in 1828 was appointed minister to Columbia, but was recalled by President Jackson. In 1840 he was elected president of the United States by the Whig party, and died in office April 4, 1841.

they let him go. And the Governor after he had encamped, sent the same Negro back to them to desire them to sleep sound and be at ease, and not approach his Sentinals lest they should be shot, and that he would not allow any of his people to go near them

The Indians however had their Piquets to prevent surprize, and often, during the night ordered the American Spies to retire from their Posts, without doing them any injury—Two young Winibiegoes, no doubt out of curiosity (for it appears the Indians had no intention to attack but to defend themselves if attacked) went near some of the American Sentinals and were shot at, and fell as wounded men, but on the Sentinals coming up to dispatch them they arose and Tomahawked them.

This insult roused the indignation of the Indians and they determined to be revenged and accordingly commenced the attack at Cock Crowing—They had the Americans between two fires, driven by the Winibiegoes, they were received by the Kikapoos, alternately, until about 9 o Clock, when the Indians gave way for want of Arrows and Ammunition. It appears, that not above one hundred Indians fired a shot, the greater number being engaged in plundering and conveying off horses.

The women and children saved themselves by crossing the river during the engagement.

The Americans burned the Prophets[1] Village and all the Corn of the Shawanees, but the Kikapoos saved theirs by having had it previously buried.—Twenty five Indians only are killed; the Kikapoo does not know the number of Americans killed, but he says their loss must have been considerable, not less than one hundred.

The Prophet and his people do not appear as a vanquished enemy; they re-occupy their former ground

---

[1] Elkswatawa, the Prophet, was the younger brother of Tecumseh, being the son of a Shawanese warrior and a Creek mother. In 1805 he had a vision and assumed the name of Pemsquatawah or "the open door." Thenceforth he became a preacher of a doctrine of righteousness and abstinence, entreating the Indians to refrain from drunkenness, lying, stealing, and witchcraft, and endeavoured to form a great confederacy among them to oppose the encroachments of the white men on their territory. In September, 1813, he accompanied General Procter in his retreat from Amherstburg, and remained during the following winter at Burlington Heights. "The Prophet has been chosen the principal Chief of all the Western Nations. His having been presented with the Sword & pistols from His Royal Highness, the Prince Regent, gave very general satisfaction."—*Lieut.-General Drummond to Sir George Prevost, April 19, 1814; Canadian Archives, C. 257, p. 233.*

From this man's report, the Chiefs of these Tribes have determined to come here only in the Spring to make a demand of ammunition and Arms.

The Prophets brother,[1] who went to the Southward in Winter 1810-11 is reported by this man to be on his return and has reached the farthest Kikapoo Town, and is there in Council with the different Nations—He passed Vincennes on his way home, and met the Army of Governor Harrison retreating, but no insult was offered to him or his few friends who accompanied him.—

When the Messenger I sent, returns, I no doubt will receive further intelligence respecting the views of the Indians and will lose no time in transmitting it to you—or perhaps be the bearer of it myself

The following is an account of the numbers of the Different Nations killed in the action vizt

Kikapoos	9	
Winibiegoes	6	
Potewatemies	4	25.
Ottawas	3	
Creeks	2	
Shawanese	1	

From the manner in which the Kikapoo relates his story I sincerely believe his account to be correct.

P S—The Indian Forces consisted of from 250 to 300 and not more than 100 were ever engaged.

CAPTAIN A. GRAY [2] TO SIR GEORGE PREVOST.[3]

(Canadian Archives, C 676, p. 79.)

Montreal 13th January 1812

Dear Sir,

....
....
....

The next object I turned my attention to was the N. West Company. I have had several discussions with the heads of

---

[1] Tecumseh, see note on p. 33.
[2] Captain Andrew Gray, acting deputy quartermaster-general from January 3 to October 30, 1812, was appointed assistant quartermaster-general, June 29, 1812. He was appointed lieutenant February 25, 1808; promoted captain in Nova Scotia Fencibles, August 1, 1811. He was killed in action while reconnoitering the enemy's works at Sackett's Harbour, May

the Companies, for it appears there are two, One called the N. West, and another denominated the S. West, or the Michilimackinack Company—The result is in substance as follows— That the Heads of the Companies are exceedingly grateful to your Excellency for taking an interest in the protection of their Trade, that they will enter with zeal into any measure of Defence, *or even offence,* that may be proposed to them. To render this Statement clear I must refer your Excellency to Smith's Map of Upper Canada. In the event of War the Route by Detroit and the River Sinclair must be abandoned, and that by York adopted. From York they will proceed by Lake Simcoe to Gloucester Bay, in Lake Huron, and along the North Shore of the Lake to the Straits, or falls of St Mary's, and from thence into Lake Superior. The only part of this Route that they feel any apprehension of being interrupted, or cut off by the Enemy, is upon Lake Huron. An armament may be fitted out at Detroit to intercept them in their return from the N. West (when their Cargoes are more valuable) It is therefore upon this line of Communication they will probably require our support. It would appear from the information I have received that we might be enabled to afford them the requisite support from York, as the communication from York to Lake Huron is much shorter than that from Detroit to the track proposed by the N. West. This is a point upon which I cannot speak with any degree of certainty at present, I merely submit such ideas as have arisen out of the conversations I have had with the Gent^n concerned in this Trade. On Lake Superior they feel every way superior to the Americans, having the compleat command of the Lake, and the country on its banks—On tracing the commun(ication) from thence downwards their first apprehensions are at the Straits of S^t. Mary's. At this point the Enemy might cut them off, if some means are not taken to prevent it. Those means could be (according to their ideas) to remove the Garrison and Post of S^t. Joseph's up to the falls of S^t. Mary, where a very eligible position may be taken up, either upon one of the Islands in the Strait, or upon

---

29, 1813. " In him the army lost a brave and intelligent officer."— *General Order, May 31, 1813.*

[3] S:r George Prevost (1767-1816), born in New York, was the eldest son of Major-General Augustin Prevost of the British army, who was a native of Geneva. He was appointed military governor of St. Lucia in 1798; civil governor in 1801; governor of Dominica in 1802; created a baronet December 6, 1805, in recognition of his services in repelling an invasion of that island by the French; lieutenant-governor of Nova Scotia in 1808; governor-in-chief and commander of the forces in British North America, October 21, 1811.

the British side. That the Post of S^t. Joseph's affords no protection whatever to their Trade, as it is upon a large Island, which has no command over the channels to the Right and left of it. That this change of Position of the Garrison, would enable them to concentrate their force upon Lake Superior at S^t. Mary, and combine their operations with our Troops. If the Enemy established himself upon any point in Lake Huron, they would Arm one of their Vessels (one of 60 Tons) and run her down the falls, and carry with them every man they could muster amounting to about 300 Voyageurs and as many Indians. This force they imagine combined with the disposable part of the Post Regulars, acting in concert with the force that it might be possible to furnish them from York, would enable them to dislodge the enemy from any Position he may take up upon the Lake, and in short exclude him entirely from any participation in the Navigation or Commerce of Lakes Superior, Huron and Michigan—To compleat this object effectually they have suggested the propriety, and practicability, of reducing Michilimackinack (an American Post at the entrance of Michigan.) This Post they describe as very weak, being commanded within Pistol shot, &c. It is to be observed that the Theatre of action of the S. West Company is the country on the Banks of Lake Michigan, and that of the N. West all the rest of the Wilderness, the Hudson Bay Company's settlm^t excepted,—There is an object that would tend materially to forward this branch of our Military System; that is forming the two Companies into two Volunteer Corps, by giving the Heads, and Confidential Clerks &c. Commissions, according to an order of Rank that they might settle among themselves. That is making the first person of each Comp^y Lt Col. Comm. and keeping a regular gradation downwards according to their influence and standing in the Comp^y.[1] They express every wish to be useful in the common cause, and I am persuaded require only to be directed how to proceed, to become a formidable Body, which I will have the honor of explaining more fully when I return—One great advantage that would result from Commissioning the Officers of these Companies, would be the protection it would ensure them in the event of any of them falling into the hands of the enemy—Without Com(mission)s they might be treated as free-

---

[1] The North West Fur Company raised the Corps of Canadian Voyageurs about October, 1812, which was disbanded at Lachine in March, 1813. They participated in engagements at St. Regis and LaColle.

booters, or plunderers. They have an impression of that kind upon their minds—They have tendered all their Vessels for the Service of Gov^t if the exigencies of the war should make it necessary to call for them—In short they are full of Loyalty and Zeal, and manifest a degree of public spirit highly honorable to them. By means of these Companies, we might let loose the Indians upon them throughout the whole extent of their Western frontier, as they have a most commanding influence over them.

MEMORANDA ON THE DEFENSIVE STRENGTH AND EQUIPMENT OF THE NORTH WEST COMPANY.

(Canadian Archives, C 676, p. 76.)

Memorandum,—From the Agents of the North West Company for the information of Capt Gray.—

The N W Co have on Lake Superior 1 vessel of 120 Tons —could be armed with 6 @[1] 8 guns—also 1 of 60 Tons which might be run down the Falls of St Marys to be made use of on the Lakes Huron and Michigan; They have also 2 vessels at Moy, (Sandwich) viz: the *Caledonia* and *Nancy* each from 100 @ 120 Tons, and Each Carrying 4 Guns.—

25 Canoes will start from La Chine the first week in May for Lake Superior—having on board 3 Agents viz: Messrs Shaw McLeod and McKenzie— 9 clerks, 10 Guides and 300 men or Engages to be at the Entrance of the French River about the 20th to 25th May—at S^t. Marys 1st @ 4th June, and at Fort William on the N. W. part of Lake Superior about 22^d @ 25th June—

To assemble at S^t. Marys for the purpose of taking down the Companys property to Montreal about the latter end of August, or Early in September in 30 @ 40 Canoes viz.—3 Agents—2 Proprietors—8 Clerks—10 Guides—250 men or Engages—also if required, as many Indians as the Company have influence over in that quarter, say from 300 @ 500—

The Agents of the N W Co beg leave to observe that they will on all occasions be ready not only to protect their own property, but to Exert all the influence they possess over the Canadians and Indians to induce them to follow their Example —at the same time they take this opportunity of Expressing their gratitude to his Excellency for having taken the means

---

[1] The sign generally used for 'at' is in this memorandum used in the sense of 'to.'

necessary for the protection of the Fur Trade into such early Consideration.—

Montreal 13th Jany 1812.

The above was furnished by the Agents of the N. West Compy at my request.

A. GRAY
Actg Depy Qr Mr Genl

MEMORANDA OF GENERAL BROCK ON PLANS FOR DEFENCE OF CANADA.

(Canadian Archives, C 728, p. 68.)

Memoranda[1] to be submitted to His Excellency the Govr. in Chief by desire of Major Genl. Brock—

To reinforce the 41st by sending up their Recruits and to send the Regt to Amherstburg, together with 50 Artillery.

To send Ordnance suited to the Reduction of Detroit (4 to 6 eight Inch Mortars)

To explain the nature of the Offensive operations proposed in that quarter

Militia on the Detroit side 300 men mostly Canadians. Kentucky population 400,000 Souls. Amherstburg population furnishes 700 Militia. Indians in the vicinity from 2 to 3000, —At the Grand River 2 to 300.

To send the 49th or some other effective Regt to the Niagara Frontier with a proportion of Artillery.

To Send a Regt to Kingston together with a Detacht of Artillery.

To send an Officer of Rank to Kingston to take charge of that Frontier.

It is proposed to select from the Militia 2 Companies from each Regt as flank Companies which will produce as Volunteers about 1800 Men.

It is proposed to raise Corps of Volunteers which may produce 1200 Men

To lay up the Ships next winter at York and by degrees remove the Naval Yard.

To provide Materials for ten More Batteaux at Kingston and at Amherstburg

To Build one Gun Boat (as an experiment) at Long Point.

To send Plans of the Quebec Boats to York. The Gun to unship and lie in the hold in bad weather.

---

[1] In the margin of this memo. are many pencilled comments, unsigned.

To Fortify the Harbour of Amherstburg.

The co-operation of the N. West and S. West Companies—To take the Post of Michilimackinack and remove S^t. Joseph's to it.

A small Work to protect the Anchorage of Vessels at Long Point, and to have 6 Gun Boats at D°. (Yong Point) if the Plan succeeds

The Co-operation of the Indians will be attended with great expence in presents provisions &c.

To send a person from Kingston to Reconnoitre Sackets Harbour. And to send from Niagara to examine the Harbours and Country on the South shore of Lake Ontario to see what preparation and if arming the Merchant Vessels

Captn Gilkinson[1] at Prescot. To enquire if he will take a Naval Command.

Captn Fish to Command the New Schooner to be built at York—

To superanuate Commodore Grant[2] and appoint Lt Hall[3] Senior Officer

Lt Barwiss[4] to command the New Schooner and 2^d Lieu^t. Rollette[5] to be appointed first and to Command the *Hunter*

---

[1] Captain William Gilkinson was appointed assistant quartermaster-general for the Johnstown and Eastern Districts, March 4, 1813.

[2] Alexander Grant (1727-1813), was the fourth son of the seventh laird of Glen Moriston in Inverness. He had been appointed acting master and commander on Lakes Erie and Huron in 1759, and was retired March 30, 1812, because of age and infirmity. He was appointed a member of the Legislative and Executive Councils of Upper Canada in September, 1791; and acted as President of the Executive Council from September 11, 1805 until August 25, 1806.

[3] George Benson Hall was appointed to command the Provincial Marine on Lake Erie, succeeding Commodore Grant, with the rank of captain, April 25, 1812. After his supercession by Captain R. H. Barclay in June, 1813, he was appointed superintendent and storekeeper of the dockyard at Amherstburg, and on December 25, 1813, naval storekeeper at Montreal. On September 21, 1813, he had been gazetted major of the 1st Essex Regiment of militia. In 1817 he was elected a member of the Legislative Assembly of Upper Canada for the county of Essex. He died at Amherstburg, January 9, 1821.

[4] Lieutenant Thomas Barwis of the Provincial Marine.

[5] Charles Frederic Rollette was born in the city of Quebec in 1783, and entered the Royal Navy at an early age. He received five wounds in the battle of the Nile, and also participated in the battle of Trafalgar. He was appointed second lieutenant in the Provincial Marine, October 4, 1807, and promoted to be first lieutenant and to command the brig *Hunter*, April 25, 1812. He was severely wounded at Frenchtown, January 22, 1813; and taken prisoner in the battle on Lake Erie, September 10, 1813. At the conclusion of the war he was presented with a sword of honour by a number of the citizens of Quebec. He died in that city, March 17, 1831.

To Superanuate Commodore Steel[1] and appoint Capt[n] Earle[2] Senior Officer and to Command the *Royal George*.

To appoint   and to Command the *Moira*.

To mount 6.24 p[r]. Carronades on Field Carriages to be used as occasion may require

To Send two Companies of the Newfoundland Reg[t] to act as Seamen and Marines

To Augment the Establishment by sending an addition of 100 Sea-men to the Lakes.

To purchase all the Cordage from Cap[t] Mills[3] at Amherstburg as this tends greatly to promote the growth of hemp.

To submit the Mem[o] from Lieu[ts] Dewar and Hall.

CAPTAIN A. GRAY TO SIR GEORGE PREVOST.

(Canadian Archives, C 728, p. 77.)

York 29th Jan[y] 1812.

Dear Sir,

....
....

I have communicated to General Brock an Extract from the Letter I had the honor to write your Excellency from Montreal, relative to the protection of the Trade of the N. West and S West Companies. The General most perfectly concurrs in the ideas submitted in that Letter, and has directed me to communicate to you his anxious wish that the Post of S[t]. Joseph might be removed to the falls of S[t]. Mary. In short the General's general Policy, and plan of Defence, agrees so exactly with the ideas I had formed, previously to my communicating with him, that I can be at no loss in giving your Excellency every information on that head on my return, it may not therefore be necessary to enter more into details at present.

I propose remaining here till after the House of Assembly has met, which will be about a week from this day.

....
....

I have also the hope of meeting Lieu[t] Dewar before my departure from hence, as he has obtained leave to come to York,

---

[1] Commander John Steel of the Provincial Marine, retired March 30, 1812.

[2] Captain Hugh Earle, of the Provincial Marine, succeeded Commodore Steel, April 25, 1812.

[3] Captain William Mills of the 1st Regiment of Essex militia.

this will afford me the opportunity of giving him more ample instructions as to the Duties of the Department, than I could by Letter. There is likewise some interesting information received respecting Detroit which he and Col. Elliot(t) (who is also expected) will be enabled to confirm—It seems the Americans are collecting a vast quantity of Ordnance, at that Post, which with other indications, pretty clearly manifests their intentions in that quarter.

. . . .
. . . .

We have got a Detailed account from the Prophet's Camp. He has gained a glorious Victory. His loss is 25 Men, and his N° actually engaged did not exceed 100.

MEMORANDUM ON LOYALTY OF INHABITANTS OF MICHILIMACKINAC COUNTY.

(Canadian Archives, C 676, p. 78.)

Memorandum respecting Indians and other persons inhabiting the Posts, in the Indian Country where the Michilimackinac Company trade; who in the event of a War between Great Britain and America could be depended upon to Join the British at the Island of S^t. Joseph Lake Huron at a short notice in the Spring—

One Hundred whites English and Canadian and about three Hundred Indians.

The other Indians throughout the Country where the Company trade are all disatisfied with the American Government, and would in my opinion be glad of a good opportunity to Commence hostilities against them.

Montreal 13th January 1812

T. POTHIER[1]

Agent for Michilim^a Comp^y.

---

[1] Toussaint Pothier held a commission as major in the second battalion of Montreal militia. He was appointed a member of the Executive Council of Lower Canada in 1838. He died October 12, 1845.

MAJOR-GENERAL BROCK TO SIR GEORGE PREVOST.

(Canadian Archives, C 676, p. 86.)

York U. C February 6th 1812

Sir,

I entered so fully in my dispatch of the 3d December into the state of this Province that I shall Confine myself on this occasion to very few observations The primary object to which I am anxious to call the attention of your Excellency is the inadequacy of the Military force to the defence of such extended frontier—In making this representation I am aware at this juncture of the necessity of limiting as low as possible the force to be employed on this Service

The more information I receive the stronger I am impressed with the necessity of being formidable at Amherstburg —Were we in a condition to act offensively in that quarter the greatest good would be Sure to result from it—The Indians in the vicinity would, in that case, willingly co-operate wth us; their example would, if I am correctly informed, be soon followed by the numerous tribes living on the Missoury, who are represented as very inveterate against the Americans By these means an important diversion would be made, and points very assailable preserved from attack—The greatest efforts are making at Detroit to put the Fort in a complete state of defence, and I am persuaded it is already too strong to carry by assault, and without the aid of mortars anything we could do against it would probably be unavailing—They have there a large depôt of Ordnance

....

MAJOR-GENERAL BROCK TO SIR GEORGE PREVOST.

(Canadian Archives, C 676, p. 92.)

York U. C February 25th 1812

Sir,

....

Every day hostilities are retarded the greater the difficulties we shall have to encounter—The Americans are at this moment busily employed in raising Six Companies of Rangers for the express purpose of overawing the Indians, and are besides collecting a regular force at Vincennes probably with the view of re-inforcing Detroit, indeed report states the arrival of a large force at Fort Wane intended for the former Garrison—Their intrigues among the different tribes are carried on openly and with the utmost activity, and as no expense is spared, it may reasonably be supposed that they do not fail of Success—Divisions are thus uninterruptedly sowed among our Indian friends, and the minds of many estranged from our interests—Such must inevitably be the consequence of our present inert and neutral proceedings in regard to them—

It ill becomes me to determine how long true policy requires that the restrictions now imposed upon the Indian department ought to continue But this I will venture to assert that each day the officers are restrained from interfering in the Concerns of the Indians—each time they advise peace, and withhold the accustomed supply of Ammunition, their influence will diminish, till at length they lose it altogether—It will then become a question whether that country can be maintained—

. . . .
. . . .

CAPTAIN J. B. GLEGG[1] TO MR. ROBERT DICKSON.[2]

(Canadian Archives, C 256, p. 209.)

Copy.

27th Feby 1812.

Sir,

As it is probable that war may result from the present *state of affairs,* it is very desirable to ascertain the degree of coopera-

---

[1] John Fahevoyle Glegg was born in England in 1773. He was awarded a gold medal for his services at Detroit, and granted the brevet rank of major October 8, 1812. He was present at the actions of Queenston, Fort Erie, and Lundy's Lane, and received favourable mention in despatches. He was appointed an assistant adjutant-general July 14, 1814, and promoted to be major in the 49th regiment March 9, 1820. He was granted the brevet rank of lieutenant-colonel May 27, 1825, and retired from the army, having served thirty-nine years. He died at Thursteston Hall in Cheshire, England, April 28, 1861.

[2] Robert Dickson was born in Dumfriesshire in Scotland in 1768, and became a trader among the western Indians when a very young man. He was one of the first white men to ascend the Missouri river to its source, and soon acquired a remarkable influence among the Sioux and other warlike nations of the far west. He died at Drummond Island, June 20, 1823.

"Among the individuals who exerted themselves on the occasion with so much spirit and ability, the first place is generally allowed to Mr.

tion that you and *your friends,* might be able to furnish, in case of such an Emergency taking place.

You will be pleased to report[1] with all practicable expedition upon the following matters.

1st. The number of your friends, that might be depended upon.

2. Their disposition towards us.

3. Would they assemble, and march under your orders.

4. State the succours you require, and the most eligible mode for their conveyance.

5. Can *Equipments* be procured, in *your Country.*

6. An immediate direct communication with you, is very much wished for.

7 Can you point out in what manner, that object may be accomplished.

8. Send without loss of time a few *faithful* and very *confidential* Agents Selected from *your friends.*

9 Will you individually approach the Detroit frontier next spring. If so, state the time and place, where *we* may meet.

Mem°. Avoid mentioning names, in your *written communications.*

I owe you acknowledgements for *two letters.*

Recollect to whom you promised to procure *Shrubs* and *small trees.*

Robert Dickson, who, besides his own men, brought forward a strong body of Sioux Indians, whose example had a most important effect in encouraging the Indians of the neighbourhood. Mr. John Askin took the command of the Ottawa Indians, and Mr. Jacob Franks assisted Mr. Dickson with the Sioux. The Canadian *voyageurs* or canoe-men, were formed into three companies of volunteers, or militia, of which Mr. Lewis Crawford acted as colonel; Mr. Toussaint Pothier, as major; Messrs. John Johnson, Charles Ermatinger, and John Baptist Nolan, as captains; Joseph Porlier, Paul Lacroix, Joseph Rolette, and Xavier Brion, as lieutenants. Mr. Henry Forrest took command of the Brig *Caledonia,* with the assistance of Mr. John Law as lieutenant: the captain of the vessel being an American, had refused to act; the vessel was the property of the North-West Company, and with five of the common sailors, formed the whole of the contribution of that company to the success of the expedition."—' *A Sketch of the British Fur Trade in North America,' by the Earl of Selkirk, London, 1816, p. 31.*

[1] For this report see p. 31.

BRIG.-GENERAL HULL TO THE SECRETARY OF WAR.[1]

(Report of the Trial of General Hull; New York, 1814; App. I, p. 29.)

(Copy.)

Washington, 6th March, 1812.

Sir,

The prompt manner in which you have adopted measures for the protection of Detroit and the other settlements in the territory of Michigan, inspires me with confidence that such ulterior arrangements will speedily be made as the peculiar situation of that section of the United States may require.

How far the measures already adopted will give security to that part of the country in the event of war with Great Britain, is a subject worthy of consideration.

Officers of a company have been appointed with orders to recruit in the territory.

The secretary acting as governor has been authorized to make a detachment of four companies of militia and call them into actual service.

The commanding officer of fort Detroit has been directed to erect batteries on the banks of the river Detroit for the protection of the town.

These, as incipient measures I very much approve, and was particularly pleased with the decisive manner they were adopted. It must be apparent however they add no *physical* strength to that section of the country. The force already there is only better organized and prepared to be called into action. By comparing this force with the force which may be opposed to us, will evince the necessity of additional means of defence, if the territory is worth preserving.

In the fort of Detroit I understand by the last returns there are less than one hundred regulars—the population of the territory is less than five thousand—and this population of the territory principally of Canadian Character—Connected with the post of Detroit, and three hundred miles North, is the island of Michilimackinac, where is a fort garrisoned by a company of regulars. Near the South bend of Lake Michigan on the Westerly side is fort Dearborn, likewise garrisoned by a company of regulars.

---

[1] In Vol. C 690, p. 37 of the Military Correspondence in the *Canadian Archives* there is a rough draft of this letter unaddressed and without signature or date which was probably found among the papers captured in the schooner *Cuyahoga*.

This is all the force on which we can at present calculate for the safety of our frontier and for the protection of the Indians which the United States are bound by treaties to afford.

No support can be derived from the Indian Nations, even in the event of war, because our officers are instructed to advise them to remain neutral—and not to accept their services if they should be offered.

I will now consider the British force opposed to this part of the United States.

A fort at Amherstberg at the mouth of the Detroit river, garrisoned by about one hundred British troops—another fort on the island of St. Joseph's at the mouth of the river St. Mary's, garrisoned by about fifty British troops—two armed ships on Lake Erie, which command the waters and would prevent all communication from the States through that channel —a population of at least fifty thousand in that part of Upper Canada which is connected with the Detroit river and Lake Erie, and could easily be brought to operate against our settlements—about four thousand men, principally Canadian employed in the Indian trade and under British influence—and lastly may be reckoned all the Indians in Upper Canada, and a large proportion of the powerful nations residing in the territory of the United States, who now hold a constant and friendly intercourse with the British agents, and are liberally fed and clothed by the bounty of the British government.

It appears from this statement that the British force which can be brought to operate against us in the territory, is more than ten to one, without including the Indians.

It requires no difficult reasoning to determine what must be the consequence—that part of the United States *must* fall into the hands of the British government, with all the inhabitants— the forts at Chicago, Michilimackinac and Detroit, and all the public stores, with the public and private vessels on the Lake. the forts at Chicaga, Michilimackinac and Detroit, and all the country North and North-west of the Miami of Lake Erie— and the settlements on the western part of the state of Ohio, will be subject to the depredations of the powerful northern nations of savages. There is nothing in my opinion (in the event of war) can prevent this state of things but an adequate force on the Detroit river, opposite to the settlements in Upper Canada. It may be asked how is this force to be placed there, and how is it to be supported? If sir, we cannot command the Ocean, we can command the inland Lakes of our country—I have always been of the opinion that we ought to have built as many armed vessels on the Lakes as would have commanded them—we have more interest in them than the British nation, and can build vessels with more convenience. If, however, there is no intention of the kind, that communication must be abandoned until we take possession of the Canadas.

The army which marches into the country must open roads through the wilderness, and the supplies and provisions of whatever else may be necessary, must pass by land through the state of Ohio. If the conquest of the Canadas is the object of the government, they will then have an army in a proper situation to commence operations, and at the same time protect the defenceless inhabitants and control the Indians within our territory. The answer probably may be, it is more expedient to leave the Michigan territory to it's fate, and direct the force to Montreal. This will prevent all communication by the St. Lawrence with Upper Canada, and it must of course surrender. In this expectation I think it probable there would be a disappointment—if a force is not sent sufficient to oppose the British force which may be collected at Amherstberg and it's vicinity, Detroit, Michilimackinac and Chicaga must fall— the inhabitants must once more change their allegiance, and the Indians become the exclusive friends and allies of the King their great Father. In the garrison at these places they will find large quantities of arms and military stores of every kind. —Upper Canada and our country of which they will be in the possession, will furnish them with provisions—How then will Upper Canada be conquered by possessing Montreal? They will be in the quiet possession of their country and a part of our's—and how are they to be approached? You cannot approach them by water, because they command the Lakes—In approaching them by land you must pass through a wilderness filled with savages under British control, and devoted to British interest. The consequences of such an attempt may probably be best learned from the history of the campaign[1] in that very country conducted by Gens. Harmar, St. Clair and Wayne. In Upper Canada they have a governor who is a Major Gen. in their army—who commands the regular troops, the militia

---

[1] General Josiah Harmar was disastrously defeated by Indians at the Miami Ford in 1790; Major-General Arthur St. Clair, who was with Amherst at Louisbourg and with Wolfe at Quebec, was overwhelmingly defeated by Indians on the Wabash in 1791; and Major-General Anthony Wayne, of reckless bravery, conducted a victorious campaign against the western tribes in 1794.

ard the Indians—the whole force of the country is therefore combined under his command and may be directed to a single point without any collision.

From the preceding state(ment) of facts and observations it must be apparent that fort Detroit and the settlements in it's neighbourhood—and likewise Michilimackinac and Chicaga under present circumstances are in the power of the British—and that their possession of them would be extremely calamitous to the United States.

In the event of peace with England I am of opinion that the northern frontier ought to be better protected than it is at present in the event of war—and the object being the reduction of the provinces of Upper and Lower Canada, I think it must be evident that the establishment of an army at Detroit, sufficient to defend that part of the country, control the Indians, and commence operations on the weakest points of defence of the enemy, would be an incipient measure indispensably necessary. With respect to the other points of attack I shall make no observations, as I probably shall have no agency in them. In considering this subject I have endeavoured to divest myself of all local feelings, and grounded my observations and opinions on public considerations alone.

Two things appear to me to be certain, one is that in the event of war, the enemy will attempt to take possession of that country, with a view to obtain the assistance of the Indians residing in our territory; and the other is, that under its present circumstances of defence, it will be in their power to do it. A part of your army now recruiting may be as well supported and disciplined at Detroit as at any other place. A force adequate to the defence of that vulnerable point, would prevent a war with the savages, and probably induce the enemy to abandon the province of Upper Canada without opposition. The naval force on the Lakes would in that event fall into our possession—and we should obtain the command of the waters without the expence of building such a force.

The British cannot hold Upper Canada without the assistance of the Indians, and that assistance they cannot obtain if we have an adequate force in the situation I have pointed out.

There is another consideration very important. It will do more to prevent a general Indian war, as far West, and beyond the Mississippi, than any other measure. The Indians cannot conduct a war without the assistance of a civilized nation.

The British establishment at Amherstberg is the great emporium from which even the most distant Indians receive their supplies. A force at the point I have mentioned would prevent all communication of the Indians with that post—indeed sir, in every point of view in which the subject can be considered, it appears to me of the first importance to adopt the measure.

BRIG.-GENERAL HULL TO THE SECRETARY OF WAR.

(Report of the Trial of General Hull; New York, 1814; App. II, p. 8.)

On the Ohio, opposite Marietta, 3d May, 1812—
6 o'clock in the morning.

Sir,

I am proceeding with all possible expedition to Cincinnati—seven days ago, 240 volunteers descended the river from this place—I understand Gov. Meigs[1] has marched the volunteers raised at and in the neighborhood of Chilicothe to Dayton, the places of rendezvous—I have heard nothing as yet of the 4th regiment, I hope to meet them at Dayton.

I met with Robert A. McCabe, an ensign in the 1st regiment, at Pittsburg—He is now with me and commands the 40 recruits on board my boats—from the best information I have obtained, the whole number of 1200 will be in readiness and principally volunteers.

LIEUT.-COLONEL T. B. ST. GEORGE[2] TO MAJOR-GENERAL BROCK.

(Canadian Archives, C 676, p. 110.)

Extract.

Amherstburg 7th May 1812

"As the *Queen Charlotte* will not be able to sail before the 12th I think it necessary to send a man with this to inform you

---

[1] Return Jonathan Meige was born at Middletown, Conn., in 1765. After graduating from Yale he commenced to practice law. In 1802 he was elected chief justice of the Supreme Court of his native state. In 1804 he was appointed to the command of the troops in the territory of Louisiana and a judge of the civil court. Three years later he was appointed a judge for the territory of Michigan. In 1808 he was elected governor of Ohio but the election was declared void. He was then appointed a senator in Congress from that state. He resigned in 1810

of a Report that we have here, which has been brought by a person in the employment of a Merchant, and who has been lately in the Interior—He reports that 1200 of the Ohio Militia were to rendezvous at Urbana the last week in April—And at the same time Colonel Kingsbury[1] was to have 1000 Regulars at Cincinnati, both, he says, were destined for the Michigan territory and Detroit—What credit the man is entitled to, I know not, he came here from Detroit, where he made the same report, and also at Sandwich—

They are making preparations on the opposite side, are embodying a Troop of Cavalry (75 men) and a company of Infantry of the same number, enlistments going on rapidly —They have erected a three Gun Battery (24 pn^{drs} in the rear of the great Store, between the wood w(h)arf and King's w(h)arf on the rise of the hill from the River—We have various reports here, and so contradictory I know not what to think— But the prevailing one is, their very great dread of the Indians, so much so, that the Inhabitants of Detroit have repeatedly applied to their Government for Troops. Provisions by all accounts, are very scarce there.

MAJOR-GENERAL BROCK TO SIR GEORGE PREVOST.

(Canadian Archives, C 676, p. 112.)

York U.C. May 15th, 1812

Sir,

I have this day been honored with Your Excellency's confidential Communication dated the 30th Ult°—

and was elected governor of Ohio. In March, 1814, he was appointed postmaster-general and retained that office until 1823. He died at Marietta, Ohio, March 29, 1825.

[2] **Thomas Bligh St. George** was commissioned as ensign in the 27th Regiment of Foot, July 25, 1771. He was present at all the actions near Toulon in 1793, and at San Fiorenzo, Bastia and Calvi in Corsica in 1794. He was promoted to be captain in November, 1794; and major in December of the same year. He served in the expedition to the coast of France in 1795; and was promoted to be lieutenant-colonel in the 63rd Regiment, March 14, 1805. He was awarded a gold medal for his services at Detroit, and granted the local rank of colonel September 6, 1812. He displayed great gallantry in leading an assault on the American position at the river Raisin, January 22, 1813, receiving six wounds which compelled him to return to England for medical treatment. He was promoted to be colonel June 4, 1813; received the Cross of the Bath, June 4, 1815; was promoted to be major-general in 1819; and created a Knight of the Order of the Crown of Hanover, February 18, 1835. He died in 1837.

[1] Colonel Jacob Kingsbury, 1st U.S. Regiment of Infantry.

I have long since thought that nothing but the public voice restrained the United States' Government from Commencing direct hostilities, and it is but reasonable to expect that they will seek every opportunity to inflame the minds of the people against England in order to bring them the more readily into their measures—It will be my study to guard against any event that can give them any just cause of complaint, but the proximity of the two Countries will in all probability produce collisions, which however accidentally brought about, will be represented as so so many acts of aggression—It would not Surprize me if their first attempt to create irritation was the Seizing the islands in the channel to which both countries lay claim[1]; Such was represented to Sir James Craig on a former occasion, to be their intention—

In addition to the force specified by your Excellency, I understand that Six Companies of the Ohio Militia are intended for Detroit—Our interest with the Indians will materially suffer in consequence of these extensive preparations being allowed to proceed with impunity—I have always considered that the reduction of Detroit would be the signal for a cordial cooperation on their part, and if we are not in sufficient force to effect this object no reliance ought to placed on the Indians

About forty regulars were last week added to the garrison of Niagara, and by all accounts barracks are to be immediately constructed at Black Rock, almost opposite Fort Erie, for a large force—

I returned three days ago from an excursion to Fort Erie, the Grand river, where the Indians of the Six Nations are settled, and back by the head of the Lake Every gentleman with whom I had an opportunity of conversing, assured me that an exceeding good disposition prevailed among the people— The Flank Companies in the Districts in which they have been established, were instantly completed with volunteers, and indeed an almost unanimous disposition to serve is daily manifested—I shall proceed to extend this system now that I have ascertained the people are so well disposed—but my means are very limited.

I propose detaching one hundred Rank & File of the 41st to Amherstburg almost immediately.—

---

[1] These were islands in the St. Lawrence, in the Kingston district, among them being Wolfe and Carleton.

SIR GEORGE PREVOST TO LORD LIVERPOOL.[1] (EXTRACT.)

(Canadian Archives, Q 117, pt. 2; p. 292.)

No. 46

Quebec 18th May 1812.

My Lord:

In obedience to the Commands signified in Your Lordship's Dispatch N° 7 of the 13th February, I now have the honor to report upon the Military position of His Majesty's North American Provinces, and the means of Defending them.

Upper Canada—

Commencing with Upper Canada, as the most contiguous to the Territory of the United States and frontier to it along it's whole Extent, which renders it, in the event of War, more liable to imminent attack.

Fort St Joseph—

Fort St Joseph, distant about 1500 miles from Quebec; consists of Lines of strong Pickets enclosing a Block House,— It stands on the Island St Joseph within the detour, communicating the head of Lake Huron with Lake Superior;— It can only be considered as a Post of assemblage for friendly Indians, and in some degree a Protection for the North West Fur Trade:—The garrison at St Joseph's consists of a small Detachment from the Royal Artillery, and one Company of Veterans.

Fort Amherstburg—

Fort Amherstburg situated on the River Detroit at the head of Lake Erie, is of importance from its being the Dock Yard and Marine Arsenal for the Upper Lakes:—

It is also a place of reunion for the Indians inhabiting that part of the Country, who assemble there in considerable numbers to receive Presents:—The Fort has been represented to me as a temporary Field Work in a ruinous State; it is now undergoing a repair to render it tenable:—The Garrison at Amherstburg consists of a Subaltern's Detachment of Artillery, and about 120 men of the 41st Regiment, the whole Commanded by Lieutenant Colonel St George, an Inspecting Field Officer:— The Militia in its Vicinity amounts to about 500 Men.

---

[1] Secretary of State for War and the Colonies, 1809-12.

MAJOR-GENERAL BROCK TO THE EARL OF LIVERPOOL.

(Canadian Archives, G 473, p. 53.)

N° 6.

York Upper Canada 25th May 1812

My Lord,

I have much Satisfaction in being able, on my return from an excursion thro' different Parts of this Province, to report to Your Lordship, that I found every where a good disposition, and a high degree of industry among the Inhabitants.—A very general determination has been manifested by all ranks, to defend the Province, in the event of hostilities with the United States, and every Gentleman, whose judgment and Loyalty can be relied on, assures me, that the people taken in a wide sense, are as sincere, as they are ardent in their professions.— The Flank Companies formed under the Supplementary Militia Act passed the last Session of the Provincial Parliament, were readily completed with Volunteers of the best description, to the extent my limited means permitted.—

This Force amounts to about Two thous^d and could be augmented, I am confident, to treble that number, had I sufficiency of Arms for them—Those remaining at my disposal, I think proper to retain in store, to be on any emergency issued to the Militia who occupy the points the most exposed to attack—I have thought it my duty, to make application to the Governor in Chief for a fresh supply of Arms and Accoutrements, and His Excellency has been pleased to promise to attend to my wishes the moment he possesses the means.

The Militia who are preparing for service, receive no sort of compensation either in pay or Clothing—This consideration, the handsome manner they volunteered, together with the sound policy of giving at this moment encouragement, to the Military of every description, suggested the measures to which the accompanying Documents (a.b.c.) apply.

I could not but view a question, the decision of which, may at a future period dispose of a large portion of the Waste Land of the Crown, as proper to be submitted to the consideration of His Majesty's Executive Council, and the Board having unanimously concurred with me, in the expediency of humbly soliciting His Royal Highness, The Prince Regent, for his gracious permission to act upon the principles stated in my representation, it is with increased confidence I presume to request Your Lordship to give Support to a proposition, which nothing but the advancement of the King's service, could possibly suggest—I made it my business to visit lately, the Indians of the Six Nations, who are settled on the Grand River—The(y) appeared well disposed to join His Majesty's Troops, whenever called upon.—

But unfortunately divisions exist among them, on points which some white people find an interest in keeping alive.—Mr Claus, the Deputy Superintendent General, has done everything in his power to bring about a reconciliation, but a Chief of some influence, whose Daughter is marired to a white person, by whom he is instigated, and for whom he has been long trying to procure a Grant of Five thousand Acres of the Indian land, cannot be pacified.

This party is small, but capable of doing much mischief—The Six Nations have from the beginning resisted his application—There are so many points connected with the welfare and happiness of the Indians, calling for the interference of Government, that I shall deem it my duty to collect the necessary materials as soon as possible, to enable Your Lordship to form a correct judgment of their actual Situation.

The utmost attention is continued to be paid, that no just cause of umbrage is given in our intercourse with the Western Tribes, to the United States Government, which necessarily diminishes our influence with that injured people.

Since the enactment of the Embargo by the United States, Reinforcements of Regulars and Militia have arrived at most of their Frontier Posts, but in no number to occasion the least uneasiness.

Enclosure a. In Despatch N° 6.

Major General Brock thinks it proper to submit to the consideration of His Majesty's Executive Council, whether it might not be expedient at the present juncture, when the Country is menaced with an Invasion, humbly to move His Royal Highness, The Prince Regent, for his gracious permission to place the family of every soldier, Regular and Militia; also every mariner employed on the Lakes, who may be killed in the course of the contest, upon the U. E. List—And to extend this advantage to such Mariner and Militia-man, for whom no provision is made, who may be maimed, or disabled, upon actual service.

And should the Executive Council concur in the expediency of the proposed measure, The Major General leaves it to their Judgment to determine, whether the times do not call for, an immediate disclosure of their intentions.
York 19th May 1812.

Enclosure b. In Despatch N° 6.

Extract from the proceedings in Council, dated 19th May 1812.

" His Honor, The President submitted to the Board, a written paper (A.) which being read, the Board unanimously concurred in the expediency of the measure proposed, and recommended that the intended application to His Royal Highness, The Prince Regent, should be made Public forthwith."—

(truly Extracted)

(signed)   JOHN SMALL
            Clk. of the Executive Council

Enclosure c. In Despatch N° 6.

Militia General Order.
Government House York, 25th May 1812.

The very satisfactory Report made to the President, by the Officers Commanding Corps, of the Spirit and Zeal manifested by the Men, in volunteering their services in the Flank Companies, has afforded His Honor the most lively gratification, and Confirmed the Opinion which he was always disposed to entertain, of their determination to defend bravely their Country, and in immitation of their veteran Fathers, evince by deeds, the ardent Loyalty they have so often professed— Conduct so honorable and dignified, has not failed making a deep impression on His Majesty's Provincial Government, and to increase if possible, their anxious desire to contribute every thing in their power towards the Comfort and happiness of the people.

With this view they have humbly solicited His Royal Highness, the Prince Regent, for his gracious permission to allot to the Wives and Children of such Soldiers, Militia, and Mariners, who may be killed in the present Contest, a portion of the Waste Lands of the Crown; and to afford relief to such as may be disabled in the Service, for whom no provision is otherwise provided.

By Command of the President
(signed) ÆNEAS SHAW
Adjutant Gen¹ Militia

ADJT.-GENERAL A. Y. NICOLL TO CAPTAIN NATHAN HEALD AT CHICAGO.

(Canadian Archives, C 688A, p. 60.)

Inspector Office
Washington City June 19th 1812—

Sir

War is declared against Great Britain you will make the best disposition of the means within your controul to meet the Event. All Officers and Soldiers absent from the post under your command you will order to join immediately
I am Sir
very respectfully
your most obedient Servt
(Signed) A Y. NICOLL
Adj^t & Inspector

Captain Nathan Heald
Commanding at Chicago

Fort Dearborn July 11 1812.

The above is a true Copy of the original received by the Commanding Officer last Evening per Express from Fort Wayne

signed N: HEALD Capt
Commanding

EXTRACTS FROM THE "NATIONAL INTELLIGENCER" OF WASHINGTON, D.C.

June 30, 1812—A letter from Dayton, Ohio, states:— The 4th U. S. Regiment arrived in town from Vincennes on Sunday last, June 7th, and on Monday, June 8th, proceeded on their march to join the army under General Hull which is now lying at Urbana.

July 4—A letter from Centerville, Ohio, of June 20, says:—On the 6th Governor Meigs held a council in the woods near Urbana with a number of Indian chiefs, Wyandots, Shawanese, and Mingoes from Sandusky, the Au Glaize, and Miami of the Lakes. Tarhe or the Crane, principal chief of the Wyandots was present. On the 7th, the army of the Ohio marched into Urbana and encamped in the town.

On the 8th a conference with the chiefs was held in the camp. Permission was granted to open a road through their territory from the Greenville treaty line in Champagne County to the foot of the rapids and to erect blockhouses.

On the 10th, the 4th U. S. Infantry arrived and on the 11th McArthur's[1] regiment marched for Manary's blockhouse to open the road and build blockhouses.

July 8—Cincinnati, June 27. It is expected General Hull's army will reach Detroit about the 10th of July.

ROBERT DICKSON TO CAPTAIN GLEGG.

(Canadian Archives, 256, p. 211.)

(N° 2)

June 18th 1812.

Queries contained in paper N° 1[2] answered—

N° 1. Answer. The numbers of my friends would have been more, but the unparalleled scarcity of provisions of all sorts, has reduced them to 250 or 300 of all sorts of different languages.

---

[1] Duncan McArthur held a commission of major-general in the Ohio militia in April, 1812, when he was elected colonel of the first regiment of Ohio volunteers. In early life he had gained some military experience as a scout in the campaigns against the Indians under Generals Harmar and Wayne. He subsequently became a land surveyor and acquired considerable wealth by speculations in land. Later he had served in the State legislature. He was unquestionably brave, energetic and popular. In 1813 he was appointed a brigadier-general in the United States army; and in October, 1814, commanded a brigade of mounted riflemen which advanced from Detroit as far as the ferry across the Grand River near Brantford with the intention of attacking the depot of stores at Burlington Heights and then joining the American forces at Fort Erie. In this project he failed and was obliged to return but destroyed several mills and considerable supplies of grain. Faux, an English traveller in the United States, who met him in 1818, described him as being "dirty and butcherlike, very unlike a soldier in appearance, seeming half-savage and dressed like a backwoodsman; generally considered as being only fit for hard knocks and Indian Warfare."—*Memorable Days in America, p. 184.* McArthur was elected governor of Ohio in 1830.

[2] For paper No. 1, see p. 17.

2. Answer. All of the same disposition as the accompanying note will shew.
3. ———— All ready to march when required under a proper person commissioned for that purpose.
4. ———— An Express to be sent to St: Josephs on receipt of this, with Instructions either by Indians or a vessel. Provisions and all sorts of proper goods required. Flags, one doz large medals with gorgets and a few small ones.
5. ———— Equipments if timely notice is given, can be procured in this country.
6. ———— The Bearer of this will inform you of these and other matters.
7 ———— As the article above—N° 6.
8. ———— Your wishes are complied with on this head— 79 of their friends are left where this comes from.
9. ———— St: Josephs will be the General Rendezvous and all our friends shall be there about the 30th inst.

N.B. An Expedition across to the Mississippi would be of great service and could be accomplished without much risk or difficulty—In the Event of hostilities more full communication will shortly take place—

COLONEL WILLIAM CLAUS TO MAJOR-GENERAL BROCK.

(Canadian Archives, C 676, p. 144.)

Copy.

Amherstburg 16th June 1812.

Sir,

On my arrival at this Post two days ago, the enclosed Speech from Teekumthie, in answer to the Message sent to him by the Superintendent of Indian affairs by your order, was put into my hands—I immediately sent to the Standing Stone for Esidore Chaine, a Huron, who was the bearer of the message, and received from him the following information.

‡ *Teekumthie* on hearing of Chaine being on the way with a Message advanced to Machekethe about Sixty miles West of Kickayuga, or Fort M(W)ayne, with twelve different Nations, amounting to about Six hundred men, two leading Chiefs and two War Chiefs of each Nation; they had plenty of Corn with the exception of the Shawonoes, who lost their's after the

———————

‡ The Prophet's Brother.

engagement with Governor Harrison—Teekumthie left at his Village three hundred men when he advanced to meet Chaine; they have been constantly employed in making Bows and Arrows, not having any ammunition; Teekumthie was much dissatisfied with his Brother for engaging Governor Harrison, last fall, as their plans were not sufficiently matured—he further states, that Governor Harrison held a General Council about the Full Moon in May, and called on the different Nations to deliver up their men who had committed murder on the Big-Knives, (meaning the Americans) the Patowatamies being particularly pointed at, replied, that before they could give an answer they must consult their Nation and that at the next full-moon they would give him an answer—he replied that it was very well, and that he would wait with patience, but if he did not hear from them by that time, he would march against that nation and cut them off. Chaine mentioned to me that the Indians knew the americans too well, to believe that their intention was to attack only the one nation, and if they struck a blow, it would be against the whole, and that they would not be asleep—That all the Nations are aware of the desire the Americans have of destroying the *Red people*‡‡ and taking their Country from them.

On examining the issues of Ammunition to Indians at Amherstburg, for the last six months, I find that in Powder they have received only 1,211. pounds, making a difference of nineteen hundred and twenty one pounds less than at former periods—of Lead, not one ounce has been issued to them since last December, which will account for the increased consumption of provisions*

SPEECH OF INDIANS ON THE WABASH IN REPLY TO MESSAGE OF COLONEL M. ELLIOTT, S.I.A.

Copy/

(Canadian Archives, C 676, p. 147.)

Speech of the Shawanoes, Kikapoos & Winibiegoes, delivered by Teehkumthia[1] at Machekethie, on the Wabash, in

‡‡ The English.
* Having no Lead the Indians cannot supply themselves with food by hunting.
[1] Also written Tecumtha, Tecumthai, Tecumthe, Tecumthei, Tecumpthsey, Tecumshee, Tecumseh and Tecumseth, meaning The Crouching Panther—a war chief of the small band of Shawanese Indians residing in the valley of the Wabash river in Indiana. He greatly distinguished himself in the action near Fort Meigs, May 5, 1813; and was killed at Moraviantown, October 5, 1813. In March, 1814, his young son and daughter visited the governor-general at Quebec by special invitation.

17804—3

answer to the Message I sent to them by the Hurons last Winter.

Father, & Brothers Hurons!
Brother Hurons,

You say you were employed by our Father and Your own Chiefs to come and have some conversation with us, and we are happy to see You and to hear Your and our Father's Speech. We heartily thank You both for having taken the condition of our poor Women and children to Your considerations: We plainly see that You pity us by the concern You shew for our welfare; and we should deem ourselves much to blame if we did not listen to the Counsel of Our Father and our Brothers the Hurons.

Father and Brothers! We have not brought these misfortunes on ourselves; we have done nothing wrong, but we will now point out to You those who have occasioned all the mischief—

Our Younger Brothers the Putewatemies, (pointing to them) in spite of our repeated counsel to them to remain quiet and live in peace with the Big Knives, would not listen to us— When I left home last Year to go to the Creek Nation, I passed at Post Vincennes and was stopped by the Big Knives, and did not immediately know the reason, but I was soon informed that the Putewatemies had killed some of their people; I told the Big Knives to remain quiet until my return, when I should make peace and quietness prevail—On my return I found my Village reduced to ashes by the Big Knives—You cannot blame Your Younger Brothers the Shawanoes for what has happened: the Putewatemies occasioned the misfortune. Had I been at home and heard of the advance of the American Troops towards our Village, I should have gone to meet them and shaking them by the hand, have asked them the reason of their appearance in such hostile guise—

Father & Brothers! You tell us to retreat or turn to one side should the Big Knives come against us; had I been at home in the late unfortunate affair I should have done so, but those I left at home were (I cannot call them men) a poor set of people, and their Scuffle with the Big Knives I compare to a struggle between little children who only scratch each others faces—The Kikapoos and Winibiegoes have since been at Post Vincennes and settled that matter amicably.

Father & Brothers, The Putewatemies hearing that our Father and You were on the way here for peaceful purposes, grew very angry all at once and killed Twentyseven of the Big Knives.

Brothers!—We Shawanoes, Kikapoos and Winibiegoes, hope You will not find fault with us for having detained You so long here; We were happy to see You and to hear Your and Our Father's words; and it would surely be strange if we did not listen to our Father and our eldest Brothers.

Father & Brothers! We will now in a few words declare to You our whole hearts—If we hear of the Big Knives coming towards our villages to speak peace, we will receive them; but if We hear of any of our people being hurt by them, or if they unprovokedly advance against us in a hostile manner, be assured we will defend ourselves like men.—And if we hear of any of our people having been killed, We will immediately send to all the Nations on or towards the Mississippi, and all this Island will rise like one man—Then Father and Brothers it will be impossible for You or either of You to restore peace between us.

Amherstburg 8th June 1812
(signed) M. Elliott S.I.A.

16th June 1812
    true Copy
(signed)   W. Claus D. S. G.

THE SECRETARY OF WAR TO BRIG.-GENERAL HULL.[1]

(Memoirs of the Campaign of the North Western Army, by General Hull; Boston, 1824; p. 35.)

Washington, June 18, 1812.

Sir, war is declared against Great Britain. You will be on your guard, proceed to your post with all possible expedition, make such arrangements for the defence of the country, as in your judgment may be necessary, and wait for further orders.[2]

---

[1] This letter was delivered to General Hull by a messenger from the postmaster at Cleveland, Ohio, at the Miami Rapids on the 2nd July, 1812.
[2] See last paragraph of despatch of Hull to the Secretary of War, July 7, p. 44.

BRIG.-GENERAL HULL TO THE SECRETARY OF WAR.

(Canadian Archives, C 676, p, 162.)

Copy/

Camp Necessity near Blanchards Creek
June 24, 1812

Sir,

The heavy & incessant Rains which have fallen since the Army marched from Urbana have inundated the Country and rendered it impossible to make that expedition which the state of things may require, and my own wishes strongly impel

I have opened the Road about thirteen Miles in advance, and established a Blockhouse, that station is about 40 Miles from the foot of the Rapids—500 Men are at the Station, the Army is now preparing to March, and will arrive at the foot of the Rapids by the 1st of July unless a continuation of the Rain prevents it—

There are now established on this Road five Strong Blockhouses, garrisoned principally by the Invalids of the Army, I have stated to you in my former Letters the importance of this communication—considering the fatigues to which the Army has been subjected, both officers & soldiers are in good Health and continue to be animated by a laudable spirit

Genl Brock the Governor of Upper Canada arrived at Malden on the 14th Ins^t with 100 British Troops, on the 17th he sailed for Fort Erie in the *Queen Charlotte,* and it is said She will return with a reinforcement immediately—large numbers of Indians from all the Northern Nations are collecting at Amherstburg, and at Browns Town opposite the British Fort, and likewise on the River Huron of Lake Erie, three Miles below Browns Town—they have a constant communication with the British Garrison, and are supplied with Provisions & other things necessary for them, In the event of Hostilities I feel a Confidence the force under my Command will be superior to any which can be opposed to it. It now exceeds two thousand Rank & file, I cannot by this conveyance send an accurate Return,† It is unnecessary to detail the difficulties I have to encounter in the March of the Army through this Wilderness, it is only for me to surmount them

---

†Vide Letter 26 June N° 3 sent herewith.

THE SECRETARY OF WAR TO BRIG.-GENERAL HULL.

(Memoirs of the Campaign of the North Western Army, by General Hull; Boston, 1824; p. 40; and Defence of General Dearborn, by H. A. S. Dearborn.)

War Department, June 24th, 1812.

Sir,

By my letter of the 18th inst. you were informed that war was declared against Great Britain. Herewith enclosed, you will receive a copy of the act, and of the President's proclamation, and you are authorized to commence offensive operations accordingly.

Should the force under your command be equal to the enterprise, consistent with the safety of your own posts, you will take possession of Malden, and extend your conquests as circumstances may justify.

It is also proper to inform you that an adequate force cannot soon be relied on for the reduction of the enemy's posts below you.

COLONEL EDWARD BAYNES[1] TO CAPTAIN CHARLES ROBERTS[2] AT ST. JOSEPHS.

(Canadian Archives, C 688.A, p. 65.)

Adjut. Generals Office
Quebec 25th June 1812

Sir

I am Commanded to acquaint you that by an Express received by the North West Company, the Commander of the Forces has received intelligence that the American Government has declared War against Great Britain. His Excellency therefore avails himself of the opportunity offered by the dispatch of Canoes to S^t. Josephs to write you this intelligence and to direct you to observe the greatest vigilance and Caution

---

[1] Charles Roberts, captain in the 10th Royal Veteran Battalion. He conducted the important expedition against Michilmackinac in July, 1812, the honour of having done so being his only reward.

[2] Edward Baynes, adjutant-general of the forces, and colonel of the Glengarry Light Infantry.

for the Protection of the Post and for the ultimate security of the Party Committed to your Charge.

The Gentlemen of the North West Co. has assured the Commd^r of the Forces of their Cordial and active Cooperation in aiding the exertions of His Majestys Government by every means in their Power and I am Commanded to inform you that it is His Excellencys most express Orders that you will to the utmost of your ability afford every assistance and Protection Possible to Promote the Interest and Security of the North West Company, Consistant with a due regard to the Security of the Post and in Case of Necessity the ultimate retreat of your Party

M^r. McKay the bearer of this is a Proprietor of the North West Company

BRIG.-GENERAL HULL TO THE SECRETARY OF WAR.

(Canadian Archives, C 676, p. 165.)

Copy

Camp at Fort Findlay on Blanchards-Fork
35 Miles from the foot of the Rapids of the Miami
June 26, 1812

Sir,

I have this moment received your Letter of the 18th of June Ins^t, Since the army marched from Urbana we have had constant & heavy Rains, this has rendered the progress of the army slow—since the junction of the whole Force not a moment has been, nor shall be, lost in advancing to our Post, the Road is already opened ten Miles in advance; to this place strong Blockhouses are erected within Twenty Miles of each other, to preserve the communication in the event of War, I have placed in them small Garrisons, and left the few sick & Invalids with their Arms, medical aid, and all necessary comforts, I suggest to you whether it would not be expedient to relieve the troops of this Army stationed in the Blockhouses by the Militia of Ohio—In the event of War it will be necessary to keep up this communication, I have with me a considerable number of friendly chiefs, and Head Men of the different Nations—the Indians as we progress appear to be friendly, I hope in three Days to be at the foot of the Rapids—the Army is in high Spirits and animated by a laudable zeal, there exists a perfect harmony—M°Arthurs Blockhouse stands on the Scioto, and the River is navigable for Boats to that station, from that station to Fort Findlay the distance is about Twenty seven Miles, and there is a Boat Navigation to Detroit by the Miami

It is my intention to build another Blockhouse on the carrying River; about half the distance between this and the foot of the Rapids, The friendly Indians are now making Canoes and will carry part of the Baggage of this Army from this to the foot of the Rapids—enclosed is the most correct Return* that can be made of the army, under present circumstances.

EXTRACT FROM RETURN OF HULL'S BRIGADE.

(Defence of General Dearborn, by H. A. S. Dearborn; p. 10.)

Extract from the return of the Brigade composed of the Ohio Volunteers and Militia and United States Infantry commanded by Brig-Gen. Hull of the United States Army.

Col. Findlay's[1] Regiment of Volunteers and Militia 509.
Col. Findlay's[39] Regiment of Volunteers and Militia 509.
Col. Cass's   do.   do.   do.   483.
Col. McArthur's do.   do.   do.   552.
Capt. Sloan's troop of Cincinnati Light Dragoons. 48.

Total.   2075.

W. HULL, Brig Genl.

Fort Findlay, June 27, 1812.
T. S. JESSUP,[2] Dy. Insp. and Brig. Major.

---

* The Return Corresponds with the Numbers stated in Gen¹ Hulls Letter of the 24th June No 2 sent herewith

[1] Colonel James Findlay, commanding the 2nd Regiment of Ohio Volunteers, afterwards a representative in Congress from Ohio, and an unsuccessful candidate for governor of the state in 1834. The town of Findlay stands on the site of Fort Findlay.

[2] Thomas Sidney Jessup was born in Virginia in 1788; and commissioned a second lieutenant of infantry in the United States army in May, 1808. General Hull appointed him brigade-major and acting adjutant-general of his force in June, 1812. He was promoted to be captain January, 1813; major in April, 1813; and lieutenant-colonel of the 25th Regiment of United States Infantry early in 1814. He distinguished himself by skilful leadership, and was severely wounded in the action at Lundys Lane July 25, 1814. In 1818, he was appointed adjutant-general of the United States army with the rank of colonel, and soon afterwards became quartermaster-general with the rank of brigadier-general. In 1836 he was appointed to command the forces in Florida operating against the Seminole Indians, but received a wound which compelled him to retire from the field. He then resumed the duties of quartermaster-general and held that appointment until his death which took place at Washington, June 10, 1860.

THE SECRETARY OF WAR TO MAJOR-GENERAL DEARBORN.[1]

(Memoirs of the Campaign of the North Western Army, by General Hull; Boston, 1824; p. 173.)

War Department, 26th June, 1812.

Sir,—Having made the necessary arrangements for the defence of the seaboard, it is the wish of the President, that you should repair to Albany and prepare the force to be collected at that place, for actual service. It is understood, that being possessed of a full view of the intentions of government, and being also acquainted with the disposition of the force under your command, you will take your own time and give the necessary orders to the officers on the sea-coast.

It is altogether uncertain at what time General Hull may deem it expedient to commence offensive operations. The preparations, it is presumed will be made, to remove in a direction for Niagara, Kingston, and Montreal. On your arrival at Albany, you will be able to form an opinion of the time required to prepare the troops for action.

BRIG.-GENERAL HULL TO LIEUT.-COLONEL ST. GEORGE.

(Canadian Archives, C 676, p. 132.)

N° 1   Camp, Spring Hill 3 Miles below Detroit
Copy

July 6, 1812

Sir,

Since the arrival of my army at this Encampment (five oClock P M yesterday) I have been informed that an number of discharges of Artillery and of small arms have been made by some of the Militia of the Territory, from this Shore into Sandwich

I regret to have received such information, the proceeding was authorised by me, I am not disposed to make War upon Private Property, or to authorise a wanton attack upon un-

---

[1] Henry Dearborn (1751-1829), born in New Hampshire; practiced medicine; served as a captain in Arnold's expedition against Quebec and was taken prisoner in the assault; participated in the actions at Saratoga, Monmouth, and in the siege of Yorktown; promoted to be lieutenant-colonel; elected representative in Congress from Maine; made Secretary of War, 1801-09; collector of customs at Boston, 1809-12; major-general in the United States army, 1812-15; minister to Portugal, 1822-24.

offending individuals, I would be happy to learn whether you consider private Property a proper object of seizure & detention, I allude to the Baggage of Officers particularly

The Bearer of this (is) Col: Cass,[1] an officer Commanding one of my Regiments, (he is accompanied by Captain Hickman) he is in possession of my ideas upon the subject of an Exchange of Prisoners, and is authorised to enter into stipulations for that purpose

LIEUT.-COLONEL ST. GEORGE TO BRIG.-GENERAL HULL.

(Report of the Trial of General Hull; New York, 1814; App. II, p. 19.)

Amherstburg, July 6, 1812.

Sir,

I am honoured with your letter of this days date; I perfectly coincide with you in opinion respecting private property, and any wanton attack upon unoffending individuals, and am happy to find, what I was certain would be the case, that the aggression in question was unauthorized by you.

In respect to the property of officers not on board a vessel at the time of capture I must be judged by the custom of war in like cases, in justice to the captors, and shall always be ready to meet your wishes respecting an exchange of prisoners when I receive orders on that subject from my government.

---

[1] Lewis Cass was born at Exeter, New Hampshire, on the 9th October, 1782. At the age of seventeen he crossed the Alleghany mountains on foot, and took up his residence at Marietta, Ohio, then a growing town. He studied law and soon after being admitted to practice was employed in the prosecution of Aaron Burr. He was appointed United States Marshall for Ohio in 1807; and in May, 1812, was commissioned as colonel of the 3rd Regiment of Ohio Volunteers. In 1813 he was appointed a brigadier-general in the army of the United States. Late in the autumn of the same year he was appointed governor of the reconquered territory of Michigan and held that post until 1831 when he resigned to become Secretary of War in President Jackson's cabinet. In 1836 he was appointed minister for the United States at Paris where he remained for six years. He was elected senator from Michigan in 1845 and held the seat until 1857 when he became a member of President Buchanan's administration. He resigned in 1860; and died at Detroit, Michigan, on the 17th of June, 1866.

GOVERNOR W. H. HARRISON TO THE SECRETARY OF WAR.

(Historical Narrative of the Civil & Military Services of Major-General Wm. H. Harrison, by Moses Dawson; Cincinnati, 1824; p. 270.)

Cincinnati, (Ohio) July 7th, 1812.

Sir,

I left Vincennes on the 19th ultimo, for the purpose of reviewing and arming the regiments in the eastern division of the territory. With respect to the Indians, nothing worthy of notice had occurred previously to my departure and subsequently to my last communication, excepting the arrival at fort Harrison of thirty Kickapoos, Winebagoes, and Shawanoese, who from thence sent me a speech, full of professions of friendship towards the United States, and earnestly desiring me to send them some corn to prevent their families from starving. They informed me also that twenty Potawatamies had set out seventeen days before, to commit murders on the Kaskaskias road. The substance of my answer was, " That their professions of friendship could not be believed sincere, when they admitted that they had suffered a war party to pass their camp (containing seven hundred warriors) with the avowed intention of committing hostilities upon our citizens; and that they could calculate upon no assistance from us until all the murderers of our people were delivered up." I pointed out to colonel Russell a route by which a detachment of rangers might possibly intercept the war party; but I think it highly probable that no such party is out, and that the story is a fabrication of the Indians, who communicated it for the purpose of enhancing their merit with us. There is no doubt of the truth of that part of their speech describing the extreme distress that prevails amongst them from the want of provisions. They have no corn, and their hunting ground being confined to a comparatively small district, and that, too, not the best for game, they are obliged to live on roots and bark. Under these circumstances it is not probable that they will leave their families to make a stroke in a considerable body; I am, therefore, no longer apprehensive for Vincennes until the roasting-ear season. But it is very probable that a few hundred might be prevailed upon by their British allies to reinforce the army that is said to be collecting to oppose general Hull, if it were not from the apprehension of leaving their families exposed to be captured by an expedition from Vincennes. From this circumstance, I consider the accumulation of a small force at Vincennes, as forming a very useful diversion in favor of general Hull. A company of United States infantry, and another of rangers under captain Penny, are now here, on their way to Vincennes, by order of colonel Russell. In addition to the force which the colonel has under his immediate command, I have directed the colonels commanding the regiments of militia in the vicinity of Vincennes to furnish him with any number of men he may call for. As my family are at this place, and there appears to be no immediate necessity for my being at Vincennes, I shall not return until towards the last of the present month, employing myself in the mean time in assisting to discipline the three regiments of militia which border on this state, the furthest of which is not more than sixty miles from this place. Should you have any orders for me in that time, I must request them to be sent to the office here; but as it is possible that some event may precipitately recall me to Vincennes, I must ask the favor of having a duplicate sent thither.

BRIG.-GENERAL HULL TO THE SECRETARY OF WAR.

(Report of the Trial of General Hull; New York, 1814; App. II, p. 9.)

Head-Quarters, Detroit, July 7, 1812.

(Sir,)

I have the honor to inform you that the army under my command arrived at this place on the 5th instant—at the fork of the Rapids of the Miami some part of the public stores and the officers' private baggage were put on board a small vessel to be transported to Detroit—at that time I had not received your letter informing me of the declaration of war—the vessel was taken on the passage and carried into Amherstburg—Inclosed are copies of two letters[1], one which I addressed to Col. (St.) George, (com'g) at Amherstburg, the other his answer.

The greatest possible exertions have been made to induce the Indians to join the British standard—The Tomahawk stained with blood has been presented to the natives in due

---
[1] See pp. 40 and 41.

form—The approach of this army has prevented many of them from accepting it—For a number of weeks they have issued about two thousand rations per day; from the best information their number is decreasing.

The patience and perseverance with which this army has sustained a march attended with difficulties uncommon in their nature, does honor to themselves and their country.

The British have established a por(s)t at Sandwich opposite Detroit; the militia of Detroit have manifested a laudable and patriotic spirit.

In your letter[1] of the 18th June you direct me to adopt measures for the security of the country and wait for further orders;—I regret that I have not a larger latitude.

LIEUT.-COLONEL ST. GEORGE TO MAJOR-GENERAL BROCK.

(Canadian Archives, C 676, p. 134.)

Copy,

Amherstburg 8th July 1812

Dear General,

I was favored with your letter of the 4th this morning, and I send down the *Hunter* immediately to Fort Erie.

The *Lady Prevost* will not I fear (with all our exertion) be in the water sooner than a week—In consequence of your letter of the 28th June which I received late in the evening of the 1st I made every arrangement in my power to carry into effect your orders, and between that time and about noon next day (2d) when I received your letter of the 29th June, the Schooner I mentioned to you in my last letter of that date, was captured[2]—She will I am informed be a valuable prize, having on board the correspondence between the Commander of the Army and the American Government——Being constantly on the road between this place and Sandwich, since the papers were found, I have not been able to peruse them, but have commissioned Captain Dixon[3] and Lieut Dewar[4] to open

---

[1] See p. 35.
[2] See note on p. 19.
[3] Matthew Charles Dixon, a captain in the Royal Engineers, was awarded a gold medal for his services at Detroit and granted the brevet rank of major, December 12, 1814. He was wounded at Sandusky, August 2, 1813, and taken prisoner at Moraviantown, October 5, 1813. He was promoted to be major-general in 1854; and died at Southampton, England, in 1860.
[4] Edward Dewar, lieutenant in the 100th Regiment and a deputy assistant quartermaster-general. He was an officer of much promise, but died suddenly at Amherstburg in December, 1812, from bursting a blood vessel.

and retain what is absolutely necessary for us to have here, respecting Indians or to take notes of them—and the rest I have ordered to be made up and sent to you—You will find by them what is opposed to us—No time was lost in getting the Militia of Kent to Sandwich (which was found absolutely necessary) and I thought that with them and the 2^d Essex (about 200 each) Sandwich would be safe—I went up the 4th with Lieu^t Dewar and made every arrangement possible for that purpose—on the 5th having heard that they were much alarmed and expected an immediate attack I went up again, and ordered the two six pounders to follow with a detach^t of 41st Reg^t to act as I saw occasion—on my arrival about 5 P.M. I found the place in great alarm from the Enemy having fired several shots from a 4 pnd^r opposite to Sandwich—and one or two shots from a 24 pnd^r at Detroit which went into a house opposite—I thought I had quieted the alarm and convinced them that there was nothing to apprehend from the forces opposed to them (no reinforcements of any consequence having then arrived) and that I would immediately support them in case of an attack—The next morning as I was sending up a party of the 41st and an officer to put them in some order, I was informed by Colonel Baby[1], that he was on his march to Amherstburg—I immediately sent off Captain Muir[2] and 50 of the 41st in carts with two 3 pounders to stop them, which he did, near the Canard bridge and returned with them to their former position—Whilst the militia was absent a flag of Truce arrived at Sandwich and was forwarded to me, the nature of which the enclosed copies of letters which passed on that occasion will explain (Vide N°s 1 & 2.)[3]

I have found it necessary at present to leave the detachment of the 41st with a Captain, two Subs and the two three pounders at Sandwich, and also two heavy Guns I ordered to follow the Detach^t to encourage the militia, and at present, as

---

[1] Jacques Baby de Rainville, eldest son of the Honourable Jacques Duperon Baby, was born at Detroit in 1763. He was colonel of the 1st Regiment of Kent militia, and a member for many years of the Legislative Council of Upper Canada of which he eventually became president. He died at Toronto, February 19, 1833.

[2] Adam Muir rose from the ranks to be sergeant-major of the 41st Regiment, and was appointed adjutant with the rank of ensign, September 30, 1793. He served during the operations in San Domingo in 1794, and was promoted to be lieutenant, July 12, of that year, and captain on February 9, 1814. "The detachment of the 41st Regiment serving under his command at the surrender of Detroit was composed of three captains, nine subalterns, one acting sergeant-major, thirteen sergeants, thirteen corporals, and 240 privates."—*Lomax, 'History of the 41st Foot,' p. 57.*

[3] See pp. 40-41.

the Enemy has not the means of passing in force, I think them secure from Surprize—I shall keep Sandwich as long as I can, as also keep open the communication, and prevent my Detach^t from being cut off—From the want of officers and other assistance I have not been able to get a state of the people I have collected—I have been obliged to issue Indian Arms to the Militia and shall arm every man I find disposed to make use of one for us—I have embodied the Canadians I detained in the eleven boats from Montreal (70) men belonging to the North West Company—Their cargoes I am obliged to make free with, consisting of Arms, Ammunition and Blankets— Had I not detained them they would have fallen into the hands of the Enemy—on receiving your letter of the 28th I ordered the *Nancy* belonging to the North West Comp^y of about 70 tons waiting for a wind to take her up from "Moy" to the upper lake, down here, where she remains— I have taken some brass three pounders from her to mount in the Boats before mentioned. In short I find myself so situated, that I am obliged to make use of everything I want, that falls in my way—I am much distressed at not being able to get returns of what men I have, and I fear there will be great confusion in the accounts, but I cannot help it—I must issue provisions to men who come forward, and am endeavouring to get all the Cattle I can, to this place—I am obliged to appoint assistants in the different departments to act in this confusion—I counted yesterday 460 militia at Sandwich including two Companies of Colonel Elliot(t)'s militia—Many without arms, but which I have supplied from the Indian, and private Stores —Captain Muir from whom I receive great assistance is laboring hard at Sandwich to get them in some order—When obliged to it, I hope they may make a regular retreat on this place—We have in the Fort the two Flank Comp^{ys} of Colonel Elliott's Reg^t in all about 140—The rest of that Battalion down the Lake I am endeavouring to collect—and when I am able to get a regular return I shall sent it—Men we shall certainly have and several seem willing to act if they knew how and were well supported, and had officers to shew them the way—I now think it fortunate that your letter of the 29th came too late to stop the Messengers sent out to the distant Indians—on my return from Sandwich yesterday we had a Grand Council of Chiefs &c &c from the neighbourhood, and the usual ceremonies of the Wampum &c &c were gone through ---There were present about 200 and besides those present I am informed 100 had gone to their Camp—Tecumthà (the Prophet's brother) acted a conspicuous part on the occasion. We are hard at work at the Fort, and have done a great deal since you left us—The Curtains begun on, are nearly finished: Two of the Bastions well fraised, the other two will be fraised in two days from this date—the Scarpe all the way round is deepened—Twenty pieces of Cannon well mounted: The Platforms all perfectly good—The North Curtain remains as it was, and with Timber we are giving it a thickness of 14 feet to that side—A log building is thrown up in the Fort (for) about 60 men—Another will be thrown up in half a day when we have done with more material work—The small magazine is in a state of forwardness—In short every exertion possible is made by us all—

I have appointed Captain Mockler[1] of the Newfoundland Reg^t my aid de camp—Besides from what I have heard of his character as an officer and a Gentleman (for he is quite a stranger to me) he is the only officer who could be spared—I am much mortified at the confused state in which I find myself with the men of the militia, now we have collected them together—their wants are many—I wish much for instruction respecting the pay &c &c of the Militia, and of those who have offered to serve and have been accepted by me—From what I have seen of their Country a Regular force here of even two Battalions would be quite sufficient for its security—But if it is found that we cannot support those who take up arms, I dread the consequences. Those we get into the Fort we can control, but no others—I shall be careful of my Detachment at Sandwich at all events—You may well suppose it requires vigilance at that distance—I should be under no uneasiness, if I had the Militia in any state of order—officers we want for them—I hope dear Genl you will excuse this irregular scroll, but I have been so harassed for these five days and nights, I can scarcely write—I am endeavouring to raise a Corps of Cavalry, and attach them to the Quarter Master General's Department and I must employ some of the Gentlemen in the Country capable of assisting, in getting in horses cattle &c I have taken a great deal on myself, but found I could not get anything done if I did not—The Boats, cargoes and vessel

---

[1] Captain Robert Mockler of the Royal Newfoundland Regiment was district staff-adjutant for the Western District, and subsequently aide-de-camp to Major-General Procter.

of the North West Company are a serious concern—I can detain the *Hunter* no longer.

P.S.

Co[l] Baby's reason for leaving Sandwich, was that the men seemed inclined to return home.

CAPTAIN M. C. DIXON, R.E. TO LIEUT.-COLONEL R. H BRUYERES, R.E.[1]

(Canadian Archives, C 386, p. 62.)

Fort Amherstburgh, July 8th 1812.

Dear Sir,

Since the 17th June, the Date of my last Letter to you, no opportunity whatever has offered of writing till the present moment; I have only received as yet one Letter from you, stating the necessity of some repairs &c to the Barracks here: Since we have received here the news of War with the U.S. my attention has been wholly directed to the object of putting the Fort in a decent state: The S. and E. curtains have been formed and finished with the exception of the Timber Facing: Twenty Pieces of Cannon are mounted: the Platforms all repaired; Four 12[dr] Gun Carriages made; The Four Bastions Fraized and the escarp all round as much as possible deepened; with the very considerable quantity of Timber in the Fort, a splinter proof Log Building has been thrown up and small expense magazine in the centre of the S. Fort is in a state of Forwardness. This Latter Service Gen[l] Brock ordered: The side walls I have made 5 f[t] thick & I propose a Flat log ceiling, loaded with Dry masonry to form a Bombproof; I trust, Sir, you will do me the credit of believing that no exertion or activity has been spared by me in carrying on the Service here and that my best endeavours shall be exerted for the security of this Important Post; a Few days since, B[r] Gen[l] Hull with an army of 2000 Men arrived at Detroit: Their Main Body is encamped at Sandwich; of this Total, 475 are regulars being the 4th U.S. Reg[t]: who were at the Wabash; the rest are Ohio Militia & Volunteers: The whole army has had a severe march from Cincinnati (Ohio) and their principal point has been in advancing to secure a safe communication all the Way

[1] **Ralph H. Bruveres**, lieutenant-colonel commanding the Royal Engineers, in the Canadas.

by Establishing Block Houses at the Distance of 20 miles from each other, garrisoned by the Invalids &c of the Army: The day after we received News of War, our Boats captured an American Schooner with 40 men and officers of their Army; The whole of the officers Baggage, Medical Stores of the Army, Clothing, 40 stand of Arms &c with all Governor Hull's papers of the first consequence have fallen into our hands; on examining them we got a complete insight into all his views: his official correspondence[1] with the Secretary of State was also very interesting: Co¹ S. George has thought them of such consequence as to send them to Gen¹ Brock: our Force here consists of 300 Regulars, 850 Militia and about 400 Indians, so that I think we have no reason to be afraid of our Yankey Friends; I forgot to mention that the A. Army cut the road the whole of the way, which in fact they were obliged to do as the whole march was through a wilderness: The ship is now waiting for this, so I have only to apologise for the hurry I write in, and have the honor of remaining. . .

THE SECRETARY OF WAR TO GOVERNOR HARRISON.

(Historical Narrative of the Civil and Military Services of Major-General Wm. H. Harrison, by Moses Dawson; Cincinnati, 1824; p. 272.)

Was Department, July 9th, 1812.

Sir,

By letter from Governor Edwards[2] it appears that the Indians are again collecting. Should the regular troops and rangers under colonel Russell, with the reinforcements ordered to be furnished on your requisition, be inadequate to the protection of the frontier, your Excellency will please to consult with governor Edwards, and to request from the governor of Kentucky[3], such detachments from the militia of that state, as emergencies may require.

The Governor of Kentucky will be advised of this instruction to your Excellency, and no doubt can be entertained of his cheerful co-operation.

---

[1] The draft of a despatch from Hull to the Secretary of War given on p. 19 was probably one of these.

[2] Ninian Edwards (1755-1833) was governor of Illinois territory, 1809-18, where he did much in restraining Indian hostilities during the war.

[3] Charles Scott (1733-1813) was governor of Kentucky from 1808 to 25th August, 1812. See note on Shelby, p. 202.

Should offensive measures become necessary, the command within the Indiana territory will devolve upon you; and with the consent of governor Edwards, your military command may be extended in the Illinois territory.

BRIG.-GENERAL HULL TO THE SECRETARY OF WAR.

(Report of the Trial of General Hull; New York, 1814; App. II, p. 9.)

Detroit, 9th July, 1812.

Sir,—I have received your letter of the 24th June.—The army under my command arrived here on the 5th July, inst. Every effort has been and is still making by the British, to collect the Indians under their standard;—they have a large number. I am preparing boats and shall pass the river in a few days. The British have established a post directly opposite to this place; I have confidence in dislodging them, and of being in possession of the opposite bank. I have little time to write; every thing will be done that is possible to do. The British command the water and the savages; I do not think the force here equal to the reduction of Amherstburg; you therefore must not be too sanguine.

BRIG.-GENERAL HULL TO THE SECRETARY OF WAR.

(Report of the Trial of General Hull; New York, 1814; App. II, p. 9.)

Detroit, July 10, 1812.

Sir—Mr. Beard, Augustus Porter's agent here, informed me that, in consequence of the lake being closed against us, he cannot furnish the necessary supplies of provisions. I have, therefore, authorized Mr. John H. Piatt (Pratt?) of Cincinnati, (now here) to furnish two hundred thousand rations of flour and the same quantity of beef. I have engaged to give him five per cent. on the amount of purchases and pay his necessary expences, and the expence of transportation; he will either hire or purchase pack-horses to transport the flour. I shall draw on you for the money necessary for the purpose. The communication must be secured or this army will be without provisions. Troops will be absolutely necessary on the road to protect provisions. This must not be neglected; If it is this army will perish by hunger.

LIEUT.-COLONEL ST GEORGE TO MAJOR-GENERAL BROCK.

(Canadian Archives, C 676, p. 141.)

Copy

Amherstburgh 10th July 12

Dear General,

Colonel Elliot(t) having received information relative to the Indians I send it off by Express—Since writing by the *Hunter* (which was not able to leave the Bar till yesterday Evening) I have been at Sandwich. I found the Kent and Essex not then in a better condition than when I left them two days before—they are all Armed—but I am not able to withdraw my Detachment—Their Colonels think if I do so they will not remain—even Two Companies of the Militia of this place who were ordered up on the Two Regiments retreating and who I have particular occasion for at the Petit Coté to keep up the communication, I am not able to withdraw—nor the Two heavy Guns (9 P^{rs}) I sent up on that occasion—in short I believe I must move the Two Regiments and Detachments down here, but that I shall not do until I get all the Cattle possible from the Thames, and Sandwich and drive them below Amherstburgh—I have now sent off Lieu^t. Dewar to make arrangements, and have found it necessary to employ Mr Francis Baby[1] to assist in the Q^r Mr Generals Department at Sandwich, and also Mr Caldwell[2] here—

I have got some mounted Men at Sandwich for Patrole, about 30, I hope we shall be able to get more here when the Militia of Colonel Elliot(t)s come from the Lake, of that part of his Regiment not more than 20 have yet joined—I have the greatest difficulty respecting the Officers of *all* the Regiment^{ts} as Col^l Elliott thinks his papers cannot admit of delay—

(P.S.) On my arrival at Sandwich early yesterday morning I found Genl Hull had struck his Camp at Spring Hill and marched into Detroit—should the Kent and Essex continue so much alarmed at their situation I must withdraw them from Sandwich; and as I have nothing to replace them, must also withdraw the Detachment, I am at present so disagreeably

---

[1] François Baby made assistant quartermaster-general with rank of captain, July 3, 1812.
[2] Captain William Caldwell, senior, formerly of Butler's Rangers, usually known as Colonel Caldwell from his former rank in the militia. After the death of Colonel Matthew Elliott he was appointed deputy superintendent of the Indian Department in Upper Canada, May 8, 1814.

situated from the prevailing disposition of both Officers, and Men, that I have no doubt in the case of an attack on Sandwich which the Enemy appear to be preparing for, the Force there will be obliged to retreat on this place, and before that happens, which would throw the Militia into a state of confusion liable to disorganize the whole body, before it is too late I shall most likely think it incumbent on me to bring them down to this place, and make the most of them—perhaps they will shew a better spirit when they have a larger body of Regulars to set them an example—

CAPTAIN ROBERTS TO MR. ROBERT DICKSON.

(Canadian Archives, C 256, p. 215.)

Fort St Josephs 10 July 1812

Sir,

Having volunteered your services with the Indians you have brought along with you I have to request that you will comply with such orders as you may receive from me from time to time

BRIG.-GENERAL HULL TO GOVERNOR MEIGS OF OHIO.

(Report of the Trial of General Hull; New York, 1814; App. II, p. 19.)

Detroit, July 11th, 1812.

Dear Sir,

The army arrived here on the 5th inst. I have now only time to state to you that we are very deficient in provisions, and I have authorized Mr. Pratt to furnish a supply for two months.

The communication must be preserved by your militia, or this army will perish for want of provisions. We have the fullest confidence, you will do all in your power to prevent so distressing a calamity as the want of provisions to this patriotic army.

BRIG.-GENERAL HULL TO THE SECRETARY OF WAR.

(Defence of General Dearborn, by H. A. S. Dearborn, p. 10.)

Sandwich July 19, 1812.

Sir:—

The army is encamped directly opposite to Detroit. The camp is entrenched. I am mounting the 24 pounders and making every preparation for the siege of Malden.

The British force, which was in numbers superior to the American, including militia and Indians, is daily diminishing. Fifty or sixty of the militia have deserted daily since the American standard was displayed and taken protection. They are now reduced to less than one hundred. In a day or two I expect the whole will desert. Their Indian force is diminishing in nearly the same proportion. I have now a large council of ten or twelve nations sitting at Brownstown and I have no doubt the result will be that they will remain neutral.

The brig *Adams* was launched on the 4th of July. I have removed her to Detroit under cover of the cannon and shall have her finished and armed as soon as possible. We shall then command the upper lakes.

CAPTAIN ROBERTS TO MAJOR-GENERAL BROCK.

(Canadian Archives, C 676, p. 156.)

Copy/ Fort St Joseph's 12th July 1812

Sir,

I had the honor to receive Your Orders of the 26 and 27th of June, on the 8th inst.—the best disposition my resources afforded were instantly made with the view to an immediate attack upon the Fort of Michilimackinac, when the Second Express with Your Orders of the 28 and 29 in duplicate to Suspend hostilities, arrived, which also eeming to preclude the necessity of the Express to Amherstburgh it consequently has not been forwarded—Every exertion will be made use of to put the force I have here in such a state of preparation so as to be able to act as Your Orders may direct or occasion require.

To Mr Pothier, Mr Dickson, Mr Crawford,[1] and the Gentlema(e)n at the Sault of St Mary's, I am under the greatest

---

[1] Ma or Lewis Crawford of the Canadian Voyageurs. See note on Robert Dickson, p. 17.

obligations for their ready and effectual aid and personal exertions voluntarily contributed—Mr Pothier has thrown open his Store houses to Supply my requisitions in the handsomest manner.

Mr Dickson with a chosen Band of Warriors of upwards of a hundred men in whom he appears to have the greatest Confidence has greatly assisted me with his advice—much may be looked for from him and his party in the event of an Attack upon the American Fort—

Mr Crawford, at the head of 140 Canadian Volunteers, contributes every thing in his power to accelerate the general Interest—assurances are also held out to me of ample reinforcements in Men, Arms and provisions being Speedily Sent down from the N. W. Company's Post at Fort William.

I have this morning held a Council with most of the principal Chiefs of the Outawas—It has been a Subject of much Speculation how these people would act—on this occasion it gives me pleasure to inform You that after a long and private Consultation amongst themselves, in Consequence of my Communicating to them the state of affairs, they at last decided unanimously in our favor and are just going off for their Arms, and the remainder of their Men.

I took measures for Securing the *Caledonia* in (on) her way down from the Sault—She is now here and may be of essential Service,—I have enclosed a Memorandum of Articles received from the South West Company's Stores for Your information.

The Express has been detained partly at the request of Mr Pothier as well as to give You the Sentiments of the Outawas—

No reinforcements had arrived at Mackinack when these people passed that place Yesterday.

CAPTAIN N. HEALD TO LIEUT PORTER HANKS AT MACKINAC.

(Canadian Archives, C 688A, p. 115.)

Chicago 12 July 1812.

Dear Sir

I received your Letter of the 1st Inst. per Mr Williams. Also the 6 Barrels of Pork which came in a very good time we having been out of that Article for 5 or 6 Days

The Indians have been a little troublesome to us since the Spring opened, but not half so bad as you have been informed. They killed two Citizens about 3 Miles from the Garrison in April, and have since that time killed many of our Cattle and stole several Horses. We are somewhat confined to the Fort on account of the hostile disposition of the Winebagoes and some of the Pottawattamees; and whenever we have occasion to send out 2 or 3 Miles for Wood or any other Article I take the precaution to send an armed party.

Enclosed is a copy of a Letter which I received from the Adju^t and Inspector on the 10th Instant Also my latest newspaper—I think it possible this post will be evacuated.[1]

P.S. I forgot to tell you that Baker[2] is promoted—

CAPTAIN HEALD TO LIEUT. HANKS.

(Canadian Archives, C 688A, p. 116.)

Chicago 13th July 1812.

Sir

Last night between the hours of 10 and 11 I suspected from the barking of the Dogs and other circumstances that there was a party of Indians about us, and sent out two men to reconoiter a small distance round the Garrison, they had not got more than 70 or 80 yards from the Fort when they discerned 4 or 5 Indians within 15 or 20 paces of them; The two Soldiers drew up their Muskets loaded with buck shot fired on them and returned to the Fort The Indians returned but one shot and that had no effect. But I believe the Soldiers either killed or badly wounded one of them from the signs we have discovered this morning, the party remained about us 'till three oClock in the morning and occasionally fired a Gun at a distance, probably to induce me to send out another party. They have taken off one Horse and wounded with their knives and Tommahawks four Sheep which were shut up in a Stable not far from the Fort, I suspect they are Pottawattamies.

---

[1] See Heald's letter to the Secretary of War, p. 225.
[2] Captain Daniel Baker of the 1st U. S. Regiment of Infantry.

ROBERT DICKSON TO MAJOR-GENERAL BROCK.

(Canadian Archives, C 256, p. 187.)

Copy/

Sir,

I take the liberty of addressing Your Honor on the Subject of the Indians Nations to the West, a number of whose Chiefs and Warriors have accompanied me to this place in order to Co-operate with His Majesty's Forces wherever their Services may be wanted—The situation of those nations last Winter has, from their usual Supplies being withheld, been truly deplorable—there is but little hope at present of goods being this Season carried into their Country, and unless they receive Strong Support in Ammunition & Cloathing from His Majesty, they must infallibly perish.

I had intended at this moment to have paid Your Honor a visit, in order to have had the Satisfaction of representing to You the State of the Country, and Several other interesting Subjects in the present crisés; but I have deferred this that I may be ready for the attack of Michilimackinac, so earnestly wished for, as the means of Securing the Communication to the Mississippi and retaining and Supporting all the Indian Tribes in their present happy disposition so favorable to the interests of Britain—

From Captain Roberts I have received every mark of attention that politeness could dictate, or that the good of the Service can require—The Indians are much gratified with his comportment towards them, and in him they repose the highest Confidence—

I some time since despatched from Green Bay, thirty Indians to Amherstburg—had I received earlier information, I would have with ease brought an addition of Four or Five hundred to those now here.—

We wait anxiously for Your Orders, on which the fate of this Country depends.

St Joseph's July 13th 1812

BRIG.-GENERAL HULL TO THE SECRETARY OF WAR.

(Report of the Trial of General Hull; New York, 1814; App. II, p. 10.)

Sandwich, in Upper Canada, July 13th, 1812.

Sir—from the 5th July inst. the day of the arrival of the army at Detroit, the whole was employed in strengthening the fortifications for the security of the town, and preparing boats for the passage of the river. About one hundred regulars of the British army, and, from the best accounts I have been able to obtain, six hundred Canadian militia with artillery, were in possession of the opposite bank, and fortifying directly opposite the town; seven or eight hundred Indians were likewise attached to this corps. On the evening of the 11th, before dark, the boats were ordered down the river, and a part of the army marched towards the river Rouge, with directions to return under cover of the night and proceed above the town. The object of this movement was to induce the enemy to believe that this was a preparatory measure to the passage of the river below: this indeed would have been the real movement, if a sufficient number of boats could have been collected for the passage of a body of troops at once superior to the enemy's: the necessary arrangements having been made, the latter moved above the town to Bloody bridge. The 4th U. S. regiment, M'Arthur's, Finley's and Cass's regiments of Ohio volunteers, with three six pounders under the command of Captain Dyson,[1] marched to the same point; the descent was immediately made, and the army is now encamped on the Canada shore without the loss of a man. In the course of the night the enemy abandoned their position and retreated to Amherstburg. Both the embarkation and the debarkation were conducted with the greatest regularity, and all the heavy artillery that was mounted on carriages was placed on the bank in suitable situations to have covered the landing. In less than five minutes after the first boat of a regiment struck the shore, the whole regiment was formed. The manner in which this difficult movement was executed does honor to the officers and soldiers of this army. I consider the possession of this bank is highly important. By erecting one or two batteries opposite to the batteries at Detroit, the river will be completely com-

---

[1] Captain Samuel Dyson, 1st U.S. Regiment of Artillery.

manded in the rear of the army. On the Detroit River, the River La Trenche, and Lake St. Clair is a populous and valuable part of the province; it is likewise probable that when the Indians see the American standard erected on both sides the river it will have a favorable effect.

Inclosed is a copy of a proclamation to the inhabitants, which I hope will be approved by the government. Two hundred copies have been printed and are now in circulation; all the inhabitants who have seen it appear satisfied.

PROCLAMATION OF BRIG.-GENERAL HULL.

(Canadian Archives, C 676, p. 168.)

By William Hull, Brigadier General and Commander of of the North Western Army of the United States

A PROCLAMATION

INHABITANTS OF CANADA! After thirty years of Peace and prosperity, the United States have been driven to Arms, The injuries and aggressions, the insults and indignities of Great Britain have *once more* left them no alternative but manly resistance or unconditional submission. The army under my Command has invaded your Country and the standard of the United States waves on the territory of Canada To the peaceful unoffending inhabitant, It brings neither danger nor difficulty I come to *find* enemies not to *make* them, I come to *protect* not to *injure* you.

Separated by an immense ocean and an extensive Wilderness from Great Britain you have no participtaion in her counsels no interest in her conduct. You have felt her Tyranny, you have seen her injustice, but I do not ask *you* to avenge the one or to redress the other. The United States are sufficiently powerful to afford you every security consistent with their rights & your expectations, I tender you the invaluable blessings of Civil, Political, & Religious Liberty, and their necessary result, individual, and general, prosperity: That liberty which gave decision to our counsels and energy to our conduct in our struggle for INDEPENDENCE and which conducted us safely and triumphantly thro' the stormy period of the Revolution.

That Liberty which has raised us to an elevated rank among the Nations of the world and which has afforded us a greater measure of Peace & Security wealth and prosperity than ever fell to the Lot of any people.

In the name of my *Country* and by the authority of my Government I promise you protection to your *persons, property, and rights,* Remain at your homes, Pursue your peaceful and customary avocations. Raise not your hands against your brethren, many of your fathers fought for the freedom & indepen(de)nce we now enjoy Being children therefore of the same family with us, and heirs to the same Heritage, the arrival of an army of Friends must be hailed by you with a cordial welcome, You will be emancipated from Tyranny and oppression and restored to the dignified station of freemen. Had I any doubt of eventual success I might ask your assistance but I do not. I come prepared for every contingency. I have a force which will look down all opposition and that force is but the vanguard of a much greater. If contrary to your own interest & the just expectation of my country, you should take part in the approaching contest, you will be considered and treated as enemies and the horrors, and calamities of war will Stalk before you.

If the barbarous and Savage policy of Great Britain be pursued, and the savages are let loose to murder our Citizens and butcher our women and children, this war, will be a war of extermination

The first stroke with the Tomahawk the first attempt with the Scalping Knife will be the Signal for one indiscriminate scene of desolation, *No white man found fighting by the Side of an Indian will be taken prisoner* Instant destruction will be his Lot. If the dictates of reason, duty, justice, and humanity, cannot prevent the employment of a force, which respects no rights & knows no wrong, it will be prevented by a severe and relentless system of retaliation

I doubt not your courage and firmness; I will not doubt your attachment to Liberty. If you tender your services voluntarily they will be accepted readily

The United States offer you *Peace, Liberty,* and *Security* your choice lies between these, & *War, Slavery, and destruction,* Choose then, but choose wisely; and may he who knows the justice of our cause, and who holds in his hand the fate of Nations, guide you to a result the most compatible, with your rights and interests, your peace and prosperity

              (Signed)   WM. HULL

By the General
  A F HULL[1]
    Captn. 13. U. S. Reg^t of Infant^y & A.D.C
    Head Quarters at Sandwich
        July 13th 1812

BRIG.-GENERAL HULL TO THE SECRETARY OF WAR.

                      Sandwich, July 15, 1812.
Sir,—

The Canadian militia are deserting from Malden in large parties; about sixty came in yesterday. I send them to their homes and give them protection. The probability is that the greatest part of them will desert in a few days.

The force under my command and the movement into this province has had a great effect on the Indians. They are daily returning to their villages. A very large council is now sitting at Brownstown. The Wyandots are at the head of it. The object is to induce all the nations to be neutral. I furnish them with provisions. The Crane, Walk-in-the-water, Blackhoof, Blue Jacket, &c., &c., &c., are zealous friends of neutrality. I have great hopes the object will be effected. I have reason to believe the number of hostile Indians is decreasing. The inhabitants have received my proclamation with great satisfaction so far as information has been received.

I shall march the army to Malden as soon as the necessary preparations can be made for the siege.

As the British have no naval force above Detroit and as we now command the river, I shall direct the brig *Adams* to be completed and armed as soon as possible for the purpose of supplying the posts at Michilimackinac and Chicago with provisions and the necessary stores provided we can obtain them here.

---

[1] Abraham Fulton Hull, son of General Hull, killed in action at Lundy's Lane, 1814.

LIEUT.-COLONEL ST. GEORGE TO MAJOR-GENERAL BROCK.

(Canadian Archives, C 676, p. 177.)

Amherstburg 15th July 1812

Copy

Dear General,

Since my letter of the 8th which I sent by the *Hunter*, finding that it would not be possible for me to keep Sandwich owing to the disposition in which I found the Militia; I thought it right to prepare to withdraw the force there to Amherstburg, and on the 10th Instant I sent the Assistant Quarter Master General to arrange with Mr Francis Baby (who I had appointed to assist in that Department) to drive whatever cattle &c &c could be found, to this Post—On the 11th I received a letter from Colonel Baby, stating, that from the preparation made on the opposite side, & every appearance of the Enemy crossing in great force, he had determined (with the unanimous advice of his Officers) to withdraw to Amherstburg immediately. On my arrival there, the same day I found that the heavy guns and Baggage were sent off—and from the information of those I could most depend on, that the men had shown so great a disposition to get away home, I had every reason to suppose that in the course of the night they would disperse—I thought it best to get them to Amherstburg—

The next morning early (the 12th) the Enemy crossed with the greatest part of his force near Hog Island, and occupied Sandwich—

Since that time the Militia have been going off in such numbers, that I have not more than 471 in all this morning—and in such a state as to be totally inefficient in the field—However when I find in what manner the Enemy attack, I must try them—In the mean time I am endeavouring to get them in some order—Their numerous wants I am straining every nerve to supply—yet I am stunned with complaints chiefly respecting their families left in the greatest want—Some of the oldest have been allowed to go home—Regular Returns I am unable to get from their officers—There are certainly many well disposed, but the idea of leaving their families and farms at this season occasions their principal disatisfaction—As to the Indians I wished those here to act when I could support them, but as they are so anxious I must let them on, and sustain them as I see occasion, to the utmost of my power—It is impossible to tell their numbers in our favor, as they are continually going and coming—But I shall know in a day or two how many I can have here to depend on—

I hope the Enemy will move forward by land—The Canard is so strong a position that I think (with the assistance of the Indians) I can annoy them much before they can get to this by that Road—

I am sorry I have to complain of want of information of every kind—-

The *Lady Prevost* was launched the day before yesterday.

COLONEL ELLIOTT TO COLONEL CLAUS.

(Canadian Archives, C 676, p. 180.)

Amherstburgh 15th July 1812.

Sir,

On Saturday 11th inst the enemy appeared in motion from Detroit upwards towards Hog Island on their own side of the River, where they had collected a number of boats. Our Militia stationed at Sandwich to watch their motions, and to prevent if possible their crossing, placing little reliance on their own strength, and fearing they might be cut off, immediately determined on a retreat, and accordingly did so on the same night to this post, with two pieces of cannon which had been given them for their defence—And early in the morning of the 12th the enemy crossed in a line from Hog Island to Detroit, and landed at several places at the same time from Mackintoshes to Sandwich without a Shot being fired to the number of about 6 or 800. General Hull immediately (occupied) Mr Babys brick house opposite to Detroit and placed his largest force at Sandwich where they began to entrench themselves, and they have since crossed over their cavalry and artillery with more troops and now are entrenching themselves down the settlement towards this post, erecting batteries at distances, and have also sent a detachment towards the River Thames—The Genl on landing issued proclamations to the Inhabitants, promising all those who should remain at their homes protection for their persons & property—Their Proclamations have operated very powerfully on our Militia (who had come forward with as much promptitude as could have been expected) Since their issuing our Militia have left their Posts and returned to their homes, so that since Sunday the number is reduced to about one half, and I expect that in two or three days we shall have very few of them at the post.

We expect to be attacked to day or tomorrow. The Indians with us are between 3 & 400 who have resisted every allurement which Genl Hull laid before them. Tech-Kum-thai has kept them faithful—he has shewn himself to be a determined character and a great friend to our Government.

Delay in attacking the enemy has been very detrimental to our interests and greatly cooled the former spirit of our Militia—

We have no ball remaining in the Indian store, and if more Indians come, I really do not know how to act—We have taken all (and that was very little) in the possession of the Merchants here.

The bearer of this is Guendik a faithful little man, and who will proceed with despatch with this by the way of point Pele

P.S. The people here are much dejected & have removed all their effects out of the place.

ARTICLES OF CAPITULATION OF MICHILIMACKINAC.[1]

(Canadian Archives, C 676, p. 234.)

Heights above Michilimackinac
17 July 1812

Copy

CAPITULATION agreed upon between Captain Charles Roberts, Commanding His Britannic Majesty's Forces on the one part, and Lieutenant Hankes Commanding the Troops of the United States of America on the other—

First—The Fort of Michilimackinac shall immediately be surrendered to the British Force—Granted—

Second—The Garrison shall march out with the Honors of War, lay down their Arms and become Prisoners of War, and Shall be Sent to the United States of America by His Britannic Majesty, not to Serve in this War until regularly exchanged,

---

[1] Another copy of these articles is to be found in *Canadian Archives,* C 676, p. 190. It is not attested by Brock, and differs from the one here given in that after articles one and two the word 'granted' does not appear; the American officer's signature reads 'Lieut' Hanks—not P. Hankes, &c.; and in article four the last clause runs ' as far as in my power.'

and for the due performance of this Article the Officers pledge their Word and Honor—Granted.

Third—All the Merchant Vessels in the Harbour, with their Cargoes Shall be in the possession of their respective Owners.

Fourth—Private property Shall be held Sacred as far as it is in my power.

Fifth—All Citizens of the United States, who shall not take the Oath of allegiance to His Britannic Majesty, Shall depart with their property from the Island in One Month, from the date hereof—

    (Signed) CHARLES ROBERTS
        Captain Commanding His
            Britannic Majesty's Forces—

    (Signed) P. HANKES
        Lieutenant Commanding
            the Forces of the United States—
                Fort Michilimackinac.

True Copy
  ISAAC BROCK
  M. G^r

SUPPLEMENT TO THE ARTICLES OF CAPITULATION SIGNED ON THE 17TH JULY.[1]

(Historical Register of United States, 1812-13; 2 ed., Philadelphia, 1814; Vol. II, p. 83.)

The captains and crews of the vessels *Erie* and *Freegoodwill* shall be included under the second article not to serve until regularly exchanged, for which the officers shall pledge their word and honour.

Fort Michilimackinac, 17th July, 1812.

            CHARLES ROBERTS,
      Capt. commanding the Forces of
            his Britanic majesty,
Granted,
            P. HANKS,
    Lieut. commanding the United States' forces.

---

[1] The supplementary article, as given in '*Report of the Trial of General Hull,*' App. II. p. 23, bears the date July 23, 1812.

CAPTAIN ROBERTS TO COLONEL BAYNES.

(Canadian Archives, C 676, p. 183.)

Fort Michilimackinac 17 July 1812

Sir,

On the 15th instant I received Letters by Express from Major General Brock with orders to adopt the most prudent measures either of offence or defence which circumstances might point out, and having received intelligence from the best information that large reinforcements were daily expected to be thrown into this Garrison, and finding that the Indians who had been collected would soon have abandoned me if I had not made the attempt, with the thorough conviction that my situation at S^t. Josephs was totally indefensible,[1] I determined to lose no time in making the meditated attack on this Fort

On the sixteenth at Ten oclock in the morning I embarked my few men with about one hundred and eighty Canadian Engagees half of them without Arms about three hundred Indians,[2] and two Iron six pounders, the boats arrived without the smallest accident at the place of Rendezvous at three oClock the following morning—by the exertions of the Canadians one of the Guns was brought up to a height commanding the Garrison and ready to act about Ten Oclock, a summons was then sent in a Copy of which as well as of the Capitulation which followed, I have the Honor to enclose at twelve the American Colours were hauled down and those of His Majesty's were hoisted—A Committee has been appointed to examine into the State of the Public Stores. Inclosed also are Returns[3] of the Ordnance and Military Stores found in the Fort, and the Strength of the Garrison. The greatest praize is due to every Individual employed in this Expedition to my own Officers I am indebted in particular for their active assistance in carrying all my orders into effect

The Indians are flocking in from all quarters but in a few weeks I shall be left in a great measure to my own resources, and I trust His Excellency the Governor General will see the necessity of adding to my force,

---

[1] For report on Fort St. Joseph, see p. 26.
[2] For the number of Indians in this engagement, see despatch of Hanks to Hull, p. 67; also observations of T. Pothier, p. 214. For the different tribes, see Askin to Claus, p. 67.
[3] A return of ordnance, ammunition and stores is found in *Canadian Archives*, C 676, p. 186; also in C 688 A, p. 122. A return of provisions is found on p. 161 of the last-named volume. The monthly return of the garrison for June, giving 62 as the full strength, is found in C 676, p. 189.

CAPTAIN ROBERTS TO MAJOR-GENERAL BROCK.

(Canadian Archives, C 676, p. 232.)

Copy/

Fort of Michilimackinac 17 July 1812.

Sir,

I had the honor to receive Your letter dated the 4th of July, on the 15th inst. and foreseeing that I should soon be abandoned by the Indians whose minds had been prepared for hostilities, if I did not immediately employ them, and also that the moment so favorable for making an attack upon this place so highly important at the present Crisis might soon be lost,—I embarked on the morning of the 16th with Two of the Six pounders and every Man I could muster, and at Ten o'clock the Signal being made we were immediately under weigh.

By the almost unparralleled exertions of the Canadians who manned the Boats, we arrived at the place of Rendezvous at 3 oclock the following morning.

One of these unwieldly Guns was brought up with much difficulty to the Heights above the Fort and in readiness to open about Ten oclock at which time a Summons was sent in and the Capitulation, a Copy of which I have the honor to enclose, was soon after agreed upon.—I took immediate possession of the Fort, and displayed the British Colours.—It is a circumstance I believe without precedent, and demands the greatest praise for all those who conducted the Indians, that although these people's minds were much heated, yet as soon as they heard the Capitulation was signed they all returned to their Canoes, and not one drop either of Man's or Animal's Blood was Spilt, till I gave an Order for a certain number of Bullocks to be purchased for them—I have not yet been able to obtain returns of the Stores here—they shall be forwarded by the earliest opportunity—

I cannot conclude this Letter without expressing my warmest thanks to my own Officers—to the Gentlemen of S[t] Joseph's and S[t] Mary's, and to every individual engaged in this Service.

I trust, Sir, in thus acting I have not exceeded Your Instructions, for be assured that prudential measures of the first necessity demanded the Step which has put me in possession of this Island.

JOHN ASKIN, JR.,[1] TO COLONEL WILLIAM CLAUS.

(Canadian Archives, C 676, p. 201.)

Copy/

Michilimackinac 18th July 1812

Dear Sir,

I am happy to have it in my power to announce to you that Fort Michilimackinac Capitulated to us on the 17th ins^t at 11 o'clock A.M.—Captn Roberts at our head with a part of the 10th R. V. Battalion, Mr Crawford had the Command of the Canadians which Consisted of about 200 men. Mr Dixon 113 Sie(o)ux. Follavoines & Waynebegoes—myself about 280 men.—Ottawas & Chippawas—Part of the Ottawas of L'harbre Croche had not arrived.—It was a fortunate circumstance that the Fort Capitulated without firing a Single Gun, for had they done so, I firmly believe not a Soul of them would have been Saved.—My Son, Charles Langlade, Augustine Nolin, & Michelle Cadotte Junr have rendered me great Services in keeping the Indians in order, & executing from time to time such Commands as were delivered to me by the Commanding Officer.—I never saw so determined a Set of people as the Chippawas & Ottawas were.

Since the Capitulation they have not drunk a single drop of Liquor, nor even killed a fowl belonging to any person (a thing never known before) for they generally destroy every thing they meet with.

LIEUT. PORTER HANKS[2] TO BRIG.-GENERAL HULL. (EXTRACT.)

(Report of Trial of General Hull, App. II, p. 21.)

Detroit, 4th August, 1812.

Sir—I take the earliest opportunity to acquaint your excellence of the surrender of Michillimackinac, under my command to His Britannic majesty's forces under the command of Captain Charles Roberts, on the 17th ult—the particulars of which are as follows:—On the 16th I was informed by the Indian interpreter, that he had discovered from an Indian that the several nations of Indians then at St. Joseph, (a

---

[1] John Askin, junior, an elder half brother of Charles Askin, storekeeper in the Indian Department at the island of St. Joseph; promoted captain in 1814.

[2] Lieutenant Porter Hanks of the United States Artillery was killed by a round shot at Detroit on the morning of August 16, 1812.

17804—5½

British garrison, distance forty-five miles) intended to make an immediate attack on Michillimackinac. I was inclined, from the coolness I had discovered in some of the principal chiefs of the Ottawa and Chippawa nations, who had but a few days before professed the greatest friendship for the United States, to place confidence in this report. I immediately called a meeting of the American gentlemen at that time on the island, in which it was thought proper to dispatch a confidential person to St. Joseph to watch the motions of the Indians. Capt. Daurman, of the Militia was thought the most suitable for this service. He embarked about sunset and met the British forces within ten or fifteen miles of the island, by whom he was made prisoner and put on his parole of honor. He was landed on the island at day-break, with positive directions to give me no intelligence whatever. He was also instructed to take the inhabitants of the village indiscriminately to a place on the west side of the island, where their persons and property should be protected by a British guard; but should they go to the fort, they would be subject to a general massacre by the savages, which would be inevitable if the garrison fired a gun. This information I received from Doctor Day, who was passing through the village when every person was flying for refuge to the enemy. Immediately on being informed of the approach of the enemy, I placed ammunition, &c. in the block-houses; ordered every gun charged, and made every preparation for action. About 9 o'clock I could discover that the enemy were in possession of the heights that commanded the fort, and one piece of their artillery directed to the most defenceless part of the garrison. The Indians at this time were to be seen in great numbers in the edge of the woods. At half past 11 o'clock, the enemy sent in a flag of truce, demanding a surrender of the fort and island to his Britannic Majesty's forces. This, Sir, was the first intimation I had of the declaration of war; I, however, had anticipated it and was as well prepared to meet such an event as I possibly could have been with the force under my command, amounting to fifty-seven effective men, including officers. Three American gentlemen, who were prisoners, were permitted to accompany the flag: from them I ascertained the strength of the enemy to be from nine hundred to one thousand strong, consisting of regular troops, Canadians and savages; that they had two pieces of artillery and were provided with ladders and ropes for the purpose of scaling the works if necessary. After I had obtained this information, I consulted my officers and also the

American gentlemen present, who were very intelligent men; the result of which was, that it was impossible for the garrison to hold out against such a superior force. In this opinion I fully concurred, from a conviction that it was the only measure that could prevent a general massacre. The fort and garrison were accordingly surrendered.

The enclosed papers exhibit copies of the correspondence between the officer commanding the British forces and myself, and of the articles of capitulation. This subject involved questions of a peculiar nature; and I hope, Sir, that my demands and protests will meet the approbation of my government. I cannot allow this opportunity to escape without expressing my obligations to Dr. Day for the service he rendered me in conducting this correspondence.

In consequence of this unfortunate affair, I beg leave, Sir, to demand that a court of enquiry may be ordered to investigate all the facts connected with it; and I do further request, that the court may be speedily directed to express their opinion on the merits of the case.

P.S. The following particulars relative to the British force[1] were obtained after the capitulation, from a source that admits of no doubt: Regular troops 46 (Including 4 officers;) Canadian militia 260—Total 306.

SAVAGES—Sioux 56; Winnebagoes 48; Tallesawain (Folles Avoines) 39; Chippewas and Ottawas 572—savages 715, whites 306—Total 1021.

It may also be remarked, that one hundred and fifty Chippewas and Ottawas joined the British, two days after the capitulation.

BRIG.-GENERAL HULL TO LIEUT.-COLONEL ST. GEORGE.

(*Canadian Archives, Q 118, p. 192.*)

Copy/   Head Quarters of the North Western
       Army of the United States.
            Camp at Sandwich July 16th 1812.
Sir,

Among the Articles on Board the Boat commanded by Captain Chapin which was taken into Amherstburg, were a number of papers, which it is presumed will be of no service to the British Government, nor to the Commanding Officer

---

[1] For strength of the British force, see Roberts to Baynes, July 17, p. 65.

at Amherstburg, nor to the Captors of the Boat—The papers have undoubtedly undergone an examination before this time, and the bearer Captn Brown of the 4th U. S. Regiment of Infantry is authorized to receive them.

I am anxious to learn your determination relative to the private Apparel and Baggage taken in the Boat, and belonging to Officers and Men, who were not on board at the time of the Capture. You have already reciprocated the sentiment that private property should be considered Sacred: indeed it will operate to the advantage of Canada that it should be so considered.

I have it in my power to retaliate signally any aggression on such property, or to avenge an unjust delay in the restitution of it.

N°2. Enclosure in Sir G. Prevost's N° 3 Augt 17th 1812.

LIEUT.-COLONEL ST. GEORGE TO BRIG.-GENERAL HULL.

(Canadian Archives, Q 118, p. 194.)

Copy/

Amherstburg 16th July, 1812.

Sir,

I was honoured with your favor by Captn Brown—With respect to the papers taken in the Schooner, they have upon examination, almost without exception, proved to be public Documents, the few of a private nature that may be amongst them, it would cause considerable trouble to select, more indeed than the Officer whom I have entrusted with the examination can at present spare.

As to private property, I beg to refer you to my answer to your former letter, I can add nothing to what I have express'd further than that I have not as yet heard the determination of my Government on the subject.

I regret to find in Your Excellency's letter, the words " retaliation & avenge "—You must be aware, Sir, that retaliation can be carried to a great degree on both sides 'till there is no saying where it will stop.

I hope that for both our sakes, that I shall be as little obliged to use the means in my power as you those in yours.

N° 3. Enclosure in Sir G. Prevost's N° 3. Augt 17th, 1812.

LIEUT.-COLONEL CASS TO BRIG.-GENERAL HULL.

(Historical Register of the United States, 1812-13; 2 ed., Philadelphia, 1814; Vol. II., p. 39.)

Sandwich, Upper Canada, July 17, 1812.

Sir, in conformity with your instructions, I proceeded with a detachment of 280 men, to reconnoitre the enemy's advanced posts. We found them in possession of a bridge over the river aux Canards, at the distance of four miles from Malden. After examining their position, I left one company of riflemen, to conceal themselves near the bridge, and upon our appearance on the opposite side of the river, to commence firing, in order to divert their attention, and to throw them into confusion. I then proceeded with the remainder of the force about five miles, to a ford over the river aux Canards and down on the southern bank of the river. About sunset we arrived within sight of the enemy. Being entirely destitute of guides, we marched too near the bank of the river, and found our progress checked by a creek, which was then impassable. We were then compelled to march up a mile, in order to effect a passage over the creek. This gave the enemy time to make their arrangements, and prepare for their defence. On coming down the creek we found them formed; they commenced a distant fire of musquetry. The riflemen of the detachment were formed upon the wings, and the two companies of infantry in the centre. The men moved on with great spirit and alacrity. After the first discharge the British retreated— we continued advancing. Three times they formed, and as often retreated. We drove them about half a mile, when it became so dark that we were obliged to relinquish the pursuit. Two privates in the 41st regiment were wounded and taken prisoners. We learn from deserters, that nine or ten were wounded, and some killed. We could gain no precise information of the number opposed to us. It consisted of a considerable detachment from the 41st regiment, some militia, and a body of Indians. The guard at the bridge consisted of 50 men. Our riflemen stationed on this side the river aux Canards, discovered the enemy reinforcing them during the whole afternoon. There is no doubt but their number cor siderably exceeded ours. Lieutenant-colonel Miller[1] conducted in the most spirited and able manner. I have every reason to be satisfied with the conduct of the whole detachment.

BRIG.-GENERAL HULL TO THE SIX NATIONS.

(New York Gazette, August 20th, 1812.)

Sandwich, July 18, 1812.

My Brethern of the Six Nations:—

The powerful army under my command is now in possession of Canada. To you who are friendly it will afford safety and protection. All your lands and all your rights of every kind will be guaranteed to you if you will take no part against us. I salute you in friendship and hope you will now act such a part as will promote your interest, your safety and happiness. May the Great Spirit guide you in person.

WM. HULL,
Governor of the Territory of Michigan and Commander of the Northwestern Army of the United States.

MR. MACKENZIE AT FORT WILLIAM TO MR. DUNCAN MACKINTOSH[2] AT SANDWICH—DATED JULY 19TH. (EXTRACT.)

(Report of the Trial of General Hull; New York, 1814; App. I, p. 47.)

The declaration of war reached us on the 16th instant, but we are neither astonished or alarmed. Our agents ordered

---

[1] James Miller was born at Peterborough, New Hampshire, April 25, 1776. He studied law and was admitted to practice. In 1808 on the augmentation of the United States army he was commissioned as major of the 4th Regiment of Infantry. He was promoted to be lieutenant-colonel in 1810, and was present at the action with the Indians at Tippecanoe. He was promoted to the rank of brevet colonel for good services in August, 1812, before the surrender of Detroit was known at Washington. In May, 1814, he was appointed colonel of the 21st United States Infantry and served with distinction in the actions at Chippawa, Lundy's Lane and Fort Erie. He was breveted a brigadier-general and presented with a gold medal by Congress in recognition of his gallantry in leading an assault on the British position at Lundy's Lane on the evening of July 25, 1814. In 1819, he was appointed governor of the newly created territory of Arkansas and held that office until 1825, when he was appointed collector of the port of Salem, Massachusetts. He died at Temple, New Hampshire, July 7, 1851.

[2] Son of Honourable Angus McIntosh of Moy, Hudson Bay Co. agent.

a general muster, which amounted to 1200, exclusive of several hundred of the natives. We are now equal in all to 1600 or 1700 strong. One of our gentlemen started on the 17th with several light canoes, for the interior country, to rouse the natives to activity, which is not hard to do, on the present occasion. We likewise despatched messengers in all directions with the news. I have not the least doubt but our force will, in ten days hence, amount to at least five thousand effective men. Our young gentlemen and engagees offered most handsomely to march immediately for Michilimackinac. Our chief Mr. Shaw[1] expressed his gratitude, and drafted one hundred —They are to proceed this evening for St. Joseph's. He takes about as many Indians:—could the vessel contain them, he migth have had four thousand more. It now depends on what accounts we receive from St. Joseph's, whether these numerous tribes from the interior will proceed to St. Joseph's or not.

MAJOR-GENERAL BROCK TO SIR GEORGE PREVOST.

(Canadian Archives, C 676, p. 203.)

Fort George July 20th 1812

Sir,

My last to Your Excellency was dated the 12 Instant, since which nothing extraordinary has occurred on this communication—The enemy has evidently diminished his force, and appears to have no intention of making an immediate attack—

I have herewith the honor of enclosing the Copy of two letters which I have received from Lt Colonel St George, together with some interesting documents found on board a schooner which the boats of the *Hunter* Captured on her voyage from the Meamie to Detroit

From the accompanying official correspondence between General Hull and the Secretary at War it appears that the collected force which has arrived at Detroit amounts to about two thousand

I have requested Colonel Procter to proceed to Amherstburg, and ascertain accurately the state of things in that

---

[1] Angus Shaw, a partner of the North West Company, and afterwards major in the corps of Canadian Voyageurs raised by the company in October 1812.

quarter—I had every inclination to go there myself, but the meeting of the Legislature on the 27th renders it impossible

I receive this moment a dispatch dated the 15th Inst from Lt Colonel St George giving an account of the enemy having landed on the 12th and immediately after occupying the village of Sandwich—It is strange that three days should be allowed to elapse before sending to acquaint me of this important fact I had no idea until I received Lt Colonel St George's letter a few days ago that General Hull was advancing with such a large force

The Militia from every account behaved very ill—The officers appear the most in fault. Colonel Proctor[1] will probably reach Amherstburg in the course of tomorrow—I have great dependance in that Officers decision, but fear he will arrive too late to be of much service—The enemy was not likely to delay attacking a force that had allowed him to cross the river in open day without firing a shot

The position which Lt Colonel St George occupied is very good, and infinitely more formidable than the Fort itself— Should he therefore be compelled to retire I know of no other alternative than embarking in the King's vessels—and proceeding to Fort Erie—

Were it possible to animate the Militia to a proper sense of their duty something might yet be done, but I almost despair—

Your Excellency will readily perceive the critical situation in which the reduction of Amherstburg is sure to place me— I do not imagine General Hull will be able to detach more than one thousand Men, but even with that trifling force I fear he will succeed in getting to my rear The Militia will not act without a strong Regular force to set them the example, and

---

[1] Henry Procter was born in 1763; and commissioned as ensign in the 43rd Regiment of Foot on April 5, 1789; promoted to be lieutenant in December, 1791; captain, November 30, 1792; major, 1795; lieutenant-colonel in the 41st, October 9, 1800; colonel, July 25, 1810. He took over the command of the Western District and the Right Division of the forces in Upper Canada on the departure of Brock, and defeated General Winchester at Frenchtown on the river Raisin, January 22, 1813. He was granted the local rank of brigadier-general February 8, 1813. He defeated an attempt by General Clay to raise the siege of Fort Meigs, May 5, 1813, but failed to capture that post. He was promoted to be major-general, June 4, 1813. The disastrous result of the naval action on lake Erie, September 10, 1813, forced him to abandon Detroit and Amherstburg, and the small force under his command was overtaken and defeated by General Harrison at Moraviantown, October 5, 1813. He was tried by court-martial and suspended from rank and pay for six months for negligence during the retreat. He died at Bath, England, October 31, 1822.

as I must now expect to be seriously threatened from the opposite shore, I cannot, in prudence, make strong detachments, which would not only weaken my line of defence, but in the event of a retreat endanger their safety—

I have never, as Your Excellency has doubtless noticed, been very sanguine in my hopes of assistance from the Militia, and I am now given to understand that General Hull's insidious proclamation, herewith enclosed, has already been productive of considerable effect on the minds of the people—In fact a general sentiment prevails that with the present force resistance is unavailing I shall continue to exert myself to the utmost to overcome every difficulty—Should however the Communication between Kingston and Montreal be cut off the fate of the troops in this part of the Province will be decided —I now express my apprehensions on a supposition that the slender means Your Excellency possesses will not admit of diminution, consequently that I cannot look for re-inforcements

The enemy evidently has no intention at present of penetrating into the Province by this Strait—He seems much more inclined to work on the flanks—After they are secured little will remain for him to do—

The last official communication[1] from the Lower Province is dated the 25 Ult° The adjutant General then announced the receipt of intelligence by a Mercantile house of war being declared by the United States against Great Britain, I need not entreat Your Excellency to honor me with your commands with as little delay as possible—I consider every moment exceedingly precious—

EXTRACTS FROM AMERICAN NEWSPAPERS, AUGUST, 1812.

From the " New York Gazette," 5th August, 1812.

Letters from Detroit of the 14th July say:—" The Canadian militia are deserting from Malden in large parties; sixty in one body on receiving the proclamation reported themselves to the General and retired to their farms.

" The American flag waving on both sides of the river has astonished the natives and they are retiring to their villages and already holding councils to advise the Indians to remain

---
[1] See despatch of Adjutant Baynes to Captain Roberts, p. 37.

neutral. The General has promised us a trip to Malden after which we shall detach a small party of our friends to Michilimackinac and I hope pursue our march down Lake Erie through several pleasing little settlements.

"The General is determined to adhere religiously to his proclamation and hold as sacred all the property of individuals. The citizens of Canada, for I already hail the peninsula of the lakes as a state, appear satisfied with our visit."

From the "New York Gazette," 12th August, 1812.

A letter from Detroit dated July 28th states:—" On Saturday last a scouting party of about one hundred men went down towards Malden and when arrived near the Canard, they got into a scrape with about the same number of Indians. A variety of manœuvres took place between the contending parties, each endeavoring to gain the most advantageous positions, small parties branching out from each and almost continual firing for nearly three hours when our men retired with the loss of 4 men killed, 1 wounded, and 1 taken prisoner. The Indians lost from 10 to 12 killed, the scalp of one of them I have seen. Had it not been for the dastardly conduct of the drafted Ohio militia who composed one half of the party and who took to their heels when they evidently had the advantage, the whole of the Indians would have been either killed or taken. The officers endeavored to rally them and said they would be fired at by their own party if they did not stand. They replied that they would rather be killed by them than by the damned Indians."

From the "Federal Republican" of Georgetown, D.C., 24th August, 1812.

Extract from a letter from Captain Ulery,[1] dated at Sandwich, July 26.

"We have had four engagements with the Indians and British—the first time beat them back and took the ground. The other three times we had to retreat without the loss of a man, only two slightly wounded, one out of Capt. Frazer's company, the other out of Capt. Cunningham's. Yesterday we had an engagement with a few of our men under Major James Denny, particularly with the Indians but had to leave the ground with the loss of three men out of our regiment."

---

[1] Captain Ulery was killed at Brownstown. See p. 126.

From the " National Intelligencer " of Washington, D.C.

Extract from a letter from B. F. Stickney, Indian Agent to John Johnson, Agent for Indian Affairs, dated at Fort Wayne, July 20, 1812.

"The Prophet came here a week ago with 60 Kickapoos, 20 Winebagoes, and 12 Shawanese who are still here. They said they had been invited to take the tomahawk by the British but refused and made strong professions of friendship for the Americans.

" I have been informed this morning that an Indian has been sent out from Malden in the forepart of last week with a belt of wampum three feet wide and six feet long (painted red as an emblem of war) as the dernier resort to rouse the Indians to take up the tomahawk. The bearer of this great belt is instructed among other things to advise the Indians not to attend the council at Piqua, that it is a contrivance of the United States to lead all the men from home and then fall upon their women and children and destroy their towns.

" They call the belt the King's Great Broad Axe and that it is to cut down all before it. Some friendly Indians are now in pursuit of the war-belt to stop it.

" I have invited the Prophet to attend the council at Piqua and he has promised not only to go but to send to Malden for Tecumseh to go and stand by his side."

From the " Federal Republican " of Georgetown, D.C.

Extract from a letter from Fort Wayne to Major William Ruffin, dated 27th July, 1812.

" The Prophet and party consisting of 70 Kickapoos, 20 Winebagoes, 12 Shawanese, and two Piankishaws arrived here on a visit to see their new and good father as they call him.

" The Prophet held out pacific doctrine to the agent, disclaiming everything like hostilities to his white brethern. He requested the agent to pay no attention to news of a contrary import as it might interrupt his great and good intentions to maintain peace. Yet while he was lulling the agent into a belief of the rectitude of his heart, two Indians arrived from Tecumseh who is at Malden and has espoused the cause of the British with speeches to be circulated among the Indians, wanting them to be united for the purpose of assisting him in behalf of the British. Accordingly two young men of the Kickapoo tribe were despatched from this place by the Prophet to his town to further the plan. In order to facilitate the business, they stole two horses from Captain Wells, the most valuable in the country. The two Indians that came from Malden stole a horse in the neighbourhood of the River Raisin which gave out a few miles below this place. Two days after the Prophet despatched those two young men to his village, he and his party left here, which was the 22nd."

BRIG.-GENERAL HULL TO THE SECRETARY OF WAR.

(Defence of General Dearborn, by H. A. S. Dearborn; p. 11.)

Headquarters of the Northwestern Army, Sandwich.

July 21, 1812.

Sir:—

When I marched from Urbana, I proposed a general council of the Indians at Brownstown to be held the beginning of this month. I have held frequent councils with the chiefs and my proposition to them was neutrality.

I have just received the result of the council of nine nations counting the Six Nations as one. The nations are the Ottawas, Chippewas, Pottawatomies, Delawares, Wyandots, Munsies, some Kickapoos, Six (Sioux?) and the Six Nations. Tarhe or the Crane, Miere or Walk-in-the-water, Blackhoof, Col. Lewis and Wolf have made great exertions to detach the Indians from the British standard. At the close of the council they sent speeches to all the nations informing them of the result. I have now informed them they must proceed immediately to the grand council at Piqua. Tecumseh and Marpot are the only chiefs of consequence remaining with the British.

CAPTAIN WILLIAM WELLS[1] TO GOVERNOR HARRISON.

(Historical Narrative of the Civil and Military Services of Major-General Wm. H. Harrison, by Moses Dawson; Cincinnati, 1824; p. 278.)

Fort Wayne, July 22, 1812.

Sir,

I consider it a duty that I owe to my country, particularly to the inhabitants of Vincennes, to make the following state-

---

[1] Captain William Wells was born in 1770 in Kentucky. When 12 years old he was taken prisoner by the Miamis Indians, and adopted as a son of Chief Little Turtle. In 1790 he deserted them and became a captain of scouts in Wayne's army. In 1795 when peace was made he became an Indian agent and a justice of the peace. See also letter of Captain Heald to Secretary of War, p. 225.

ment to you. On the 17th June, Tecumseh arrived at this place, and said he was on his way to Malden, to receive from the British government twelve horse loads of ammunition, for the use of his people at Tippecanoe. He went on to Malden and arrived at that place a few days before general Hull with his army arrived at Detroit, and immediately declared that he would join the British against the United States.

On the 12th instant, his brother the Prophet arrived at this place, with nearly one hundred Winebagoes and Kickapoos, who have ever since been amusing the Indian agent at this place with professions of friendship, and it is now evident that he has completely duped the agent, who has suffered him to take the lead in all his councils with the Indians, giving him ammunition, &c. to support his followers until they can receive a supply from Tecumseh.

On the 19th instant an express arrived in the prophet's camp from Tecumseh. In order that it should make the better speed, the express stole a horse from some of the inhabitants of the river Raisin, and rode night and day. The horse gave out within twenty miles of this place. This express was directed by Tecumseh to tell the prophet to unite the Indians immediately, and send their women and children toward the Mississippi, while the warriors should strike a heavy blow at the inhabitants of Vincennes; that he, Tecumseh, if he lived, would join him in the country of the Winebagoes.

The prophet found no difficulty in keeping this information to himself and one or two of his confidential followers, and forming a story to suit the palate of the agent here; and on the 20th instant, despatched two confidential Kickapoos to effect the objects Tecumseh had in view; in order that these Indians might make the better speed, they stole my two riding horses, and have gone to the westward at the rate of one hundred miles in twenty-four hours at least. To keep the agent blind to his movements, the prophet went early in the morning yesterday, and told the agent that two of his *bad* young men were missing, and that he feared they had stole some horses; the agent found no difficulty in swallowing the bait offered him, and applauded the prophet for his honesty in telling of his bad men, as he called them, stealing my horses.

To keep up appearances, the prophet has this morning despatched two men on *foot*, as he tells the agent, to bring back my horses, &c. And that he and all his party will certainly attend the commissioner of the United States next month at Piqua.

This he will do, if he finds he cannot raise the western Indians against the United States; but if he finds the western Indians will join him, you may rely on it, he will strike a heavy blow, as Tecumseh says, against the whites in that quarter. You may rely on the correctness of this statement, as I received information relative to the views of Tecumseh, last night, from a quarter that cannot be doubted; the conduct of the agent towards the prophet I have been an eye witness to.

I send this letter by an Indian to fort Harrison, and hope you will authorize me to pay him twelve dollars. General Hull is now in Sandwich, with his army: I heard from him last night. It is believed that the British will make little or no defence in Malden. The Indians have all, with the exception of Tecumseh and about one hundred, abandoned the British: it is supposed that Malden has surrendered to general Hull before this time.

P.S. The prophet and his party leave this to-day for Tippecanoe. I have no reason to believe that he has sent after my horses. He will remain at his village until he knows the intentions of the western Indians; if they wont join him, he will then go and endeavor to save himself by pretensions of peace to the commissioners at Piqua.

BRIG.-GENERAL HULL TO THE SECRETARY OF WAR.

(Report of the Trial of General Hull; New York, 1814; App. II, p. 10.)

Detroit, July 22d, (1812), 5 o'clock A.M.

Sir—yesterday afternoon I passed over to this place with Lieutenant Colonel Miller and one battalion of the 4th regiment, for the purpose of accelerating the preparations for the siege of Malden. I find that entirely new carriages must be built for the 24 pounders and mortars; it will require at least two weeks to make the necessary preparations; it is in the power of this army to take Malden by storm, but it would be attended, in my opinion, with too great a sacrifice under the present circumstances.

I am making preparations for an attempt on the "Queen Charlotte."

If Malden was in our possession I could march this army to Niagara or York in a very short time.

PROCLAMATION OF MAJOR-GENERAL BROCK.

(Canadian Archives, Q 315, p. 152.)

PROCLAMATION.

The unprovoked declaration of War, by the United States of America, against the United Kingdom, of Great Britain and Ireland, and its dependencies, has been followed by the actual invasion of this Province in a remote Frontier of the Western District by a detachment of the Armed Force of the United States. The Officer commanding that detachment has thought proper to invite his Majesty's subjects not merely to a quiet and unresisting submission, but insults them with a call to seek voluntarily the protection of his Government. Without condescending to repeat the illiberal epithets bestowed in this appeal of the American Commander to the People of Upper Canada, on the Administration of his Majesty, every Inhabitant of the Province is desired to seek the confutation of such indecent slander in the review of his own particular circumstances: where is the Canadian Subject who can truly affirm to himself that he has been injured by the Government in his person, his liberty, or his property? Where is to be found in any part of the world, a growth so rapid in wealth and prosperity as this Colony exhibits,—settled not thirty years by a band of Veterans exiled from their former possessions on account of their loyalty, not a descendant of these brave people is to be found, who under the fostering liberality of their Sovereign, has not acquired a property and means of enjoyment superior to what were possessed by their ancestors. This unequalled prosperity could not have been attained by the utmost liberality of the Government or the persevering industry of the people, had not the maritime power of the mother Country secured to its Colonists a safe access to every market where the produce of their labor was in demand.

The unavoidable and immediate consequence of a seperation from Great Britain, must be the loss of this inestimable advantage, and what is offered you in exchange? to become a territory of the United States and share with them that exclusion from the Ocean, which the policy of their present Government enforces.—you are not even flattered with a participation of their boasted independence, and it is but too obvious that once exchanged (estranged) from the powerful protection of the United Kingdom you must be reannexed to the dominion of France, from which the Provinces of Canada were wrested by the Arms of Great Britain, at a vast expense of blood and treasure, from no other motive than to *relieve* her ungrateful children from the oppresion of a cruel neighbor: this restitution of Canada to the Empire of France was the stipulated reward for the aid afforded to the revolted Colonies, now the United States; the debt is still due, and there can be no doubt but the pledge has been renewed as a consideration for Commercial Advantages, or rather for an expected relaxation in the Tyranny of France over the Commercial World.— Are you prepared Inhabitants of Upper Canada to become willing subjects or rather slaves to the Despot who rules the nations of Europe with a rod of Iron? If not, arise in a Body, exert your energies, co-operate cordially with the King's regular Forces to repel the invader, and do not give cause to your children when groaning under the oppression of a foreign Master to reproach you with having too easily parted with the richest Inheritance on Earth.—a participation in the name, character and freedom of Britons.

    The same spirit of Justice, which will make every reasonable allowance for the unsuccessful efforts of Zeal and Loyalty, will not fail to punish the defalcation of principle; every Canadian Freeholder is by deliberate choice, bound by the most solemn Oaths to defend the Monarchy as well as his own property; to shrink from that engagement is a Treason not to be forgiven; let no Man suppose that if in this unexpected struggle his Majesties Arms should be compelled to yield to an overwhelming force, that the Province will be eventually abandoned; the endeared relations of its first settlers, the intrinsic value of its Commerce and the pretensions of its powerful rival to repossess the Canadas are pledges that no peace will be established between the United States and Great Britain and Ireland, of which the restoration of these Provinces does not make the most prominent condition.

    Be not dismayed at the unjustifiable threat of the Commander of the Enemies forces to refuse quarter if an Indian appear in the Ranks.—The brave bands of Natives which inhabit this Colony, were, like his Majesty's Subjects, punished for their zeal and fidelity by the loss of their possessions in the late Colonies, and rewarded by his Majesty with lands of superior value in this Province: the Faith of the British Government has never yet been violated, they feel that the soil they inherit is to them and their posterity protected from the base Arts so frequently devised to over reach their simplicity. By what new principle are they to be prevented from defending their property? If their Warfare from being different from that of the white people is more terrific to the Enemy, let him retrace his steps—they seek him not—and cannot expect to find women and children in an invading army; but they are men, and have equal rights with all other men to defend themselves and their property when invaded, more especially when they find in the enemies Camp a ferocious and mortal foe using the same Warfare which the American Commander affects to reprobate.

This inconsistent and unjustifiable threat of refusing quarter for such a cause as being found in Arms with a brother sufferer in defence of invaded rights, must be exercised with the certain assurance of retaliation, not only in the limited operations of War in this part of the King's Dominions but in every quarter of the globe, for the National character of Britain is not less distinguished for humanity than strict retributive Justice, which will consider the execution of this inhuman threat as deliberate murder, for which every subject of the offending power must make expiation.

      ISAAC BROCK,

        Maj. Gen. and President

GOD SAVE THE KING.

Head Quarters Fort George
  22nd July, 1812.

By order of His Honor the President

J. B. GLEGG, Capt. A.D.C.

MILITIA GENERAL ORDERS.

(From an Order Book of Lt.-Colonel John Macdonell.)

Headquarters, Fort George, 22d July, 1812.

Militia Genl. Orders.

Colonel Talbot[1] will make detachments from the First and Second Norfolk and Oxford and Middlesex Regiments of Militia to consist together of two hundred men with a proportionate number of officers, the whole to be placed under the command of Major Salmon[2] of the Second Regiment of Norfolk Militia. This detachment will be assembled as soon as possible in as complete a state as circumstances will admit for service. Major Salmon will proceed with this force to the Moravian Town on the River Thames where he will await the arrival of Major Chambers[3] under whose command he will place himself.

By order of the Major-General,

J. MACDONELL, P.A.D.C.[4]

[1] Thomas Talbot, born at Malahide Castle near Dublin in Ireland, July 19, 1771, was appointed an ensign in the 66th Regiment of Foot, May 14, 1783; promoted to be lieutenant in the 24th Regiment, December 28, 1787; captain in the 85th Regiment, November 21, 1793; major, March 6, 1794; lieutenant-colonel in the 5th Regiment, June 12, 1796; aide-de-camp to Lieutenant-Governor Simcoe, 1791-94; retired December 25, 1800. He settled at Port Talbot in Upper Canada, May 21, 1803, and began the settlement named after him. He was appointed lieutenant for the county of Middlesex in 1804; elected a member of the Legislative Assembly for Upper Canada in 1809; and made colonel of the 1st Regiment of Middlesex militia on February 12, 1812. He died at London, Ontario, February 5, 1853.

[2] George C. Salmon, a native of England, was appointed major in the 2nd Regiment of Norfolk militia, February 13, 1812; on this occasion he commanded detachments of the 1st and 2nd Norfolk, 5th Lincoln and 2nd York.

[3] Peter Latouche Chambers was born in 1788; and commissioned as ensign in the 41st Regiment of Foot, June 21, 1803; promoted to be lieutenant, April 19, 1806, and captain, May 14, 1808. He was awarded a gold medal for his services at Detroit; and appointed deputy assistant quartermaster-general to the Right Division, February 14, 1813. He particularly distinguished himself by gallant conduct in a critical situation in the action at the Miami river, May 5, 1813, but was taken prisoner at Moraviantown, October 5, 1815, and detained upwards of a year in captivity. He was granted the brevet rank of major, February 25, 1815; and substantive rank, May 3, 1821. While leading a storming party in the assault of a stockade at Kemmendine in Burmah he received a severe wound in the face from a spear. He was granted the Cross of the Bath, April 12, 1826, and promoted to be lieutenant-colonel commanding the 41st Regiment, April 5, 1827. He died at Bangalore in Mysore, August 29, 1828.—"He was an officer of the first order; an extra-

CAPTAIN DANIEL SPRINGER[1] TO MAJOR-GENERAL BROCK.

(Canadian Archives, C 688A, p. 145.)

Delaware 23th (rd) July 1812

Please your Honor,

In Obedience to your letter of the 19th Instant, not having a Sufficient number of Men about me, that I Could trust to assist in apprehending the persons mentioned in your Letter, I immediately Sent to Lt Col.^{1} Bostwick[2] who was then in Oxford, on the twenty Second He and Lieu^t Merrit(t)[3] Came down to delaware, and on the twenty third made an attempt to take Ebenezer (Allan) and Some others about him who had been about his house for Several days, but did not Suceed, they apprehended two persons, John Micks (Meeks) and one

ordinary devotion to his regiment combined with a desperate valour being his chief characteristics."—*Lomax, 'History of the 41st Foot,' p. 372.*

[4] John Macdonell was born in Glengarry, Scotland, April 19, 1785. He studied law and was called to the bar of Upper Canada in Easter term, 1808. He was appointed attorney-general, November 28, 1811; and elected a member of the Legislative Assembly for the county of Glengarry at the general election of 1812. He was appointed a provincial aide-de-camp to Major-General Brock, April 15, 1812, with the rank of lieutenant-colonel in the militia. For his services in the expedition against Detroit he was awarded a gold medal. He died, October 14, 1812, of wounds received in the action at Queenston the day before.

[1] Daniel Springer was a native of Albany county, in the state of New York, who emigrated to Upper Canada in 1798. He was appointed captain of a flank company of the 1st Middlesex militia, February 13, 1812. On January 31, 1814, he was taken prisoner at his home by a raiding party guided by Andrew Westbrook, and carried off to Kentucky, but escaped in time to share in the battle of Lundy's Lane.

[2] Henry Bostwick was born in New Jersey in 1782. He studied law and was admitted to the bar of Upper Canada. Although a resident of the county of Norfolk he was selected by General Brock for the command of the 1st Regiment of Oxford militia to which he was appointed with the rank of lieutenant-colonel, February 12, 1812. He commanded a detachment of the Norfolk militia in a successful attack on a band of marauders near the mouth of Nanticoke creek, November 13, 1813. He died at his residence in the township of Woodhouse, July 27, 1816.

[3] William Hamilton Merritt, the son of Thomas Merritt, formerly an officer in the Loyalist Corps of Queen's Rangers, was born at Bedford in the state of New York, July 3, 1793. He became a resident of Upper Canada with his parents in 1796, and served through the war as an officer of the Provincial Dragoons. He was taken prisoner at Lundy's Lane, 1814. In 1824, he succeeded in forming a company for the construction of the Welland Canal, of which he became manager and head agent. He was elected to represent the county of Haldimand in the Legislative Assembly of Upper Canada, and held the seat until the union of the provinces, when he was elected for the north riding of the county of Lincoln. In 1848, he became a member of the Baldwin-Lafontaine administration as president of the Council; and in 1850 was appointed commissioner of Public Works, but resigned a few months later. He continued to represent the same constituency in the Legislative Assembly until 1860, when he was elected to represent the Niagara district in the Legislative Council. He died at Cornwall, U.C., July 5, 1862.

McClemings by name, on Suspicion of given Ebenezer and his party notice, I Certify that the Suspicion is on good grounds, they are hired men to one andrew Wes(t)brook[1] of this place who has been with Some others of his men very intimit with Ebenezer allen Since his arival from Sandwich the Said Ebenezer Allan brought with him General Hulls Proclamation whom he did read to the people, on the nineteenth this westbrook and his men was at Ebenezer allans, and remained untill Some time in the evening, and I believe Convert with Simon Z Watson[2] who was then there as appears by every Circumstance, this Wes(t)brook Publickly declare(d) that he would not take up arms against General Hulls force, that he had to(o) much at Stake, there, likewise was a petition in the Hands of one of his hired men address(ed) to General Hull representing myself to be a troublesome Person, that I was Continually urging the Inhabitants to take up arms and defend themselves, that if Consistant to have me removed from amung them, this was given under oath this day by Mary Allan, this man who had the petition was one thomas Wescoat who is gone to the americans—and this andrew Wes(t)brook was heard to Say addressing himself to another person that, Wescoat was

[1] **Andrew Westbrook**, a blacksmith, residing in the township of Delaware, was a comparatively recent immigrant from the United States. An official return of persons in the London district who had joined the enemy, dated December 13, 1814, and signed by John Bostwick, sheriff of the district, states that he owned lands in the townships of Delaware, Oxford, Dorchester and Blenheim, and in the county of York. He made his escape to the United States, and during 1814 conducted many small raiding parties from Detroit into Upper Canada, whose chief object seems to have been to destroy the property of the loyal inhabitants and to disorganize the militia by capturing and carrying off the most active officers. Lieutenant-Colonels Burwell and Francis Baby, assistant quartermaster-general of militia, Captains Brigham, Curtis and Springer were taken by these parties at different times. Thomas L. McKenney in his book, entitled '*A Tour to the Lakes*,' published in 1827, relates that he found Westbrook residing on lands granted him by the government of the United States in the neighbourhood of Fort Gratiot in Michigan, and describes him as a large, red-haired, rough-featured man who had been a noted partisan in the war with Great Britain. Major Richardson apparently selected him as the model for the character of Desborough in his novel, '*The Canadian Brothers.*'

[2] **Simon Zelotes Watson** was a land surveyor, and had been a justice of the peace in the district of Montreal in Lower Canada. In 1810 he undertook to settle three hundred families from Lower Canada and the United States in the London district. Subsequently he had a bitter quarrel with Colonel Talbot over the terms of settlement, and as Talbot was supported by the government, he became hostile to it also. The temporary or local rank of colonel or lieutenant-colonel was apparently conferred on him by General Hull, who seems to have been greatly impressed by his statements. He escaped capture when Detroit was surrendered, and on August 20, 1813, was appointed topographical engineer with the rank of major in the army of the United States for Military District No. 8, which comprised the states of Kentucky and Ohio and the territories Illinois, Indiana, Michigan and Missouri.

not a fit Person to Conduct that business that he would Hang himself, the proclamation of General Hull has Such an effect on the minds of the People that I dare not trust them on any occation whatever and Conceive myself in danger, the enemy is about two or three times a week within thirty miles of me, and Spyes Continualy among the People,—when the gard Stopt to refresh themselves Ebenezer Allan Came boldly up to them, and they made him a prisoner, Lieut. Merrit(t) took him and the two other persons into Custody, and promised to Deliver them Safe at niagara, I believe that It Can be proved that Ebenezer Allan and that Syrous Hullbird came in Company with Simon Z Watson and one norton from the american troops

DEPOSITION OF ANNA BICROFT.

(Canadian Archives, C 688A, p. 142.)

Upper Canada } London district } Personally appeared before me Daniel Springer Esquire one of his majestys Justices of the peace in and for the Said District, anna bicroft, who maketh oath and Saith that on the night of the twenty Second Instant, (she) heard John meeks and one McClemings Say that one burns(?) had told them that there was thre(e) flank Companys of British troops at McMillens and Saith that on the twenty third Instant at the breake of day the Said John meeks and McClemings Came and got Some powder and ball from this deponent, and whent off, and further this deponent Saith not.

Sworn before me
  this 23^d Day of July 1812   ANNA X BICROFT.
  Daniel Springer J.P

DEPOSITION OF WILLIAM HAMILTON MERRITT.

(Canadian Archives, C 688A, p. 143.)

Upper Canada } London district } Personally appeared before me Daniel Springer Esquire one of his majestys Justices of the peace in and for the Said district Lieu^t William Merrit(t), Who maketh oath and Saith, that on meeting John Meeks and one McCleming, and that they, immediately on Seeing this deponent fled into the woods—and Saith that he took McClemings laying under a Log, and asked McCleming who was with him, he replied no body, this deponent told him, that it was no use to deceive him that he had Seen another man with him, the Said McCleming then replied, that the man had gone on the other Side of the road and in to the woods, this deponent then asked him where he was going, answered to Williams, a little forwards, John Meeks was taken a little distance from McClemings, and this deponent asked him where he was going answered to McMillens, this deponent, asked him what he was going there for, meeks made answer that he had heard there was a Company of Militia or horse, this deponent asked him Whither they were americans or brittish—and that he would not give him a decent answer and further this deponent Saith not

Sworn before me
this 23^d day of July 18(1)2   W^m. H. MERRITT.
  Daniel Springer J.P

ARCHIBALD McMILLEN TO ANDREW WESTBROOK.

(Canadian Archives, C 688B, p. 9.)

Friday 28th Augt 1812

D^r friend

I understand there are some of the guards in Delaware who are Determined to take me if possible in order to get the letter I have for you from your friend in Sandwich therefore I dare not be seen I wish you to meet me at the mouth of Allens Cove at nine Oclock tomorrow morning I got a friend to slip this in the hand of the express for fear he should see me—as it will be much in your favour to Receive those letters of advice from your friend before you are taken—I have hopes you will Not fail to Meet me at the time & place appointed

Arch^d McMillen

(Addressed)
  Mr Andrew Wes(t)brook
    Woods

DEPOSITION OF CHARLES NICHOLS.

(Canadian Archives, C. 688B, p. 13.)

Upper Canada } Personally appeared before me Daniel London district } Springer Esquire one of his majestys Justices of the peace in and for the Said district, Charles Nichols who maketh oath and Saith, that he Saw Andrew Westbrook at detroit before it was given up, and heard the Said Andrew Westbrook Say, that he wished that the americans had taken the whole province of Upper Canada at the time they Crossed the detroit river and this deponent further Saith that it was generally reported in Detroit that the Said Andrew Westbrook applied to General Hull for permission to Come up the river thames with a detachment of men to assist in takin(g) the province of Upper Canada, and Saith that he heard the Said Andrew Westbrook Say that he had Volunteered in Detroit Militia in order to go down the river on an expedition

CHARLES NICHOLS

Sworn before me the 29th Day }
of August 1812— }
Daniel Springer.

COLONEL PROCTER TO MAJOR-GENERAL BROCK.

(Canadian Archives, C 676, p. 242.)

Copy

Amherstburg July 26th 1812

Dear Sir

After much vexatious delay from very windy weather &c.[a] I arrived here at day break this morning. You received by the *Hunter* a correct statement of the Enemy's force and have since been informed that he crossed the River on the 12th instant and took post above Sandwich—On the evening of the 16th he attacked a Picquet, and I regret to say, cut off two Sentries of the 41st Regiment, who were on the other side (of) the Bridge on the River Canard, and killed one & wounded the other, both refusing to surrender. There has been Skirmishing two or three times on the Canard which is about five miles from here, in which the Enemy have lost men—On the 25th they advanced to a Fork of the River were attacked by the

Indians and retreated with the loss of some killed; the Indians having one killed and another wounded. I send you a Return of the Strength of the Garrison of Amherstburg by which you will perceive how much the Militia have diminished—It is said and I hope many of them will return when they have gotten in their harvest, but neither the Militia nor the Indians who are very deficient of the number you would suppose will ever remain with us if a considerable reinforcement does not arrive here. Five hundred of the 41st would I am confident, soon decide matters—The Enemy's Arts and Misrepresentations have operated strongly on both the Indians and People of this country, among whom their agents now appear. You have received Mr Hull's infamous Proclamation, and I herewith send you a copy of what I conceive to be very interesting Letters from him, intercepted and which I regret were not sent sooner. The originals shall be sent by the *Lady Prevost* I do not apprehend that this Post is in any immediate Danger, but I am fully convinced of the necessity of a Reinforcement. I conceive it only prudent to keep the *Queen Charlotte* here, she is a very considerable check on the Enemy. I inclose a Return of Prisoners and request to know whether they are to be sent down. You will be surprised to know that the greatest number of Indians, among whom were several Boys, that the utmost exertions of the Indian Department could collect did not exceed Two hundred and thirty—this was on the 18th instant and they have rather decreased since—

P.S. The Return is inclosed to the Brigade Major

MAJOR-GENERAL BROCK TO SIR GEORGE PREVOST.

(Canadian Archives, C 676, p. 208.)

Fort George July 26th 1812

Sir,

Since my dispatch to your Excellency of the 20th Instant, I have received information of the enemy having made frequent and extensive inroads from Sandwich up the River Thames. I have in consequence been induced to detach Captain Chambers with about 50 of the 41st Regim^t to the Moraviantown where I have directed two hundred Militia to join him—From the loud and apparently warm professions of the Indians residing on the Grand River, I made no doubt of finding at all times a large majority ready to take the field, and act in conjunction with our troops, but accounts received this morning state that they have determined to remain neutral, and had in consequence refused (with the exception of about 50) to join Captain Chambers' detachment

I meditated, the moment I could collect a sufficient number of Militia, a diversion to the westward, in the hope of compelling General Hull to retreat across the river, but this unexpected intelligence has ruined the whole of my plans—The Militia which I destined for this service, will now be alarmed, and unwilling to leave their families to the mercy of 400 Indians, whose conduct affords such wide room for suspicion—and really to expect that this fickle race would remain in the midst of war in a state of neutrality is truly absurd—The Indians have probably been led to this change of sentiment by emissaries from General Hull, whose proclamation to the six nations is herewith enclosed—[1]

I have not deemed it of sufficient importance to commence active operations on this line by an attack on Fort Niagara—It can be demolished when found necessary in half an hour, and there my means of annoyance would terminate—To enable the Militia to organize some degree of discipline without interruption is of far greater consequence than such a conquest—

Every thing shall be done in my power to overcome the difficulties by which I am surrounded but without strong reinforcements, I fear the Country cannot be roused to make exertions, equal, without support, to meet the present crisis—

I proceed immediately to York to attend the meeting of the Legislature—I hope to return on Wednesday—The charge of this frontier will in the mean time devolve on Lt Colonel Myers,[2] who appears worthy of every confidence—

The actual invasion of the Province has compelled me to recall that portion of the Militia whom I permitted to return home and work at harvest—I am prepared to hear of much discontent in consequence—The disaffected will take advantage of it and add fuel to the flame but it may not be without reason that I may be accused of having already studied to the injury of the service, their convenience and humour

---

[1] For text of this proclamation, see p. 72.
[2] Lieutenant-Colonel Christopher Myers, 70th Foot. He was made a deputy quartermaster-general, 1810; was wounded three times, and made a prisoner during the war.

I should have derived much consolation in the midst of my present difficulties had I been honored, previous to the meeting of the Legislature, with Your Excellency's determination in regard to this Province—That it cannot be maintained with its present force is very obvious, and unless the enemy be driven from Sandwich it will be impossible to avert much longer the impending ruin of the Country — numbers have already joined the invading army, commotions are excited, and the late occurrences at Sandwich have spread a general gloom

I have not heard from Lt Colonel St George, nor from any individual at Amherstburg, since I last had the honor of addressing Your Excellency, which makes me apprehensive that Colonel Procter has been detained on his journey too long for the good of the service—

The enemy's cavalry amounts to about fifty. They are led by one Watson, a surveyor from Montreal, of a desperate character, This fellow has been allowed to parade with about 20 men of the same description as far as Westminster, vowing as they went along the most bitter vengeance against the first characters of the Province—Nothing can more strongly shew the state of apathy which exists in that part of the Country— I am perhaps too liberal in attributing the conduct of the inhabitants to that cause

Mr Couche[1] has represented to the head of his department the total impracticability of carrying on the public service without a remittance in specie, or a government paper substitute—He was once in expectation of making arrangements with some individuals that would have enabled him to proceed, but I much fear the whole project has fallen to the ground— The Militia on this Communication was so clamourous for their pay that I directed Mr Couche to make the necessary advances. This has drained him of the little specie in his possession—

My present Civil office not only authorizes me to convene General Courts Martial for the trial of offenders belonging to the Militia but likewise the infliction of the sentence of death —whilst in regard to the Military my power is limited to the mere assembling of the court. I beg leave to submit to the consideration of Your Excellency whether in time like the present I ought not to be invested with equal authority over each service—

---

[1] Edward Couche, deputy commissary-general.

I herewith have the honor to transmit two letters one from Captain Roberts Comm^g at St Josephs, and the second from Mr Dickson a gentleman every way capable of forming a correct judgment of the actual state of the Indians Nothing can be more deplorable than his description Yet the United States' government accuse Great Britain of instigating that people to war—Is not the true cause to be found in the state of desparation to which they are reduced by the unfriendly and unjust measures of that Government towards them?

COLONEL THOMAS TALBOT TO MAJOR-GENERAL BROCK.

(Canadian Archives, C 688A, p. 153a.)

Oxford Monday 27th July 1812.

My dear General

I arrived at this place this morning from Long point where I had been two days, one spent in endeavouring to procure 100 Volunteers from the Norfolk Militia, and I am sorry to inform you that notwithstanding the apparent readiness manifested by the Flank Companies of those Batt^{ns} on former occasions, that when it was understood that the men required, were absolutely to proceed to The River Thames, very few turned out for that service, after much explanation of the expectations of the Government and the disgrace that would attend their Reg^{ts} I made out about 60 men, I then ballotted 40 more and ordered the detachment to march to join Major Chambers as yesterday morning, when I reached the ground from whence the Detachment was to march, I found a large assembly of the Farmers with their Women, who upon my approach addressed me, by declaring that their men should not March, upon this I enquired if there were any Magistrates present, the answer was, several, I required one to come forward, on which Mr Bemer appeared, I asked him, how he as a Magistrate could permit such proceedings, he offered no excuse, but said that he conceived the measure of withdrawing any of the Militia from Long point was highly improper. I then ordered the party to March, when about a half obey'd anl after proceeding a short distance the men fell out, all but about 20, who continued their march, and even those few appeared unwilling, I therefore thought it most prudent to allow those few to return as I could not flatter myself with any material benefit that could result from their weak and uncertain assistance—Major

Salmon who was present, I directed to proceed to Head Quarters and state the circumstances as they occurred to you.

Major Chambers is at this place with the Flank Companies of the Oxford Militia, Lt Col. Bostwick reports that they have generally volunteered, there are about 60 Rank & file, but I confess I am not disposed to place much reliance on their offers or services—not an Indian as yet and Major Chambers informs me that Norton[1] gave him to understand that 40 or 50 men would be the utmost that he could promise himself from the Grand River Tribes. Middlesex might furnish about 60 men but from Mr Bostwicks information, that those of Delaware and Westminster had sent a petition to Genl Hull for protection, you will be enabled to value the support that may be expected from that part of Middlesex—In fact, My dear Genl the prospect is dismal, unless there is some other resource that I am not acquainted with—I have advised Major Chambers not to advance his small and valuable party until he received orders from you or obtained such strength as might justify such movement—I have thought of going to Port Talbot for a day to oversee my affairs there, I'm most anxious to know your determination, if you should be forced to send to Genl Hull do let me know as those in promise of land on performing their settlement duties should be included in such conditions as may be entered into and something relative to myself—Mr Crooks[2] who is begging to be off requires my concluding by assuring you My Dear Genl that I am (&c.)

LIEUT.-COLONEL BOSTWICK TO MAJOR CHAMBERS.

(Canadian Archives, C 688A, p. 151.)

Oxford 27th July 1812

Sir,

In consequence of information communicated to me by Danl Springer Esqr of Delaware, I have thought proper to detain Andrew Westbrook at this place until the pleasure of Genl Brock can be known respecting him. Mr Springer informed me that Westbrook had been very officious in causing

---

[1] John Norton was a native of Scotland who had been adopted into the Mohawk nation of Indians under the name of Teyoninhokarawen, or the Snipe. He was granted the local rank of major in the army, February 15, 1816, in consideration of his good service during the war.

[2] Probably Captain William Crooks of the 4th Regiment of Lincoln militia. See pp. 236 and 237.

a Petition to be circulated, addressed to Gen¹ Hull, requesting him to save them & their property, stating that they would not take up Arms against him,———Also that Westbrook had declared that he (Westbrook) had too much property to risk it, by opposing the Americans, and further that Westbrook's nightly attendance was very frequent at the House of Ebenezer Allen, during the time Watson was there—and that he had advised the people of Delaware to commit the management of the Petition to Gen¹ Hull, to a more proper person than the one who had it.—

P.S. Mr Springer informed me that the Petition had been transmitted to Gen¹ Hull by One Westcoat—

H.B.

LIEUT.-COLONEL THE HON. JAMES BABY TO CAPTAIN GLEGG.

(Canadian Archives, C 676, p. 219.)

Copy

Dundas Street 30 miles from York 27th July
9 o'clock P.M.

Sir,

I am just arrived at this place—I hasten to write as I understand it is likely General Brock will go back to Niagara immediately—Should it be his pleasure to see me before he goes, I will be in York tomorrow as soon as I can—I have not been able to procure a fresh horse, mine is completely tired after a jaunt by the way of Pointe Pélé. I coasted the lake to Colonel Talbot's Settlement—I left Amherstburg in the afternoon of last monday. I met Colonel Procter on thursday, bound by the wind six or seven miles above Colonel Talbots—

From the weather we have had, he must be now at Amherstburg—On last saturday sen'night a party of about one hundred and fifty Americans came to the River Canard and skirmished with a party of our People, they wounded two men of the 41st one died, the other was expected also to die—the Americans were repulsed—The next day, Sunday, they returned to the same place, and began the skirmish; they were again repulsed, lost four men and had several wounded; they retreated with great precipitation and were followed by a few Indians some considerable distance; some of our Boats went as far as Turkey Creek, the Americans had already got beyond it, on their way to Sandwich—About eleven or twelve at noon on Monday last, the *Queen Charlotte* anchored opposite the mouth of the Canard, made signal that a large party was coming again to the Canard Bridge—A party of the 41st were on the South side of the Bridge and a good number of Indians had gone to join them—An Express came from the place where a third action had taken place, and informed that our party with two field pieces had repulsed the Americans who had brought four pieces with them—I have no doubt but they were more completely beaten than before—We were forced to come away before the issue—We had not more than about 230 Indians when I left Amherstburg—A report prevailed that about 300 were expected from the River Huron near the mouth of the River, and a like number from St: Josephs under Mr Robert Dixon. God grant they may be there— There were still between three and four hundred militia when I came away—A great number had withdrawn themselves to go to the harvest—I have no letters from Colonel St: George for the General, tho' he told me he would write—I called, and sent for his letter, but did not get it—He had gone to the river Canard. I am sorry to say that the volunteers of Long Point whom I saw yesterday have refused to march, not one is gone to join Major Chambers—I fear those of Oxford will follow their bad example—I parted with Colonel Talbot yesterday about four or five o'clock P.M. he was going to Burford—I should not omit to say there is a great want of balls for the Indians—The Hurons have done all they could to dissuade the other nations from Joining us—I heard that Norton instead of 150 or 200 of the six nations could hardly get fifty to go up to the westward—We want immediate assistance in that quarter, I write this from Dundas Street at John Clever's, and send it by a Missisagé to overtake you, before you go over—In case the General would wish for more information than I can give on this paper—I have written in the dark therefore excuse this scrawl—If the General goes round the Lake I may meet him at the Credit—

I give you this rough detail for his information—

SIR GEORGE PREVOST TO MAJOR-GENERAL BROCK.
(Canadian Archives, C 1218, p. 339.)

Quebec 27 July 1812

Sir/
I have the honor to acknowledge the receipt of your Letter of the 12th instant. I can readily understand the temper and disposition of your Militia, and can justly estimate the reluctance with which you submit to the seperation of any portion of them, after the difficulty of Assembling them for training and defence, from the experience I have lately aquired in bringing the Embodied Militia of Lower Canada into a proper state of subordination. With regard to your deficiency of Arms I have to lament my inability to meet your Wants, beyond the late supplies which have been forwarded to Upper Canada, as they consisted of a full proportion of what I possessed.

The loss of the *Cambo* Transport on board of which 6,000 stand of Arm's were embarked in England last autumn for this place, is a serious inconvenience, It has been stated to me, that this vessel left Bermuda in April last under convoy of His Majesty's Ship *Julia,* parted Company in a heavy gale and has not since been heard of.

You will ere this have received a supply of Materials probably sufficient to Clothe about 2,000 of your Militia, and I have now lirected the Commissary General[1] to purchase here immediately, (if they are to be had) 1000 or 1500 pairs of shoes, and to send them up as soon as possible.

In addition to the Cannon that has reached (you), four short 6 Pounders have been ordered to Kingston from Montreal.

Lieut: Col: Myers the Dep^y Quarter Mr General and Colonel Lethbridge[2] an Inspecting Field Officer of Militia have been sent to Upper Canada; the latter officer will I hope be found fit for the Command of the Eastern District.

To supply the Want of specie, recourse is about to be had in Lower Canada to a paper Money, as a Circulating Medium, and with the Assistance of the Legislature, who have met my wishes on the subject, I trust the Arrangement for putting in operation the substitute for specie, will speedily be com-

---
[1] William H. Robinson, afterwards knighted, took office October, 1811.
[2] Robert Lethbridge, who was made a major-general, June, 1813.

pleted,—when it takes effect I shall direct a Statement of the Plan to be transmitted for your information

The Scanty Reinforcement sent from England in the 103rd Regiment composed of about 750 very young Soldiers and Boy's, does not hold out an expectation of adding materially to your strength at present, but to support to the utmost your exertions for the preservation of the communication between Upper & Lower Canada, thereby securing in an extreme case of being attacked by an overwhelming Force, a retreat for the Regulars and Loyalists Embodied into this Province, Major Heathcote[1] with two Companies of the Royal Newfoundland Reg^t & a further supply of Stores will embark from hence for Kingston on Thursday.

At the same time as many Veterans as are fit for service belonging to the Companies in Upper Canada are under Orders to proceed with the Newfoundland Regiment.

From the Accounts you have transmitted me of the recent communication had with the Indians, they have appeared to be tractable beyond my expectations, however I am well aware their Faith is not to be relied on.

COLONEL TALBOT TO LIEUT.-COLONEL JOSEPH RYERSON.[2]

(Canadian Archives, Militia Papers, M. D., Vol. 31.)

Oxford 28th July 1812

Dear Sir

I was so much mortified at the behaviour of the Men belonging to The Norfolk Flank Companies in refusing to march, that I had nearly determined never to take any further command of The Militia of that County—but on my arrival at this place finding that a general disposition of zeal and Loyalty prevailed in the Flank Companies of this County and feeling the necessity of a firm attempt to force the body of the Enemy that has entered our Country to recross The River to Detroit, I conceive that if the Body of the Militia were assembled and the situation of the regulars and The Oxford Flank Companies under the Command of Lt Co^l Bostwick were explained to the men, that still there might be a

---

[1] Roland Heathcote, later made lieutenant-colonel.
[2] Lieutenant-Colonel Joseph Ryerson of the 1st Regiment Norfolk militia. He had been a lieutenant in the Prince of Wales' American Volunteers.

considerable number turn out to assist in this cause of relief to the Province I therefore request that you will assemble your Reg^t and use y^r influence in getting as many as you can and forward them under good officers to this Place, Cap^n Bostwick[1] who is going with me to Port Talbot will be back in a couple of days & he will accompany any of his men who may offer their services—

MAJOR-GENERAL BROCK TO SIR GEORGE PREVOST.

(Canadian Archives, C 676, p. 217.)

York July 28th 1812

Sir,

I consider the enclosed letter this instant received from the Honble James Baby of sufficient importance to forward by express—

I conceived the Long Point Militia the most likely to shew the best disposition of any in this part of the Country, and their refusal to join Captain Chambers indicates the little reliance that ought to be place(d) in any of them—My situation is getting each day more critical I still mean to try and send a force to the relief of Amherstburg, but almost despair of succeeding—The population, though I had no great confidence in the majority, is worse than I expected to find it. And all Magistrates &c &c appear quite confounded, and decline acting. The consequence is the most improper conduct is tolerated. The officers of Militia exert no authority, every thing shews as if a certainty existed of a change taking place soon But I still hope the arrival of re-inforcements may yet avert such a dire calamity. Many in that case would become active in our cause who are now dormant

I have the honor herewith to transmit a Copy of my Speech to the two houses delivered yesterday A more decent House has not been elected since the formation of the province—but I perceive at once that I shall get no good of them

They, like the magistrates and others in office, evidently mean to remain passive. The repeal of the Habeas Corpus

---

[1] Captain John Bostwick, a brother of Lieutenant-Colonel Henry Bostwick, was sheriff of the London district, and commanded a flank company of the 1st Norfolk regiment. He was wounded in action at Frenchman's Creek, near Fort Erie, on the night of November 28, 1812, and again at Nanticoke, November 13, 1813. He was promoted to be major, August 1, 1816, and lieutenant-colonel of the 3rd Middlesex militia, June 13, 1822.

will not pass. and if I have recourse to the Law Martial I am told the whole armed force will disperse Never was an officer placed in a more awkward predicament—The Militia cannot possibly be governed by the present Law—all admit the fact, yet the fear of giving offence, will prevent any thing effectual from being effected—I entreat the advice of Your Excellency! Some letters rec^d from individuals represent the conduct of the 41st above all praise—I cannot get a line from Colonel St George—Colonel Procter was provokingly delayed on his journey—I entreat Your Excellency to excuse the haste with which I presume to address you

CAPTAIN ROBERTS TO MAJOR GLEGG.

(Canadian Archives, C 688A, p. 154.)

Fort Michilimackinac 29^{tb} July 1812

Sir,

Although I am persuaded that the General's letter of the 4th of july leaves me at liberty to act in a great degree at discretion, yet it will be very satisfactory to learn that (in) what has been done here I may not be thought to have acted prematurely—The Prisoners of War and the American Citizens sailed from hence on the 26th inst. one of the vessels which surrendered under the capitulation has been employed as a cartel for this purpose—I have taken every precaution in my power for their safety, an Interpreter and three Indians well acquainted with the River St: Clair tribe, have been sent with them. Hugh Kelly, deserter from the 49th Regiment, ˙Alexander Parks from the Royal Artillery and Redmon(d) Magrath from the 5th were amongst the number that laid down their Arms, the two last I have employed being an excellent drum and fife, but they are all under confinement until the General's decision relative to them shall be known. Eighteen Canadians have taken the oath of allegiance and after much solicitation, volunteered to serve for a limited˙ period; these with two old men discharged from the late Canadian Volunteers, formed part of the American Garrison here.

Having no power to enlist, I have only taken them for the moment to strengthen me, but I find them so extremely awk(w)ard and ill inclined that I almost repent of accepting of their Services—Two small sloops on their way from the American Post at Chicago chiefly laden with furs have fallen into our hands, several letters sent by them have been intercepted, some of which I send you, that the state of that Garrison may be known, they are in general of little importance.

The Conduct of the Ottawas has been marked with suspicion throughout the whole of this business, the Bearer of these despatches was the person I sent from St: Josephs with orders for them to join us immediately, they did not arrive until several days after the surrender, and it is now evident they were encamped all this time at no great distance, waiting to hear the result of our attack.

Time I hope will inspire these people with more confidence, this lukewarm behaviour in them is more to be regretted as they must be considered our principal support. If I can accomplish my design of bringing over all the Chippewas from the neighbourhood of St: Josephs and settling them near this place, it will render us independant of these Ottawas, in whom I shall never have any reliance—I am now employed in organizing the Indians, one hundred, chiefly Riflemen are stationed at the Loopholes—a strong Guard is immediately to be sent to Bois blanc Island either to cut off if possible, or give timely notice of the approach of an Enemy—The remainder will be disposed of, as circumstances may require, my own men will be barely sufficient for manning the Guns in the Blockhouses, however you may rest assured, that every nerve shall be strained for the defence of this Post—There has been an immense consumption of provisions for some time past, but I am now getting rid of the supernumeraries, as fast as possible—

If the Importance of this (post) is viewed below, with the same anxiety, which prevails here, I should hope a Reinforcement will be spared, and I must beg leave to observe that none but active Aroops are fit to be employed here at this moment—The men I have here, tho' always ready to obey my orders are so debilitated, and worn down by unconquerable drunkenness, that neither the fear of punishment, the love of fame or the honor of their Country can animate them to extraordinary exertions, it is painful to me to be obliged to draw such a picture, but truth and justice demands it—The Establishment of Artillery should if possible be augmented to a Sergeant and nine—One Smith the Bearer of despatches from Detroit was taken by the Express I sent to Amherstburg about fifteen leagues from hence, they have taken him and his papers to that place, I wish he may not prove too cunning, and either make his escape or perhaps carry my despatches to Detroit—A Committee has been appointed, who have taken Inventories of all Property in the public Stores, a large portion is claimed as belonging to our own Subjects, but as this is a point I am unable to decide upon it must be left for regular investigation—Copies of all these documents shall be forwarded as soon as possible—The Stores in what the Americans called their Factory have been given over to the Indian Department and will barely recompense the Indians I brought with me, if the goods for these people do not soon arrive, I fear there will be great murmuring—

An officer has been left with six men at St Josephs to take care of the buildings, and an acting Interpreter appointed for that Post—On examination by an Engineer Officer, I apprehend many parts of these works will be found to require repair, and I should beg leave strongly to recommend that at a Post so distant from all aid, a certain number of artificers should be attached—I enclose you a return[1] of the American Garrison as it stood at the time of its surrender, and also a Return[2] of the Ordnance and ammunition, the brass guns, and Howitzers were taken it appears at York Town, and have an Inscription upon them, stating that fact—In the statement I have made above of the Indian force I have now employed, I must explain that altho' I can at this moment command double the number mentioned, yet such is the fluctuating disposition of these people that in a week hence, I might not be able to collect more than one hundred men.

The distant Indians who came with Mr Dickson, leave this tomorrow.

I am fully aware that there is a want of regularity and correctness in the style of this communication, which would be unpardonable at any other time, but the multiplicity and variety of matter which demands my constant attention will I trust be thought a sufficient excuse—As the situation I am now in, is entirely new to me and having to decide upon so many cases which occur almost daily, I shall feel greatly obliged to you if your time admits of it, for such information in matters of civil jurisdiction as the General may see necessary to put into immediate force—Report states the Americans to be in great force at Detroit, we have been so long without the arrival of a vessel or advice from that quarter that I am

---

1 and 2. See note 3, p. 65.

apprehensive our communications are obstructed—As the cargoes of the vessels from Chicago which were taken after the capitulation, and are I imagine of course legal prizes, are of a perishable nature, I shall be much obliged to you for advice how to act, so that this property may not be lost, I have appointed a prize Agent, but beyond this, I am totally in the dark as to what is next to be done.

Mem°. A Return[1] of provisions is herewith annexed

BRIG.-GENERAL HULL TO GOVERNOR SCOTT OF KENTUCKY.[2]

(Report of Trial of General Hull; New York, 1814; App. II., p. 12.)

Sandwich, U.C. 29th July, 1812.

Sir—in my letter of this date to the secretary of war, I have requested a reinforcement of 2000 men; 1500 from the state of Kentucky, and 500 from the state of Ohio. I hope, sir, you will consider yourself authorized to call them into service, and order them to the place of destination, before you receive particular instructions from the secretary of the department of war. I have just received information that Michilimackinac (situate 300 miles from here) has been taken by the British, ailed by about 1000 Indians.[3] The operations of this army has been hitherto successful, and it is of the greatest importance that the objects should be effected. I refer you to Mr. Carneal for every information respecting the situation of the army and the state of things. The men must be armed; we have no spare arms here.

MAJOR-GENERAL BROCK TO SIR GEORGE PREVOST. (EXTRACT.)

(Canadian Archives, C 676, p. 236.)

York July 29th 1812

Sir,

I have the honor to transmit herewith a dispatch this instant received from Captain Roberts announcing the surrender by Capitulation on the 17th Instant of Fort Michilimackinac—

The conduct of this officer since his appointment to the command of that distant part of the Province, has been dis-

---

[1] See note 3, p. 65.
[2] A copy of this letter was sent to Governor Meigs of Ohio.
[3] For the number of Indians in the engagement see despatch of Roberts to Baynes, 17 July, p. 65.

tinguished by much zeal and judgment, and his recent eminent display of those qualities, Your Excellency will find, has been attended with a most happy effect—

The Militia stationed here volunteered this morning without the least hesitation their services to any part of the Province—I have selected one hundred whom I have directed to proceed without delay to Long point—where I propose collecting a force for the relief of Amherstburg—This example, I hope, will be followed by as many as may be required—By the Militia law a man refusing to march may be fined five pounds, or confined three months, and although I have assembled the Legislature for the express purpose of amending the act, I much fear nothing material will be done. Your Excellency will scarcely believe that this infatuated House of Assembly have refused by a majority of two to suspend for a limited time the Habeas Corpus—

The Capture of Michilimackinac may produce great changes to the Westward—The actual invasion of the Province justifies every act of hostility on the American territory—

It was not until this morning I was honored with Your Excellency's dispatches dated the 7th and 10th Instant—Their contents, I beg to assure your Excellency, have relieve(d) my mind considerably—I doubt whether General Hull had instructions to cross to this side the river—I rather suspect he was compelled by a want of provisions—I embark immediately in the *Prince Regent* for Fort George, I return here the day after tomorrow, and probably dissolve the Legislature—

GARRISON ORDER.

(Toronto of Old, by Henry Scadding; Toronto, 1873; p. 79).

(York, 29th July, 1812.)

" In consequence of an order from Major-General Brock, commanding the forces, for a detachment of volunteers, under the command Major Allan,[1] to hold themselves in readiness to proceed in batteaux to the Head of the Lake to-morrow at 2 o'clock, for the purpose of being fitted with caps, blankets and haversacks, as well as to draw provisions. On their arrival at the Head of the Lake, regimental coats and canteens will be

---

[1] Major William Allan, 3rd Regiment of York militia, alterwards, 1816, a lieutenant-colonel.

ready to be issued to them, Capt Howard,[1] Lieut. Richardson, Lieut. Jarvis,[2] Lieut. Robinson.[3] Sergeants Knott, Humberstone, Bond, Bridgeford."

"Major-General Brock has desired me (Captain Stephen Heward) to acquaint the detachment under my command of his high approbation of their orderly conduct and good discipline while under arms: that their exercise and marching far exceeded any that he had seen in the Province. And in particular he directed me to acquaint the officers how much he is pleased with their appearance in uniform and their perfect knowledge of their duty."

EXTRACTS FROM AN AMERICAN NEWSPAPER, AUGUST AND SEPTEMBER, 1812.

A letter from Lt. Col. McArthur to Major Morris, dated Canada, July 24th, states:—I was detached up the Thames with 115 men and 20 cavalry. The men are sickly and some have died. The weather has been changeable; from the 5th to the 12th of July very hot, but lately we have had cold storms of rain and hail and very cold nights. When at the Canard on Sunday the *Queen Charlotte* fired several shots at us. Nobody was hurt but some badly scared.

Capt. Cook of the 4th U. S. Regiment writes from Sandwich on July 28th:—Since we have crossed into Canada we have had a few skirmishes. We have had three killed and one slightly wounded. The British had 1 killed and 1 wounded and taken prisoner. We expect to be ready to attack Fort Malden in 15 or 20 days. We are now about 2,000 strong and expect 2,000 reinforcements from Ohio. The enemy's

---

[1] Stephen Heward was captain of a flank company of the 3rd York militia. He was promoted to be major, May 31, 1816, and subsequently lieutenant-colonel commanding the 1st East York regiment.

[2] Samuel Peters Jarvis, son of Wm. Jarvis, Provincial Secretary. He was colonel of the Queen's Rangers during the Rebellion of 1837-38.

[3] Sir John Beverly Robinson, Bart., was born at Berthier, Lower Canada, July 26, 1791. He was appointed lieutenant in Captain Heward's flank company of the 3rd Regiment of York militia in April, 1812, and commanded the company in the action at Queenston. He was promoted to be captain, December 25, 1812. He acted as attorney-general of Upper Canada from the death of John Macdonell until the return of Hon. D'Arcy Boulton in 1815. He was solicitor-general from 1815 until 1818; attorney-general from 1818 until 1829; represented the town of York in the Legislative Assembly from 1820 until 1829; and was chief justice from 1829 until 1862. He died in Toronto, January 31, 1863.

strength is 270 English and about 500 Indians and Canadians; 360 have deserted *from Malden since* we have been here.

Major James Denny[1] writes from Sandwich on August 2d to Mr. J. Carlile:—Nearly all the inhabitants had left when we crossed over and the few that remained had removed all their best property to the woods and swamps.

A letter from a gentleman in Illinois dated August 20th states:—The Northwest trade is almost exclusively in the hands of British subjects who have routes by which to transport their goods. The first is through Lake Superior and westwardly and northwestwardly; the second through Lake Michigan to Green Bay, thence up Fox River, down the Ouisconsin and up the Mississippi and its various branches; the third is through Lake Michigan to the Illinois river and down it to its mouth. By the river Ottawa a great quantity of goods were last year brought to St. Joseph's, smuggled into this country by merchants in St. Louis as well as by the celebrated Dickson[2] and others.

On the first of May last two Indians were apprehended at Chicago on their way to meet Mr. Dickson at Green Bay. They had taken the precaution to put their letters in their moccasins and bury them in the ground and nothing being found on them, they were permitted to proceed. A Mr. Frazer from Prairie du Chien who went with Dickson to the portage of the Ouisconsin and who was present when the letters were received states that Dickson was informed by them that he might soon expect to see the British flag flying on the American garrison of Mackinac.

MAJOR-GENERAL BROCK TO COLONEL BAYNES.

(Canadian Archives, C 676, p. 239.)

York July 29th 1812

Dear Colonel,

I was not favored with your letters of the 8th and 10th Instant until this morning. I had not before received any official communication of war being declared, and I assure you began to fear I was wholly forgot. My situation is most

---

[1] Major James Denny of the 1st Regiment of Ohio Volunteers.
[2] Robert Dickson—see note p. 17.

critical, not from any thing the enemy can do, but from the disposition of the people—the population, believe me is essentially bad—a full belief possesses them all that this Province must inevitably succumb—this pre possession is fatal to every exertion—Legislators, Magistrates, Militia Officers, all, have imbibed the idea, and are so sluggish and indifferent in their respective offices that the artful and active Scoundrel is allowed to parade the Country without interruption, and commit all imaginable mischief—They are so alarmed of offending that they rather encourage than repress disorders or other (im)- proper acts. I really believe it is with some Cause they dread the vengeance of the democratic party, they are such a set of unrelenting villains, but to business—several of my letters must have miscarried, otherwise you would long since have been aware that I requested you to re-instate Lieu^t Johnston in the Glengarry Regiment. He may not be very efficient but then consider the claims of his family—Indeed the proposition came originally from you. Should Johnston be rejected, I am under previous engagements to *Lamont*[1] therefore cannot give ear to FitzGibbon's[2] application.

I have necessarily so many detachments along my widely extended frontier that I cannot possibly spare an Officer, I have therefore detained Lt Kerr of the Glengarry I am obliged to mix regulars with the Militia, otherwise I could not get on at all—It is a pity you did not understand his wishes in regard to the recruiting business.

What a change an additional regiment would make in this part of the Province!! Most of the people have lost all confidence. I however speak loud and look big—Altho' you may not be able to cast a look this far, you must not omit Johns- (t)o(w)n and Kingston, Some regulars will be highly necessary   I wish very much some thing might be done for Mr Grant Powell,[3] He was regularly brought up in England as a Surgeon I intended to have proposed to Sir George to appoint him permanent Surgeon to the Marine department, but I scarcely think the situation would now answer   His abilities I should think might be usefully employed now that so many troops are called out—

[1] Thomas Lamont, 49th Regiment, promoted to a lieutenancy in March, 1814.
[2] Lieutenant James Fitzgibbon of the 49th Regiment, afterwards distinguished for his able conduct in the action at Beaver Dams, June 24, 1813.
[3] A son of Wm. Dummer Powell, afterwards chief justice of Upper Canada.

Mess[rs] Dickson, Pothier and Crawford behaved nobly at the capture of Michilimackinac—This event may give a total change to the war in the West—Captain Roberts is spoken of in the highest terms—

COLONEL PROCTER TO MAJOR-GENERAL BROCK.

(Canadian Archives, C 676, p. 245.)

Copy/

Amherstburg July 30th 1812

Dear Sir,

The morning after my arrival I sent off Express to You the trusty Canadian by whom You had received Lieutenant Colonel S[t] George's Letter of the 11th inst, and on the evening of the 28th I had the disappointment of his return back, having narrowly escaped the Enemy near Point Aux Pins.—His Majesty's Schooner *Lady Prevost* sails this morning, as does also the Schooner *Nancy,* that these may be at Fort Erie, (as) Conveyance for an effectual Reinforcement, which from the Confidence it must inspire, would cause the return of many who have left the Militia, and also ensure a powerful Aid from the Indians of whom the Enemy are much in dread.—It would be imprudent to send away the *Queen Charlotte,* especially as the *Adams* is I understand nearly ready.—

M[r] Hull I believe awaits the defection of the Militia and Indians, and which I am confident will occur if we do not Soon receive a reinforcement.—The Enemy expects a Reinforcement, which, if received after we are enabled to Act, may be of less importance to him.—I am sorry to observe that the Individuals of the Indian Department are too Old for Actual Service, or does ability and Cordiality appear in the performance of its duties.—I have been under the necessity of Sanctioning the appointment of some active Interpreters.— With respect to the Militia Officers, I feel myself at a loss how to act; they are in number out of all proportion to the Strength of their Corps, and in general unequal to the performance of their Duties—If they should be retained in proportion to the strength only of their Corps, most of them would be driven, having no Support, to seek their property where the Enemy are, and their Corps, to which I still hope to see many return, would be disbanded.—I hope soon to hear of the Completion of the Arrangement for the payment of the Militia.—I found no sources ascertained for procuring certain information respecting the Enemy and which I might reasonably have expected, where it must have been so easily effected, if attended to in time, by residents in the interest of Government—

P.S. I have conceived it expedient to send by this Opportunity the four Officers who were detained Prisoners of War on the 2nd instant.

SIR GEORGE PREVOST TO THE EARL OF LIVERPOOL.

(Canadian Archives, C 1218, p. 347.)

N° 59

Quebec 30th July 1812—

My Lord/

I do myself the honor to report to your Lordship that I have this Morning received despatches from Major General Brock commanding in Upper Canada, conveying to me the intelligence that an American Army of *2000* Men under the Command of B. Gen¹ Hull had made its appearance at Detroit, and that a large Detachment from it had crossed on the 12 inst to our possessions in Upper Canada, and are now occupying the village of Sandwich a few Miles above Fort Amherstburg;

At Sandwich several Hundreds of the Militia with a small Detachment of regular Troops from the 41st Regiment and two Field pieces were collected to defend it, but the Enemy landing in several points so superior a force, occasioned our Troops and the Militia to retreat to Fort Amherstburg;

Immediately on the Enemys taking up his position at Sandwich B: Gen¹ Hull issued an artful and insidious proclamation,[1] (a copy of which I enclose for your Lordships information) and which I have reason to apprehend has already been productive of considerable effect on the minds of the People,—a general sentiment prevails in that part of Upper Canada, that with the present Force of the Enemy resistance is unavailing and great Numbers of the Militia have returned to their homes, under the promise held out to them by General Hull that if they remain at their Homes, their Persons and private Property will be respected, Lieut Colonel St George commanding at Fort Amherstburg states that not more than 470 of the Militia were with him on the 15th instant and those in such a state as to be totally inefficient in the Field; Lieut

---
[1] For this proclamation, see p. 56.

Colonel St George has also about 300 of the 41st Reg^t with him at Fort Amherstburg.

Were it possible to animate the Militia in that part of the Upper Province with a proper sense of their Duty something might yet be done, for its defence, Lt Col. St Georges position at Fort Amherstburg is very good and formidable—but should he be compelled to retire there is no alternative for him, than Embarking in the Kings Vessels and proceeding to Fort Erie;

By the report of the Captain of Engineers I sent to Amherstburg, I am informed that 20 pieces of Cannon are mounted in the Fort—the Platforms and Gun Carriages are all repaired—the four Bastions fraized and the escarp all round deepened—they have a large quantity of Timber in the Fort,—

a splinter proof Log Building has been thrown up and a small expence Magazine is in a state of forwardness.—

Major General Brock has enclosed to me the Copies of some interesting documents (3) found on board a schooner (captured by the Boats of His Majestys Schooner *Hunter*) on her Voyage from Miami to Detroit, which I have the honor to transmit herewith for your Lordships information.—

SIR GEORGE PREVOST TO THE EARL OF LIVERPOOL.

(Canadian Archives, C 1218, p. 345.)

N° 60

Quebec 30th July 1812

My Lord/

In addition to my dispatch N° 59 of this date, I have the honor to represent to your Lordship that the exhausted state of the Military Chest of the Canadas and the impossibility of replenishing it but from England, exposes His Majesty's service to serious difficulties, which will not altogether be removed by the operation of the Army Bill Law, which has passed the Honse of Assembly and is now with the Legislative Council;

I cannot doubt its affording much relief to our embarrassed Finances, altho' I shall have to contend in enforcing it with the deep rooted projudice of Canadian against a paper money;

I cannot more fully bring the subject before your Lordship than by enclosing a representation which has been made to me by the Commissary General of the embarrassments in his Department from the difficulties experienced in obtaining the smallest supply of Money.

Letter from Commissary General Robinson enclosed in the above.

Commissary Generals Office
Quebec 30th July 1812

Sir/

I have the honor to acquaint your Excellency that in addition, to the embarrassments I have lately laboured under in this Province, from the total want of specie so well known to you that I need not here detail them, I have this morning received a Letter from Deputy Commissary General Couche which occasions me the greatest alarm, he informs me that Major General Brock has ordered out one third of the Militia of Upper Canada (about 4000 Men) and he begs to be informed in what Manner they are to be paid.—The expence attending this measure will be about Fifteen Thousand Pounds a Month, a sum which it will be impracticable to find in that Country, Nor have I the means of affording effectual Assistance at this moment, and if the Militia are not regularly paid, great evil will ensue, indeed Mr Couche represents some symtoms of discontent have already appeared; Besides this expence, various other payments are also at a stand, tho' I have paid drafts of my sub accountants to a large amount lately, and more are daily presented to me, but still a sufficiency of Money cannot be raised in this Way, from the scarcity of specie; The prospect of a paper medium being immediately established here will be a relief to this Province, but without the concurrence of the Legislature of Upper Canada it cannot be counted upon as a certain assistance there. Yet I submit to your Excellency the expedience of trying the experiment by sending a Packet of our Notes as soon as they can be issued, with such recommendations to Genl Brock upon the subject, as you may deem adviseable

In Mr Couches former Letter of the 3rd instant, which I had the honor to lay before you; he had held out a prospect of relief from the establishment of a Paper Currency upon a limited scale, and under the auspices merely of the Merchants, upon which in his last Letter he is silent, therefore I conclude it has not produced the beneficial effects he expected.

Under all these Circumstances, I beg leave to suggest to your Excellency the Necessity of recommending to His Majesty's Government to use every endeavor to send out specie from England before the Navigation Closes, which for the reasons I have mentioned is requisite towards the aid of the other Province, and will also be extremely desirable in this, notwithstanding the prospect of a Paper medium, as I have reason to think the Lowest Note intended to be recognized by the Legislature is Four Dollars and these payable on demand in Cash.

DISTRICT GENERAL ORDER.

(Canadian Archives, Militia Papers, M.D., Vol. 31.)

Fort George 31st July 1812

D.G.O

The Major General Commanding is happy to announce to the Troops, under his Command, the Surrender of Michilimackinac, together with the ordnance Stores &ca. to His Majestys arms; the Garrison Prisoners of War. Too much praise cannot be given to Captain Roberts who commanded as well for his firmness and judgement during the preparations made for the attack as to ·his prudence which controled the feelings of his force, after the Enemy surrendered. The Major General Thanks those Gentlemen &ca in the neighbourhood who so honorably contributed to Capt. Roberts' exertions and is pleased and is pleased with the Conduct of the Indians, who on this Occasion directed by the Generous feelings of Britons; spared that Enemy which otherwise they could have annihilated.—

N° 2. The Major General announces with pride and satisfaction, the complete repulse of the Enemy, by that part of the army stationed at Amherstburgh on two seperat(e) Occasions and thanks them for their Gallantry—The Militia behaved honorably; the Indians with the most determined Spirit: but the conduct of the 41st Regiment, commanded the admiration of all who witnessed their heroic Valour. If the Enemy is thus made to sustain severe losses at the Threshold of our Territory by a small but determined band of United Troops what has he to expect from the whole Physical Force of the Province actuated by an ardor and Loyalty worthy their Sires—

N° 3   Commanding Officers will be attentive in ascertaining that all General Orders are read to the Troops composing the Militia Force

N° 4   Mr James Cummings is appointed to act in the Commissariat Department with the pay of 10/ per day and Forage for One Horse to Commence from the 24th Instant—

By order
    (Signed)   Thomas Evans[1]
                                B. Major—

SIR GEORGE PREVOST TO MAJOR-GENERAL BROCK.

(Canadian Archives, C 1218, p. 349.)

Quebec 31st July 1812

Sir/

I have received your Letter of the 20th instant accompanied by the copy of two Letters from Lieut Col. St George, who is in command at Amherstburg, and some interesting documents found on Board a Schooner which had been taken by the Boats of the Schooner *Hunter;*

In consequence of your having desired Colonel Procter to proceed to Amherstburg and of your presence being Necessary at the Seat of Government to meet the Legislature of Upper Canada, I have taken upon myself to place Major Genl Sheaffe[2] on the Staff to enable me to send him to assist you in the arduous task you have to perform, in the able execution of which I have great confidence; He has been accordingly directed to proceed without delay to Upper Canada, there to place himself under your Command.

I believe you are authorized by the Commission under which you administer the Government of Upper Canada to declare Martial Law in the event of Invasion or Insurrection it is therefore for you to consider whether you can obtain any thing equivalent to that power from your Legislature, I have not succeeded in obtaining a Modification of it in Lower Canada and must therefore upon the occurrence of either of

---

[1] Afterwards, 1855, General Evans. He served through the War of 1812, being wounded four times, and mentioned in despatches ten times.

[2] Major-General Roger H. Sheaffe took command at Queenston when Brock was mortally wounded. He administered the government of Upper Canada from October 1812 to June 1813.

those calamities declare the Law Martial unqualified, and of course shut the Doors of the Courts of Civil Law.

The Report[1] transmitted by Captain Dixon of the Royal Engineers to Lieut Colonel Bruyeres of the state of defence in which he had placed Fort Amherstburg, together with the description of Troops allotted for its defence, give me a foreboding that the result of Genl Hulls attempt upon that Fort will terminate honorably to our Arm's.

If Lt Col: St George is possessed of the talents and resources required to form a Soldier he is fortunate in the opportunity of displaying them.

Should Genl Hull be compelled to relinquish his operations against Amherstburg, it will be proper his future movements should be most carefully observed, as his late march exhibits a more than ordinary Character of enterprize.

Your supposition of my slender means is but too correct, Notwithstanding you may rely upon every exertion being made to preserve uninterrupted the communication between Kingston and Montreal, and that I will also give all possible support to your endeavors to overcome every difficulty.

The possession of Malden which I consider means Amherstburg appears a favorite object with the Government of the United States,—I sincerely hope you will disappoint them.

Should the intelligence which arrived yesterday by the way of Newfoundland prove correct, a remarkable coincidence will exist in the revocation of our orders in Council as regards America, and the declaration of War by Congress against England, both having taken place on the same day in London and at Washington, the 17th June.[2]

MAJOR P. L. CHAMBERS TO LIEUT.-COLONEL CHRISTOPHER MYERS AT NIAGARA.

(Canadian Archives, C 688A, p. 162.)

31st July 1812

From every account I can Collect I am led to imagine Watson has gone to the American army and Wes(t)brook is on

---

[1] For this report, see 48.
[2] War was declared on June 18th by the United States Congress. The orders-in-council were revoked in Great Britain on the 23rd of June, with the provision that such revokation become null and void if the American government refused to revoke certain acts against British armed vessels, and against commercial intercourse between the two countries.

his Way to the Same Place. I have therefore decided to move on to Delaware as there are a Number of Cattle and Plenty of Provisions to be procured there and it is doubtless the Intention of Watson to Return with such a Party as Shall be Sufficient to despoil that Part of the Country and of course prevent our advancing

Westbrook has twelve head of Cattle and above one Hundred Bushels of Corn.

Delaware is More Centrical and it is easier to Establish an Intercourse with Col Procter from that Place than here I shall move on today with ten Light Horse and some Militia— the Remainder of the Flank Companies with Major Touzely[1] goes off tomorrow with the 41st and Light Horse. I hope this arrangement may meet the General's approbation

We have accounts from Amherstburgh by an Indian of a Battle or rather Skirmish having taken Place in which the Indians behaved well and the Americans Lost about Thirty Men. I hope it may be true as a Trifling circumstance of that kind may Infuse ardour and confidence I shall write on my arrival at Delaware. I have seen Mr Springer a Magistrate highly spoken of by Colonel Talbot—on consideration we have thought better not to send the man alluded to in a Former Part of my Letter as we find he will be of some consequence in giv(ing) us Information. the Name of the man is Stiles. I am in hopes to have Intelligence shortly worthy of Communication.

BRIG.-GENERAL HULL TO THE SECRETARY OF WAR.

(Report of Trial of General Hull; New York, 1814; App. II., p. 11.)

Sandwich, U.C. August 4th, 1812.

Sir—At the time when the army under my command took possession of this part of the province of Upper Canada every thing appeared favourable, and all the operations of this army have been successful; circumstances have since occurred which seem materially to change our future prospects. The unexpected surrender of Michilimackinac and the tardy operations of the army at Niagara are the circumstances to which I

---

[1] Major Sykes Tousley, commanding flank companies of 1st Regiment Oxford militia.

allude. I have every reason to expect in a very short time a large body of Indians from the north, whose operations will be directed against this army. They are under the influence of the North and South-west Companies,[1] and the interest of these companies depends on opening the communication of the Detroit river this summer. It is the channel by which they obtain their supplies, and there can be no doubt but every effort will be made against this army to open that communication. It is the opinion of the officers and the most intelligent gentlemen from Michilimackinac, that the British can engage any number of Indians they may have occasion for, and that (including the *Engages* of N. W. and S. W. Companies) two or three thousand will be brought to this place in a very short time. Despatches have been sent to Malden and the messengers have returned with orders. With respect to the delay at Niagara, the following consequences have followed: a Major Chambers of the British army with 55 regulars and 4 pieces of brass artillery, has been detached from Niagara, and by the last accounts had penetrated as far as Delaware, about 120 miles from this place; every effort was making by this detachment to obtain reinforcements from the militia and Indians; considerable numbers had joined; and it was expected this force would consist of 6 or 700: the object of this force is to operate against this army. Two days ago all the Indians were sent from Malden with a small body of British troops to Brownstown and Maguag(a) and made prisoners of the Wyandots at those places. There are strong reasons to believe that it was by their own consent, notwithstanding the professions they had made. Under all these circumstances you will perceive that the situation of this army is critical. I am now preparing a work on this bank, which may be defended by about 300 men. I have consulted with the principal officers and an attempt to storm the fort at Malden is thought unadvisable without artillery to make a breach. The pickets are 14 feet high, and defended by bastions on which are mounted 24 pieces of Cannon.

I am preparing floating batteries to drive the *Queen Charlotte* from the mouth of the River Canards, and land them below that river; and it is my intention to march down with the army, and as soon as a breach can be made, attempt the place by storm. Circumstances, however, may render it necessary to re-cross the river with the main body of the army, to preserve the communication for the purpose of ob-

---

[1] See despatch from Gray to Prevost, p. 8, and memoranda, p. 11.

taining supplies from Ohio. I am constantly obliged to make a strong detachment to convoy the provisions between the foot of the Rapids and Detroit. If nothing should be done at Niagara, and the force should come from the north and the east, as is almost certain, you must be sensible of the difficulties which will attend my situation. I can promise nothing but my best and most faithful exertions to promote the honor of the army and the interest of my country.

GENERAL ORDERS.

(Report of Trial of General Hull; New York, 1814; App. II., p. 19.)

Detroit, August 4, 1812.

If Major Van Horne[1] should deem a larger force necessary to guard the provisions from river Raisin to Detroit, than the detachment under his command, he is authorized to order Captain Lacroix and fifty of his company to join him, and march on the whole or part of the way to Detroit. It must, however, be so arranged that his march back will be safe, if the company does not proceed the whole distance.

(Signed)   W^m. HULL.
Brig. Gen. Commanding.

LIEUT.-COLONEL JOHN ANDERSON, COMMANDING THE 2ND REGIMENT OF MICHIGAN MILITIA, TO BRIG.-GENERAL HULL.

(Report of Trial of General Hull; New York, 1814; App. II., p. 19.)

River Raisin, August 4, 1812.

Hon'd. Sir,

According to your order of the 10th July, I have this day called into actual service all the 2d regiment, except Captain D. Hull's[2] company, at the Miami. It appears that we are

---

[1] Major Thomas B. Van Horne of Findlay's Regiment of Ohio Volunteers, afterwards lieutenant-colonel of the 26th U.S. Infantry. He was mentioned in despatches for distinguished conduct in the action at Maguaga. See p. 140.

[2] Captain D. Hull, commanding a company of the 2nd Regiment of Michigan militia enrolled in the settlement near the rapids of the Miami.

invaded on all sides; a number of our citizens has been taken prisoners or killed between the river Huron and Swamp Creek (Swan Creek?), and they have been at Sandy Creek up the settlement, and skulking about. I now wisk to know if I will call Captain Hull's company into service, and how I will organize the regiment, and whether I will take the command as my present rank—if Captain Lacroix will be under my command or not. I am fearful this settlement will be all cut off, since the Wyandots have gone over; but I am determined to give them a brushing if they come here. I send Mr. Wm. Knaggs express to wait your answer; I refer you to him for further news. Wishing to hear what news the mail would give us, I thought proper to detain Mr. Knaggs until its arrival; but finding it did not arrive by nine o'clock this night (the 5th) I have closed my letter.

I am doubtful if the mail is not taken, but I hope not; I do all in my power to keep up the spirits of the inhabitants, which is all but exhausted. There is 40 men on guard and patrole at this place, and ten at the Other (Otter) Creek and will continue the same until further orders. We are short of ammunition if attacked, please to keep a little for us if possible. I wish to know how many men will entitle a captain to command. I understand, by good authority, that numbers of Indians is passing on the heads of this river and river Huron, on their way to Malden; and, I think, that if some plan is not taken soon, that they will be in thousands at that place before long; but we must not despair in the goodness of providence. I wish you to send Mr. Knaggs out as soon as possible to let us know the news, &c.

P.S. In behalf of the inhabitants, I request you will not order away any of the people from this place, for we are too few for its defence; if it was possible, to be succored would be best.

MAJOR-GENERAL BROCK TO COLONEL BAYNES.

(Canadian Archives, C 677, p. 1.)

York August 4th 1812

My dear Colonel

I shall probably not have to trouble Sir George by this conveyance. He must by this time be in full possession of the state of this Province—He must be sensible that considerable reinforcements are absolutely necessary, and that without them my Situation will very soon become very critical

The House of Assembly have refused to do any one thing they are required—The truth is that, with of course few exceptions, every body Considers the fate of the Country as already decided, and is afraid to appear conspicuous, in the promotion of measures in the least calculated to retard the catastrophe.

I cannot hear what is going on at Amherstburg. I begin to be uneasy for Procter, should any accident befall him I shall begin to despond for the fate of Amherstburg—I am collecting a force at Long point with a view to afford him relief, but until I receive information of the state of affairs in that quarter, I cannot move. The last letter f^m Col. St George is dated the 15th written three days after Gen. Hull crossed the River with his army—Mr. Baby com^g the Militia who has arrived here to attend his parliamentary duties, brought accounts to the 20th on which day, and at the very moment he was setting off, an attack was making on our post, the particulars of which he, of course, is unable to relate, but he heard that Some one had arrived from the field and stated that the enemy was retiring—An Indian has Since reported that he counted 30 dead bodies, and that the Americans had besides many wounded—This attack must have been made in great force—the instructions contained in the Governor's Commission authorize me to proclaim Martial Law in the event of invasion and by the 4th art of the 24 Sec: of the Mutiny Act "the General, Governor, or *Officer Commanding in Chief* for the time being is to appoint General Courts Martial " &c. I am in doubt whether I come within the above description—I neither Command in Chief, nor have I the King's Sign Manual to enable me to approve of the sentence of Courts Martial—These are delicate considerations—I believe I should resort to the experiment of declaring Martial Law, but for the above doubts, which cause me to hesitate— Do Militia Officers act during Martial Law indiscriminately with officers of the line? I am told the instant the law is promulgated the Militia will disperse. It may be so, but on the other hand I am convinced that unless strong coercive measures be adopted to restrain the infamous proceedings of the disaffected the province will be lost even without a struggle —A petition has already be(en) carried to Genl Hull signed by many inhabitants about Westminster inviting him to advance with a promise to join him—What in the name of heaven can be done with such a vile population—The ungrateful and infamous conduct of the Indians on the Grand River is still more mortifying. These fellows give me every inquietude. They afford the Militia a plausible pretext for staying at home —They do not like leaving their families within the power of the Indians—The moment Government be in a condition to do itself justice, the first step ought to be to expel the Indians from their present residence and place them out of the reach of doing mischief—My thoughts have been directed to the measures necessary to be adopted to Secure in case of necessity a retreat. The 41st is necessarily so Much scattered that I find the utmost difficulty to arrange any plan—I scarcely think the enemy will attack my front. He probably will prefer making a discent at Sugar Loaf, and another of greater magnitude half way to the head of the Lake or Burlington bay—I shall find the utmost difficulty to concentrate my small force for the instant I quit any part of the frontier a force it is reasonable to expect, will be in readiness to cross and press my rear—The Indians will then shew their true disposition, And as human nature in all instances in which it determines to forsake and act against a benefactor is found infinitely more rancorous and cruel, every thing horrid must be expected to be committed

I intended to have restored Lt Cartwright[1] to the Society of the 41st but the officers requested that I should save them the mortification. The fact is the general conduct of that officer has not given satisfaction—I of course could not press the measure, I have recommended his going to Quebec.

Do, my dear Colonel, write frequently independently of the post, and give me hopes of more troops—A regiment between Kingston and Montreal, and another here would change the face of affairs materially.

MAJOR-GENERAL BROCK TO SIR GEORGE PREVOST.

(Canadian Archives, C 677, p. 5.)

York, August, 4th 1812

Sir,

I have the honor to enclose a statement made by me yesterday to His Majesty's Executive Council which will fully

---

[1] Probably Lieutenant Edward Cartwright of the 41st Regiment, who was appointed adjutant of the Corps of Voyageurs, October 2, 1812, and a staff-adjutant, November 13, 1813.

apprize Your Excellency of my situation—The Council adjourned for deliberation, and I have no doubt will recommend the prorogation of the Assembly, and proclamation declaring Martial Law, but doubts occurred in contemplation of such an event, which I take the liberty to submit to your Excellency, and request the aid of your experience and Superior judgment—

1st In the event of declaring Martial Law can I without the Sign Manual approve and Carry into effect the Sentence of a General Court Martial—

2d Can I put upon a General Court Martial, after Martial Law is proclaimed, any Person not a Commissioned Officer in His Majesty's regular forces—In other words, can Militia Officers sit in conjunction with those of the line—?

Your Excellency, I feel confident, will readily excuse the direct manner which I presume to put my queries—Should Militia Officers be debarred sitting, the proclamation of Martial Law will be a perfect nullity—There is now a want of a sufficient number of Officers at any one place in this widely extended Province to compose a Court Martial and unless Militia Officers be admitted as members, the Law cannot operate—

I have the honor to be (&c.)

I am this instant informed that a motion was made in the House of Assembly and lost only by two voices that the Militia should be at liberty to return home if they did not receive their pay on a fixed day in each Month—Your Excellency will be sensible of the necessity of furnishing the Officer of the Commissariat at each post with the means of satisfying their demand—A paper medium would, I think, answer every purpose

A vessel has just anchored from Niagara from which I learn that Mrs Procter had received letters from the Colonel dated Amherstburg—

I had no idea of being detained here so long, and my dispatches being forwarded where I expected to be, prevents my announcing their contents to your Excellency by this opportunity—

I. B.

5th Augt

CAPTAIN J. B. GLEGG, A.D.C., TO COLONEL BAYNES.

(*Canadian Archives, C 677, p. 10.*)

York Wed: night 5th Augst 9 o'clock

Dear Sir,

Despatches from Amherstburg to the 30th Ult^o inclusive having reached this Post just as the General was preparing to prorogue the House of Assembly, the duty of enclosing copies of the most important documents for the information of His Excellency the Commander of the Forces has again devolved on me, during his unavoidable absence and occupation with the necessary arrangements to be adopted during the present crisis—The accompanying communications speak so fully respecting the actual state of our operations and resources near the scene of warfare that I shall refrain from intruding any remarks that private information has furnished—The General gave his assent this afternoon to a few Bills (none of them of any particular importance) and immediately prorogued the Assemblies until the 10th of Sep^{tr}—Their conduct in the past augured, very little for the future, and the absence of a *few* of the members from their respective Districts, was of too much importance to be prolonged under circumstances where so little real public advantage could be expected—The General will embark in a merchant vessel in one hour for the head of the Lake where it is propable he will arrive early tomorrow morning, and as arrangements are already made, it is probable he will reach Long Point tomorrow evening—It is probable a force will be found there, amounting to three hundred *picked* volunteers and 60 of the 41st with one 6 prd^r detached from the Car Brigade.

With this force it is highly probable every effort will be immediately made, to reinforce our friends at Amherstburg, and I am happy in being able to add that a great proportion of boats are now in readiness to carry that measure into execution. I cannot refrain from intruding an assurance that the General's presence at Long Point and elsewhere at the Head of the army will have the very best effect, and such is his popularity amongst the best *classes* of our population, that I feel confident in saying, that provided Genl Hull, has not overwhelmed our small, but gallant force at Amherstburg before the arrival of this Reinforcement, our united troops will give a good account of his army. On arriving at Long

Point I shall again do myself the honor of reporting, provided the General is occupied with other duties.

P.S. Your liberality will make every allowance for my numerous inaccuracies, as I have not time to make a fair or correct copy.

GOVERNOR HARRISON TO THE SECRETARY OF WAR. (EXTRACT).

(Historical Narrative of the Civil and Military Services of Major-General Wm. H. Harrison, by Moses Dawson; Cincinnati, 1824; p. 272.)

Cincinnati, 6th August, 1812.

Sir,

I have this day received, by express from governor Scott, the enclosed letter, and I shall immediately obey the summons. The information received a day or two ago from Detroit is of the most unpleasant nature; the loss of Mackinac will be probably followed by the capture of fort Dearborn, and the suspension of offensive measures by Hull's army, will, I fear, give great strength to the British party amongst the Indians. The assemblage of Indians mentioned by governor Edwards, upon the Illinois river is also calculated to excite apprehensions for the safety of the settlements of Kaskaskias or Vincennes. It is, however, my opinion, that it will be the object of the British to draw as many of the Indians as possible towards Malden to cut off the supplies from, and ultimately to capture general Hull's army. To prevent this, even if there should be no real intentions of carrying on offensive operations from Vincennes or Kaskaskias, feints from either or both would be highly useful to keep the Indians at home. I shall do myself the honor to write to you from Frankfort and communicate the result of the interview with governor Scott.

GENERAL ORDER. (EXTRACT.)

(Canadian Archives, C 1168, p. 233.)

Adjutant General's Office
Quebec 6th August 1812

General Orders/

The Commander of the Forces takes great pleasure in also announcing to the Troops, that the Enemy under Brig^r Genl

Hull have been repulsed in three Attacks made on the 18th 19th & 20th of last month, upon part of the Garrison of Amherstburg, upon the River Canard, in the neighbourhood of that place, & in which attacks His Majesty's 41st Reg^t have particularly distinguished themselves. In justice to that Corps, His Excellency wishes particularly to call the attention of the Troops to the heroism & self devotion displayed by two Privates, who being left Centinels when the Party to which they belonged had retired, continued to maintain their station, against the whole of the Enemy's force, untill they both fell, when one of them, whose arm had been broken, again raising himself, opposed with his bayonet those advancing against him, until he was overwhelmed by numbers; An Instance of such firmness and intrepidity, deserves to be thus publickly recorded, and His Excellency trusts that it will not fail to animate the Troops under his Command, with an ardent desire to follow so noble an example, whenever an opportunity shall be hereafter afforded them.

(Signed) R^t. M^{c}DOUALL[1]

Assis^t. Adj^t. General

WM. STANTON [2] TO LIEUT.-COLONEL JOHN MACDONELL, A.D.C.

(Canadian Archives, C 688A, p. 165.)

7 Augt 1812

Dear Sir/

The Servants Start with the Generals Horses and yours this morning (Monday) at 9 A M—

I put into the hands of your Servant five Dollars to pay for the Generals Horses feeding

Cutts I fear is not to be trusted with money where Drink is to be purchased.

---

[1] Captain Robert McDouall of the 8th Regiment, aide-de-camp to the governor-general; major in the Glengarry Light Infantry, February 1813; lieutenant-colonel, July 29, 1813; commandant at Mackinac, May 1814; major-general, 1841; died at Stranraer, November 15, 1848.

[2] William Stanton, paymaster of militia in the Home district.

GENERAL ORDER.

(History of the Late War in the Western Country, McAfee, p. 76.)

Sandwich, August 7, 1812.

Doctor Edwards will take charge of the medical and surgical departments until further orders and will immediately make every preparation to take the field against the enemy. All the tents and baggage not necessary will be immediately sent to Detroit. The boats not necessary for the movement of the army will be sent to Detroit. An officer with twenty-five convalescents will remain at the fort at Gowie's with a boat sufficient to cross the river if necessary. All the artillery not taken by the army will be sent immediately to Detroit. The army will take seven days' provisions. Three days' provisions will be drawn to-morrow morning and will be cooked; the residue will be taken in waggons. Pork will be drawn for the meat part of the ration. One hundred axes, fifty spades, and twenty pickaxes will be taken for the army and a raft of timber and plank suitable for bridges will be prepared and floated down with the batteries. Only one day's whiskey will be drawn each day and twelve barrels will be taken in waggons. All the artificers and all men on any kind of extra duty will immediately join their regiments.

W. HULL, Brig. Gen.

BRIG.-GENERAL HULL TO THE SECRETARY OF WAR.

(Historical Register of the United States, 1812-13; ed. 2, Philadelphia, 1814; Vol. II., p. 47.)

Sandwich, August 7, 1812.

Sir,—on the 4th inst. major Vanhorn, of colonel Findley's regiment of Ohio volunteers, was detached from this army, with the command of 200 men, principally riflemen, to proceed to the river Raisin, and further, if necessary, to meet and reinforce capt. Brush, of the state of Ohio, commanding a company of volunteers, and escorting provisions for this army. At Brownstown, a large body of Indians had formed an ambuscade, and the major's detachment received a heavy fire, at the distance of fifty yards from the enemy. The whole detachment retreated in disorder. Major Vanhorn made every exertion to form, and prevent the retreat, that was possible for a brave and gallant officer, but without success. By the return of killed and wounded, it will be perceived, that the loss of officers was uncommonly great. The efforts to rally their companies was the occasion of it.

Report of killed in Major Vanhorne's defeat.

Captains Gilchrist, Ullery, M'Callough of the spies, Bœrstler severely wounded, and not expected to recover (since dead); lieutenant Pentz; ensigns Roby and Allison; 10 privates. Total 17. Number of wounded, as yet unknown.

BRIG.-GENERAL HULL TO THE SECRETARY OF WAR.

(Report of Trial of General Hull; New York, 1814; App. II., p. 12.)

Detroit, 8th *August,* 1812.

Sir—I have received your letter of the 26th July. Under existing circumstances I have, from private feelings, re-crossed the Detroit River with the main body of the army, without making an attempt on the British fort at Malden. My reasons were that I did not consider it could be done consistent with my orders, viz. the safety of the posts in our own country. Contrary to my expectations, the Wyandots have become hostile, and the other nations connected with them are following their example. Since the fall of Machana (Mackinack) the Indian force has been fast encreasing in this part of the country. From all the information, a large Indian and Canadian force may be expected from Mackinack, and the force from Niagara, which I mentioned in my former letter, is advancing. My communications with the state of Ohio, on which the supplies of this army depended, is cut off, and having been defeated in an attempt to open that communication, as appears by my letter of the 7th inst. I considered it indispensibly necessary to open that communication. Perhaps the reduction of Malden would have been the most effectual mode. The bridges were broke down and the nature of the country was such that the officers of the artillery gave it as their opinion that the heavy pieces could not be brought before the work without much time and great labour; more time than would have been safe to have employed. Time does not admit of a detail of all the difficulties which every hour were encreasing. I have built a work nearly opposite Detroit, garrisoned by 230 infantry and 25 artillerists. In pursuance of my system, Lieutenant Colonel Miller is now commencing his march with six hundred of the best troops of the army to meet Captain Brush from Ohio with two hundred volunteers, escorting 300 head of cattle and a quantity of flour on pack-horses.

MAJOR-GENERAL DEARBORN TO THE SECRETARY OF WAR.

(Memoirs of the Campaign of the North Western Army, by General Hull; Boston, 1824; p. 180.)

Headquarters, Greenbush, Aug. 9th, 1812.

Sir,—Colonel Baynes, Adjutant General of the British army in Canada, has this day arrived at this place, in the character of a Flag of Truce, with despatches from the British government, through Mr. Foster,[1] which I have enclosed to the Secretary. Colonel Baynes was likewise the bearer of despatches from Sir George Prevost which is herewith enclosed. Although I do not consider myself authorized to agree to a cessation of arms, I concluded that I might with perfect safety, agree that our troops should act merely on the defensive, until I could receive directions from my government;[2] but as I could not include General Hull in such an arrangement, he having received his orders directly from the department of war, I agreed to write to him, and state the proposition made to me, and have proposed, his confining himself to defensive measures, if his orders, and the circumstances of affairs with him, would justify it. Colonel Baynes has written similar orders to the British officers in Upper Canada, and I have forwarded them to our commanders of posts, to be by them transmitted to the British commanders.

I consider the agreement as favourable at this period, for we would not act offensively, except at Detroit, for some time, and there it will not probably have any effect on General Hull or his movements, and we shall not be prepared to act offen-

[1] Augustus J. Foster, British envoy at Washington.
[2] On August 26, General Dearborn notified General Prevost that 4 days after his despatch reached the commandant at Montreal this agreement for the suspension of hostilities would become void.

sively in this quarter, before you will have time to give me orders for continuing on the defensive or act otherwise.

We shall lose no time, or advantage, by the agreement, but rather gain time without any risk. It is mutually understood, that all preparatory measures may proceed, and that no obstructions are to be attempted, on either side, to the passage of stores, to the frontier posts; but if General Hull should not think it advisable to confine himself to mere defensive operations, the passage of military stores to Detroit, will not be considered as embraced in the agreement last noticed.

Col. Baynes informs me, that a party of British troops and Indians, had taken possession of Michilimackinac, and that our garrison were prisoners. I made no particular enquiry as to the circumstances, as I entertained some doubts as to the fact. I have no expectation that the government will consent to a cessation of hostilities, on the strength of the communication forwarded by Mr. Foster; but all circumstances considered, it may be well to avail ourselves of the occasion, until we are better prepared for acting with effect; at all events, we can lose nothing by the arrangement, I have consented to, it being explicitly understood, that my government will not be under any obligations to agree to it, unless that despatches from the British government should be such, as to induce the President to propose an armistice, as preparatory for negotiations for peace. I informed Colonel Baynes, that our government would readily meet any such overture from Great Britain, as clearly indicated a disposition for making peace on satisfactory terms; but after what had occurred, in relation to the adjustment with Mr. Erskine,[1] it could not be expected that any other than the most explicit and authentic directions to their agent in this country, would produce any change in our measures. It is evident that a war with the United States is very unpopular in Canada.—Colonel Baynes arrived at our frontier post, at Plattsburg, and was conducted to this place by Major Clark, an officer in the detached militia of this state, he returned this day with the same officer.

---

[1] David Montague Erskine, British envoy to United States, 1806. He was recalled in 1809 for having exceeded his instructions with regard to overtures towards peace.

MAJOR-GENERAL DEARBORN TO BRIG.-GENERAL HULL.

(Memoirs of the Campaign of the North Western Army, by General Hull; Boston, 1824, p. 182.)

Headquarters, Greenbush, Aug. 9th, 1812

Sir,—Having received from Sir George Prevost, Governour General, and commander of the British forces in Upper and Lower Canada, despatches from the British government said to be of a conciliatory nature, which I have forwarded to Washington, and a letter from Sir George Prevost to me, by his Adjutant General, Colonel Baynes, proposing a cessation of hostilities on the frontiers; I have so far agreed to his proposals as to consent that no offensive operations shall be attempted on our part, until I have received further instructions from our government; but as you received your orders directly from the department of war, I could not agree to extend the principle to your command, but I agreed to write to you, and state the general facts; and propose to you a concurrence in the measures, if your orders and situation would admit of it; of course you will act in conformity with what has been agreed upon, in respect to the other posts on the frontiers, if not incompatible with your orders, or the arrangements made under them, or the circumstances under which this letter reaches you. Any preparations for offensive operations may be continued, and when it is agreed to suspend any offensive operations no obstacles are to be opposed to the transportation of military stores. In all cases where offensive operations cease, by virtue of the aforementioned agreement, four entire days are to be allowed, after either party shall revoke their orders, before any offensive operations shall commence. A letter from Colonel Baynes, to the commanding officer at Amherstburg, has been forwarded by me to the commanding officer at Niagara, to be by him transmitted to Detroit. The removal of any troops from Niagara to Detroit, while the present agreement continues, would be improper, and incompatible with the true interest of the agreement. I have made no arrangement that should have any effect upon your command contrary to your own judgment.

LIEUT.-COLONEL JOHN MACDONALD TO DUNCAN CAMERON.[1]

(Life and Times of Major-General Sir Isaac Brock, by D. B. Read; Toronto, 1894; p. 150.)

Port Talbot, 10th August, 1812.

My Dear Sir,—

We left Dover on the 8th, between three and four o'clock p m., and got to this place about six this morning, when the wind blew so strong upon the shore that we found it would be quite impracticable to weather the point about thirty miles ahead, and between which and this place there is no possibility of landing, so were forced to beach and haul our boats into a fine creek, where, from present appearances, it is probable they will remain till to-morrow morning, and how much longer I cannot say. It has rained almost constantly since we encamped last night, and, although the men have been completely drenched, they continue in excellent spirits and behave in the most orderly and obedient manner. Peter Robinson,[2] with his riflemen, joined us about twelve o'clock to-day, and our fleet now consists of twelve sail of all kinds, in one of which is a six-pounder (dismounted) with ammunition, etc. The want of boats obliged the General to send a detachment, consisting of about 100 men of the Oxford and Norfolk militia, in a small vessel which happened to be at Dover, which must have reached Amherstburgh this morning.

Upon our arrival at Dover, it was said that a sufficient number of boats to embark the whole of the force assembled there had been got ready; but upon examination we found that hardly one was in a state for service, and it was not till about four o'clock next day, with every exertion, that we got ten boats under way. Many of these are in so bad a state that we are constantly delayed and detained by them, and will no doubt prevent our arriving so soon as we otherwise would.

---

[1] Duncan Cameron, assistant secretary for the Indian Department in Upper Canada; captain commanding a flank company of the 3rd Regiment of York militia.

[2] Peter Robinson, a brother of Sir John Beverley Robinson, was captain of the rifle company of the 1st York militia, and afterwards lieutenant-colonel commanding the 1st Northumberland Regiment. He represented the east riding of the county of York in the Legislative Assembly of Upper Canada from 1816 to 1820, and the counties of York and Simcoe from 1820 until 1824. At a later date he was instrumental in bringing many emigrants from Ireland into the province, and founded the town of Peterborough. He was appointed commissioner of Crown Lands. He died in 1838.

Had there been boats enough, we probably would have had with us about 100 men more than we have. Our force at present, including the men sent in the vessel, will be upwards of 350, besides twenty Indians under Cadotte,[1] who has fallen behind. There will be sixty men of the 41st sent from Fort Erie, which will, I trust, be found sufficient reinforcement to the garrison of Amherstburgh to enable us to effect the desired object. Not having heard a word from Amherstburgh since we left you, we must suppose things remain in the same state.

I am sorry to say that poor Chambers was taken so ill just as we were about to embark, that Mr. Rolph[2] thought it absolutely necessary to detain him....................
....

Chambers, I am glad to tell you, has arrived apparently perfectly recovered—not from his illness, but from his fear of being left behind, which, I believe, gave him more uneasiness than all his other complaints.

GOVERNOR HARRISON TO THE SECRETARY OF WAR.

(Historical Narrative of the Civil and Military Services of Major-General Wm. H. Harrison, by Moses Dawson; Cincinnati, 1814; p. 273.)

Lexington (ky.) 10th August, 1812.

Sir,

Upon my arrival at Frankfort on Saturday last, I was favored by governor Scott with the perusal of a late communication from governor Edwards covering a number of documents which unequivocally prove the existence of a combination amongst the Indian tribes, more formidable than any previous one. And as the only obstacle to the commencement of offensive operations on their part, (the want of ammunition,) has been removed by the taking of Macinac, I have determined to order four companies of Indiana militia to march from the counties bordering on the Ohio, to Vincennes, and they will soon be followed by a regiment from this state. I have also informed governor Scott that all the remaining part of the quota of this state will be required for active service northwest

---

[1] Probably Jean B. Cadot, an interpreter in the Indian Department of Upper Canada, holding the rank of lieutenant for the Western Nations from 1814.

[2] Probably Dr. John Rolph, afterwards noted as a political ally of William Lyon Mackenzie.

of the Ohio. Previously to the taking of any other steps, however, I have thought it proper to recur to you for further instructions, and most respectfully to offer you the result of my reflections on the subject of the employment of the disposable force in this quarter of our country. As it appears, from your letter of the 19th ult. that the government had determined on offensive measures against the belligerent Indians, the fact, then, to be considered is the nature and extent of those measures. Two species of warfare have been used by the United States in their contests with the tribes upon the north-western frontier, viz: rapid and desultory expeditions by mounted men, having for their object, the surprise and destruction of particular villages; or the more tardy, but effectual, operations of an army composed principally of infantry, penetrating the country of the enemy, and securing the possession by a chain of posts. In the war which was terminated by the peace of Greenville, both of these plans were used, but the former as auxiliary only to the latter, which was regarded as the effectual means for procuring and preserving peace. If, under the present circumstances, the government should think proper to rely upon desultory expeditions only, they would naturally be directed against those villages of the enemy which are nearest, and which, of course, would most annoy our settlements. But the direction to be given to an army of the other description, requires more attentive consideration. In the present posture of affairs, it appears to me that one of the plans which I have the honor to submit, might be adopted with advantage. The first is to establish a chain of posts upon the Illinois river, from the Mississippi to Chicago, and the other, to march immediately a considerable body of troops to fort Wayne. If it were certain that general Hull would be able even with the reinforcement which is now about to be sent to him, to reduce Malden and retake Macinac, there would be no necessity of sending other troops in that direction. But I greatly fear that the capture of Macinac will give such éclat to the British and Indian arms, that the northern tribes will pour down in swarms upon Detroit, oblige general Hull to act entirely upon the defensive, and meet, and perhaps overpower, the convoys and reinforcements which may be sent him. It appears to me, indeed, highly probable that the large detachment which is now destined for his relief, under colonel Wells[1] will have

[1] Samuel Wells, appointed colonel of the 17th Regiment of United States Infantry, July 6, 1812.

to fight its way. I rely greatly upon the valor of those troops, but it is possible that the event may be adverse to us, and if it is, Detroit must fall, and with it every hope of re-establishing our affairs in that quarter until next year. I am also apprehensive that the provisions which are to be sent with colonel Wells are by no means equal to the supply of the army for any length of time, increased, as it will be, by this detachment. They must then depend upon smaller convoys, which can never reach their destination in safety, if the British and Indians think proper to prevent it. Commanding, as they do, the navigation of the lake, the British can, with the utmost facility, transfer their force from one side of it to the other, meet our detachments, and overpower them, if they are small, whilst performing a laborious and circuitous march through a swampy country, at any point they think proper. To prevent these disasters, or to remedy them, should they occur, a considerable covering army appears to me to be the only alternative; for should any of my apprehensions be realized, it is out of the question that troops could be collected in time to render any essential service. There are other considerations which strongly recommend the adoption of this measure. I mean the situation of Chicago, which must be in danger, and if it is not well supplied with provisions, the danger must be imminent. It is possible, sir, that every thing may yet go well, that no considerable number of Indians may be collected at Malden, and that our detachments and convoys may reach their destination in safety; the reverse, however, appears to me to be the most probable; and I am fully persuaded that the opinions and wishes of the people in the western country, are unanimously in favor of the most vigorous and effectual measures. In this state, particularly, the spirit of the people is arrived to the highest pitch, and the government may rely on their utmost efforts. To be furnished with arms, and to be allowed to exert their energies to establish our affairs upon the north-western frontier, is earnestly desired by every description of persons. An army going in the proposed direction, particularly if it was sent to fort Wayne, would serve as a considerable check upon the tribes of the Wabash, and those of the west and south of lake Michigan. Supplies could be easily procured in the highly cultivated part of the Ohio between the Miami and Scioto rivers. If the plan here proposed should be adopted, some display of military force, by way of demonstration, would be highly useful, both at Vincennes and in the neighborhood of Cahokia or St. Louis. Indeed, some troops are necessary for the defence of those places and the adjacent settlements.

The only objection to the scheme of erecting a chain of posts from the Mississippi to the Chicago arises from the lateness of the season, which would, perhaps, render it impossible to collect the supplies which are necessary for the very large force that this expedition would require. It could not be undertaken with a probability of success with less than 5000 men. Moving in the manner proposed, the Indians would be apprised of the object and there can be no doubt that every effort would be made to defeat it, and as little, that they would be enabled to collect a force at least equal to that which I have stated is the necessary amount for ours. If the advanced season should prevent the plan from being completed, it might, at least, be so far effected as to occupy Peoria (an important point,) and erect an intermediate post between it and the mouth of the Illinois river. A slight inspection of the map of that country, and reference to the position of the various tribes, will at once explain the great advantage to be derived from a prosecution of the plan. It would as completely cover our settlements as a chain of posts can cover them; and it would have the effect so highly desirable, of bringing the Indian tribes to a general and decisive action.

From the enclosed letter[1] of captain Wells, it appears that the prophet had abandoned all idea of remaining upon the Wabash, and that it was his intention to return, after making a stroke at our settlements, to the country of the Winebagoes. As the order of Tecumseh was given, however, under the impression that Malden would shortly fall into our hands, it is highly probable that the procrastination of that event, and the suspension of offensive operations upon the part of general Hull's army, has inspired other hopes, and given rise to other schemes. If this should be the case, and he remains upon the Wabash, and neither of the other plans which I have recommended is adopted, a second expedition against him might be undertaken from Vincennes, or the driving him off might form part of the plan to be executed by the army proposed to be collected at fort Wayne. With the opinion I entertain of the situation of affairs at Detroit, I give a decided preference to the fort Wayne expedition. I do think it highly probable that the Indians have been collected in very considerable numbers to relieve their friends at Malden, but I have no further evidence of it, nor, indeed, of the extensive com-

---

[1] For this letter, see p. 78.

bination which I suppose to exist amongst the Indian tribes than what is, or will be, before you at the time you receive this.

Your favor of the 9th inst. I have submitted to governor Scott, Mr. Clay,[1] Mr. Bledsoe, and other conspicuous friends of the administration here, and they have all recommended that I should not put any other part of the troops in motion until I hear from you, excepting the few companies that have been ordered for the protection of Vincennes. Should the government think proper to authorise the employment of a larger force than the amount of the quota ordered from this state, no fears need be entertained of its not being obtained. I will pledge myself to raise in ten days, two thousand men, for any expedition which may be authorised, wholly independent of the regular militia, or of the quota which has been organized. I am constantly solicited to suffer independent companies to be raised, of both horse and infantry. I should be thankful to be informed of the proportion of cavalry which I may command. It is a description of force to which I am very partial in Indian warfare. If a sufficiency of swords and pistols cannot be procured, I would recommend that some of the dragoon companies be armed with the small rifles now used by the United States rifle corps.

COLONEL PROCTER TO MAJOR-GENERAL BROCK.

(Canadian Archives, C 677, p. 18.)

Amherstburg Aug 11th 1812

Dear Sir

Since the 25th Ult° the Enemy has made no Attempt on this side the River. On the 2^d Ins^t the Wyndots having at last decided on joining the other Nations of Indians, of whom they are the bravest, & eldest, against the Americans; a considerable Body of Indians accompanied the Chief Tecumseth, to the Village of the Wyndots (Brownstown), nearly thirty Miles on the opposite Shore from Detroit, and five from hence. I sent a Detachment of a hundred Men under the Command of Captain Muir to enable the Wyndots to Bring off their Families, Cattle & Effects. This was effected much to the Disappointment of Mr Hull who has given them a considerable Sum

---

[1] Henry Clay represented Kentucky in Congress from 1809, and was speaker in that body 1811-14.

of Money in the Hope of retaining them in the American Interest. Tecumseth who has generally many Indians with him remained, by which Mr Hull's Communication with his Government was interrupted. On the 5th Ins^t a select Detachment of two hundred Riflemen from several Corps were sent to escort the Mail from Detroit, which however they lost, and about fifty killed. I had sent a Detachment but they unfortunately could not reach the Scene of Action until the Affair was finished. The Indians lost only one Man, an Interpreter. I enclose a Copy of Mr Hull's Letter to Secretary at War:

Saturday (the 8th,) being the usual Day of the Post's Arrival at Detroit, every Road & Indian Path, was occupied on the 7th, 8, & 9th Ins^{ts} in the hope of intercepting the Mail for Detroit, as well as expected Supplies. On the 9th on finding that a considerable Body of the Enemy were on the March to Brownstown I sent a Reinforcement under Captain Muir which completed the Force there to 150 Men besides Indians, whose Numbers it is not possible on any Occasion exactly to ascertain. In this Affair we have not entirely succeeded. The Enemy had some Artillery, which their Numbers enabled them to make a Road for. The Ground on which the Americans had been so roughly treated on the 5th Ins^t was not as it ought to have been, occupied, & some Mistake was made, the Party retreated, the 41st has lost three Dead, thirteen wounded, & two Missing. Militia one killed & two wounded, Indians two killed & six wounded. Captain Muir is slightly wounded, Mr Sutherland[1] seriously wounded. I can ill spare Captain Muir's Services, for ever so short a Time. He is a brave good Officer. It was a warm Action, & the Officers behaved well, some Militia Officers were volunteers & acted with Spirit. The Enemy's Loss has been considerable. We are all in good Spirits.—I detained the Express in hopes of sending some Information from the Mail. I have heard from Captain Chambers, & from Norton whom I hope soon to see here.

(P.S.) The Militia are coming in, and Indians also.

---

[1] Charles Sutherland, lieutenant in the 41st Regiment.

DISTRICT GENERAL ORDERS.

(Order Book of Lt.-Colonel John Macdonell.)

Headquarters, Banks of Lake Erie,
15 Miles S.W. of Port Talbot.
August 11th, 1812, 6 o'clock, p.m.

D. General Orders.

The troops will hold themselves in readiness and will embark in the boats at twelve o'clock this night precisely.

It is Major General Brock's positive orders that none of the boats go ahead of that in which is the Headquarters, where a light will be carried during the night.

The officers commanding the different boats will immediately inspect the arms and ammunition of the men and see that they are constantly kept in a state for immediate service, as the troops are now to pass through a part of the country which is known to have been visited by the enemy's patroles.

A captain with a subaltern and thirty men will mount as piquet upon the landing of the boats and a sentry will be furnished from each boat, who must be regularly relieved, to take charge of the boat and baggage, &c.

A patrole from the piquet will be sent out on landing to the distance of a mile from the encampment.

By order of the Major General.

J. B. GLEGG, Capt'n, A.D.C.

J. MACDONELL, P.A.D.C.

LIEUT.-COLONEL CASS TO GOVERNOR MEIGS.

(McAfee, History of the Late War in the Western Country, p. 83.)

Detroit, August 12, 1812.

Dear Sir.

From causes not fit to be put on paper but which I trust I shall live to communicate to you, this army has been reduced to a critical and alarming situation. We have wholly left the the Canadian shore and have abandoned the miserable inhabitants who depended on our will and power to protect them, to their fate. Unfortunately the General and our principal officers could not view the situation in the same light. That

Malden might have been easily reduced I have no doubt. That the army were in force and in spirits enough to have done it, no one doubts. But the precious opportunity has fled and instead of looking back we must now look forward. The letter from the Secretary of War to you, a copy of which I have seen, authorizes you to preserve and keep open the communication from the State of Ohio to Detroit. It is all important that it should be kept open; our very existence depends upon it. Our supplies must come from our State. This country does not furnish them. In the existing state of things, nothing but a large force of 2,000 men at least will effect this object. It is the unanimous wish of the army that you should accompany them. Every exertion that can, must be made. If this reaches you safely by Murray, he will tell you more than I can or ought here to insert.

Endorsed.

Since the other side of this letter was written, new circumstances have arisen. The British force is opposite and our situation has nearly reached its crisis. Believe all the bearer may tell you. Believe it however much it may astonish, as much as if told by one of us. Even a c........ is talked of by the........ The bearer will supply the vacancy. On you we depend.

(Signed by Cass, Findley, McArthur, Taylor,[1] and E. Brush,[2]),

DISTRICT GENERAL ORDERS.

(Order Book of Lt.-Colonel John Macdonell.)

Headquarters, Point aux Pins.
Lake Erie, August 12th, 1812.

D. General Orders.

It is Major General Brock's intention, should the wind continue fair to proceed during the night. Officers commanding boats will therefore pay attention to the order of sailing as directed yesterday. The greatest care and attention will be requisite to prevent the boats from scattering or falling behind.

A great part of the bank of the lake where the boats will

---

[1] General James Taylor, quartermaster-general of General Hull's force.

[2] Colonel Elijah Brush of the 1st Regiment of Michigan militia, and attorney-general of the Michigan territory; his wife was Adelaide Askin, daughter of Colonel John Askin and sister of Charles Askin.

this day pass is much more dangerous and difficult of access than any we have passed. The boats will therefore not land excepting in the most extreme necessity, and the greatest care must be taken to choose the best places for landing.

The troops being now in the neighbourhood of the enemy, every precaution must be taken to guard against surprise.

By order of the Major General.

J. B. GLEGG, A.D.C.

BRIG.-GENERAL HULL TO THE SECRETARY OF WAR.

(Historical Register of the United States, 1812-13; 2 ed., Philadelphia, 1814; Vol. II, p. 47.)

Detroit, August 13, 1812.

Sir, the main body of the army having re-crossed the river at Detroit on the night and morning of the 8th inst. six hundred men were immediately detached under the command of lieutenant-colonel Miller, to open the communication to the river Raisin, and protect the provisions, which were under the escort of captain Brush. This detachment consisted of the 4th United States' regiment and two small detachments under the command of lieutenant Stansbury and ensign M'Labe, of the 1st regiment; detachments from the Ohio and Michigan volunteers, a corps of artillerists, with one six pounder and an howitzer, under the command of lieutenant Eastman, and a part of captains Smith and Sloan's cavalry, commanded by captain Sloan of the Ohio volunteers. Lieutenant-colonel Miller marched from Detroit on the afternoon of the 8th instant, and on the 9th, about 4 o'clock, P.M., the van guard, commanded by captain Snelling[1] of the 4th United States' regiment, was fired on by an extensive line of British troops and Indians at the lower part of Maguago, about fourteen miles from Detroit. At this time the main body was marching in two columns, and captain Snelling maintained his position in a most gallant manner, under a very heavy fire, until the line was formed and advanced to the ground he occupied, when the whole, excepting the rear guard, was brought into action. The enemy were formed behind a temporary breast-work of logs,

---

[1] Joseph Snelling was appointed first lieutenant in the 4th Regiment of United States Infantry in April 1809; promoted captain, June 1809; brevet-major, August 1812; inspector-general, April 1813; lieutenant-colonel of the 4th Regiment of Riflemen, February 1814; colonel of the 5th Regiment of Infantry, 1819; died at Washington, D.C., August 20, 1828.

the Indians extending in a thick wood on the left. Lieutenant-colonel Miller ordered his whole line to advance, and when within a small distance of the enemy made a general discharge, and proceeded with charged bayonets, when the whole British line and Indians commenced a retreat. They were pursued in a most vigorous manner about two miles, and the pursuit discontinued only on account of the fatigue of the troops, the approach of evening, and the necessity of returning to the care of the wounded. The judicious arrangements made by Lieutenant-colonel Miller, and the gallant manner in which they were executed, justly entitled him to the highest honour. From the moment the line commenced to fire, it continually moved on, and the enemy maintained their position until forced at the point of the bayonet. The Indians on the left, under the command of Tecumseh, fought with great obstinacy, but were continually forced and compelled to retreat. The victory was complete in every part of the line, and the success would have been more brilliant had the cavalry charged the enemy on the retreat, when a most favourable opportunity presented. Although orders were given for the purpose, unfortunately they were not executed.

Majors Vanhorn and Morrison, of the Ohio volunteers, were associated with lieutenant-colonel Miller, as field officers in this command, and were highly distinguished by their exertions in forming the line, and the firm and intrepid manner they led their respective commands to action.

Captain Baker of the 1st United States' regiment, captain Brevort of the second, and captain Hull of the 13th, my aide-de-camp, and lieutenant Whistler of the 1st, requested permission to join the detachment as volunteers. Lieutenant-colonel Miller assigned commands to captain Baker and lieutenant Whistler, and captains Brevort and Hull, at his request, attended his person, and aided him in the general arrangements. Lieutenant-colonel Miller has mentioned these officers in terms of high approbation. In addition to the captains who have been named, lieutenant-colonel Miller has mentioned captains Burton and Fuller of the 4th regiment, captains Saunders and Brown of the Ohio volunteers, and captain Delandre of the Michigan volunteers, who were attached to his command, and distinguished by their valour. It is impossible for me in this communication to do justice to the officers and soldiers, who gained the victory which I have described. They have acquired high honour to themselves, and are justly entitled to the gratitude of their country.

Major Muir of the 41st regiment commanded the British in this action. The regulars and volunteers consisted of about four hundred, and a large number of Indians. Major Muir and two subalterns were wounded, one of them since dead. About forty Indians were found dead on the field, and Tecumseh their leader was slightly wounded. The number of wounded Indians who escaped has not been ascertained. Four of Major Muir's detachment have been made prisoners, and fifteen of the 41st regiment killed or wounded. The militia and volunteers attached to his command were in the severest part of the action, and their loss must have been great—it has not yet been ascertained.

Return of killed and wounded in the action fought near Maguaga, August 9, 1812.

4th United States' regiment—10 non-commissioned officers and privates killed, and forty-five wounded; capt. Baker of the 1st regiment of Infantry; lieutenant Larrabee of the 4th; lieutenant Peters of the 4th; ensign Whistler of the 17th, doing duty in the 4th; lieutenant Silly, and an ensign, whose name has not been returned to me, were wounded.

In the Ohio and Michigan volunteers, 8 were killed and 13 wounded.

DISTRICT GENERAL ORDERS.

(Order Book of Lt.-Colonel John Macdonell.)

Headquarters, Fort Amherstburg,
August 14th, 1812.

D. General Orders.

Major General Brock announces his arrival to the troops quartered in the Western District, and directs officers in command will immediately transmit returns of their respective corps.

The Major General congratulates the troops on the evacuation of the country by the enemy. He is persuaded that nothing but the spirit manifested by those who have remained doing duty, and the judicious measures adopted by Colonel Procter have compelled him to so disgraceful a retreat.

Colonel Elliott and Major McKee[1] and the officers of the Indian Department are entitled to his best thanks for their judicious management of the Indians, and for the example of gallantry which they have uniformly shown before the enemy.

The Major General cannot avoid expressing his surprise at the numerous desertions which have occurred from the ranks of the militia, to which circumstance the long stay of the enemy on this side of the river must in a great measure be ascribed. He is willing to believe that their conduct proceeded from an anxiety to get in their harvests and not from any prediliection for the principles or Government of the United States. He requests officers commanding corps to transmit to him the names of such militiamen as have remained faithful to their oath and duty, that immediate measures may be taken to discharge their arrears of pay.

The enemy being still in the neighbourhood, the whole physical force of the country will be employed to drive him to such a distance as will ensure its tranquillity.

Officers commanding militia corps are responsible that every individual bound to embody himself do immediately repair to this station, in default of which he will be treated as a deserter and subjected to all the penalties of the new Militia Act.

Captains Muir, Tallon[2] and Chambers, 41st Regiment, Captain Glegg, 49th Regiment, Captain Mockler, Newfoundland Regiment, and Captain Dixon, Royal Engineers, are appointed to the rank of Major as long as the local service on which they are employed continues.

The troops in the Western District will be formed into three brigades: The first under Lieut. Colonel St. George, to

---

[1] Thomas McKee was born in 1770 being the son of Alexander McKee, Indian agent at Fort Pitt. He was commissioned as ensign in the 60th Regiment, March 29, 1791; promoted to be lieutenant, February 5, 1795; and captain February 20, 1796. He was appointed deputy superintendent for the western Indians in 1799 on the recommendation of Lieutenant-Governor Hunter, a post for which he was remarkably well qualified by his knowledge of Indian languages and customs. He resigned his commission in the army in 1805. He was elected to represent the county of Kent in the Legislative Assembly in 1800, and elected for the county of Essex in 1801. During the war of 1812 he held a commission as major of the 2nd Regiment of Essex militia. He died at the Cascades in Lower Canada on October 20, 1814, a victim of his intemperate habits.

"Whilst I was at Amherstburg with Baskwell he pointed out to me the stump of a very large button-wood tree, which Captain McKee of the 60th regiment had cut down with one hand for a wager between sunrise and sunset on a long summer's day. The stump measured nearly three feet and a half in diameter. Captain McKee was at this time (1800) superintendent of Indian affairs for the district of Amherstburgh; he was six feet four inches high, and exceedingly powerful, his mother consist of detachments of the Royal Newfoundland Regiment and of the Kent and First and Second Regiments Essex Militia. The Second under command of Major Chambers consisting of fifty men of the 41st Regiment and the whole of the detachments of the York, Lincoln, Oxford and Norfolk Militia. The Third Brigade, under the command of Major Tallon, will consist of the remainder of the 41st Regiment.

Colonel Procter will have charge of the whole line under the orders of the Major General.

James Givins,[1] Esquire, late Captain 5th Regiment, is appointed Provincial Aid-de-Camp, with the rank of Major in the Militia.

By order of the Major General.

J. B. GLEGG, Major, A.D.C.

SIR GEORGE PREVOST TO THE EARL OF LIVERPOOL.

(Canadian Archives, C 1218, p. 365.)

Montreal 14th August 1812

N° 65.

My Lord,

I have the honor to transmit herewith for Your Lordships information, the copy of a Report which has been forwarded to me by Major General Brock of the surrender by Capitulation of the American Post of Michilimackinac to a Detachment of His Majesty's Troops from St Josephs, under the command of Captain Roberts of the 10th Royal Veteran Battalion;

The Report is accompanied by a Return of Prisoners taken, and of the Stores which were found in the Fort;

---

was an Indian, and he himself retained a slight tinge of the olive colour of the natives, but he was one of the best tempered fellows and most entertaining companions I have ever met with."—'*Landmanns Adventures and Recollections.*' Vol. II, p. 150.

[2] Joseph Tallon, a captain in the 41st Foot. He commanded the 41st Regiment and the right wing of the British force in the action at Frenchtown on the river Raisin on January 22, 1813. He was severely wounded, and for his good conduct on that occasion received the thanks of General Procter. He was engaged in the action at the Miami, 1813; taken prisoner at Moraviantown, 1813; and detained in prison for several months as a hostage.—*(Canadian Archives, C 912, p. 26.)*

[1] James Givins was appointed an ensign in the Queen's Rangers in 1791; promoted to be captain in the 5th Foot, November 19, 1803. He was shortly afterwards appointed Indian agent at York and resigned his commission. He was gazetted provincial aide-de-camp to Major-General Brock, August 14, 1812, with the rank of major in the militia.

In addition to these I have a further report of the Crews of two Vessels amounting to the Number of 43, (who were in the Fort) having fallen into our hands together with 700 packs of Furs.

My Despatch N° 59 will have acquainted your Lordship of a large Detachment from the American Army having taken possession of Sandwich on the 12th ultimo;—

Brig^r. Genl Hull I find, commenced his Operations against Amherstburg a few days after the Detachment of the 41st Reg^t have behaved with great gallantry, in repelling three attacks made by the Americans to approach the Fort, by the River Canard; These successes with the diversion on the flank of the Enemy, by the possession of Michilimackinac on the 17th ulto' may be attended with Consequences favorable to the Security of Upper Canada.

MAJOR-GENERAL BROCK TO BRIG.-GENERAL HULL.

(Historical Register of the United States, 1812-13; 2 ed., Philadelphia, 1814; Vol. II, p. 50.)

Head-Quarters, Sandwich, August 15, 1812.

Sir,

The force at my disposal authorises me to require of you the immediate surrender of fort Detroit. It is far from my intention to join in a war of extermination, but you must be aware, that the numerous body of Indians who have attached themselves to my troops, will be beyond controul the moment the contest commences. You will find me disposed to enter into such conditions as will satisfy the most scrupulous sense of honour. Lieut.-colonel M'Donnell and major Glegg are fully authorised to conclude any arrangement that may lead to prevent the unnecessary effusion of blood.

BRIG.-GENERAL HULL TO THE MAJOR-GENERAL BROCK.

(Historical Register of the United States, 1812-13; 2 ed., Philadelphia, 1814; Vol. II, p. 50.)

Head-Quarters, Detroit, August 15, 1812.

Sir,

I have received your letter of this date. I have no other reply to make, than to inform you, that I am prepared to meet any force which may be at your disposal, and any consequences which may result from any exertion of it you may think proper to make.

I avail myself of this opportunity to inform you that the flag of truce under the direction of captain Brown, proceeded contrary to the orders, and without the knowledge of col. Cass, who commanded the troops which attacked your pickets, near the river Canard bridge.[1]

I likewise take this occasion to inform you that Cowie's house was set on fire contrary to my orders, and it did not take place till after the evacuation of the fort. From the best information I have been able to obtain on the subject, it was set on fire by some of the inhabitants on the other side of the river.

DISTRICT GENERAL ORDERS.

(Order Book of Lt.-Colonel John Macdonell.)

Headquarters, Fort Amherstburg,
August 15th, 1812.

D. General Orders.

The troops will be in readiness to embark at McGee's (McKee's?) Point at three o'clock to-morrow morning. Colonel Elliott will proceed during the night to the eastern shore of the River Rouge, and upon his communicating with the Major General the troops will immediately commence crossing the river and land between River Rouge and Spring Wells.

Colonel Elliott will place the Indians in a position to take the enemy in flank and rear, should he be disposed to oppose the crossing.

Lientenant Colonel St. George will march his brigade this evening and canton the men in the houses close to the spot at which the embarkation is to take place.

The officers of the commissariat will make the necessary arrangements to supply the troops employed on the opposite shore with provisions and every article required by the different departments. During the operations of the troops in the field each man will receive one gill of spirits per day. The number

---
[1] See despatch, Hull to Prevost, September 8, p. 212, and the following despatch.

for which provision is to be made may be calculated at two thousand.

By order of the Major General.

J. B. GLEGG, A.D.C.

ARTICLES OF CAPITULATION OF FORT DETROIT AND DEPENDENCIES.

(*Casselman's 1902 reprint, p. 67, of "Richardson's War of 1812," 1842.*)

Camp at Detroit, 16th Aug., 1812.

Capitulation for the surrender of Fort Detroit, entered into between Major-General Brock, commanding His Britannic Majesty's forces, on the one part, and Brigadier General Hull commanding the North Western army of the United States, on the other part.

1st. Fort Detroit as well as with all the troops, regulars and militia, will be immediately surrendered to the British forces under the command of Major-General Brock, and will be considered prisoners of war, with the exception of such of the militia of the Michigan territory, who have not joined the army.

2d. All public stores, arms, and all public documents, including every thing else of a public nature, will be immediately given up.

3d. Private persons, and property of every description will be respected.

4th. His Excellency, Brigadier-General Hull, having expressed a desire that a detachment from the State of Ohio, on its way to join his army as well as one sent from Fort Detroit, under the command of Colonel M'Arthur, should be included in the above capitulation, it is accordingly agreed to. It is, however, to be understood, that such part of the Ohio Militia as have not joined the army, will be permitted to return to their homes, on condition that they will not serve during the war; their arms will be delivered up if belonging to the public.

5th. The Garrison will march out at the hour of 12 o'clock this day, and the British forces will take immediate possession of the Fort.

    J. MACDONELL, Lieut.-Col. militia, P.A.D.C.,
    J. B. GLEGG, Major, A.D.C.,
    JAMES MILLER, Lieut.-Col. 5th U.S. Infantry,
    E. BRUSH, Col. com'g 1st regt. of Michigan Militia,

Approved,
    W. HULL, B. Gen'l. Com'g the N. W. Army,

Approved,
    ISAAC BROCK, Major-General.

An article supplemental to the articles of Capitulation, concluded at Detroit, the 16th of August, 1812.

It is agreed that the Officers and soldiers of the Ohio Militia and Volunteers shall be permitted to proceed to their respective homes, on this condition, that they are not to serve during the present war, unless they are exchanged.

    W. HULL, B. Gen'l. Com'g N. W. Army, U.S.
    ISAAC BROCK, Major-General.

An article in addition to the supplemental article of the capitulation, concluded at Detroit, the 16th of August, A.D. 1812.

It is further agreed that the officers and soldiers of the Michigan Militia and Volunteers, under the command of Major Wetherell, shall be placed on the same principles as the Ohio militia and volunteers are placed by the supplemental article of the 16th instant.

    W. HULL, B. Gen'l Com'g N. W. Army, U.S.
    ISAAC BROCK, Major-General.

PRIZE PAY LIST—SURRENDER OF FORT DETROIT.

(From original in the Royal Hospital, Chelsea.)

Prize pay list of those entitled to share in the property captured from the enemy at Fort Detroit, in Royal Hospital, Chelsea.

	Officers.	N.C.O.	Privates.
General and Staff Officers	9		
Field Train Department	1	1	
Commissariat	1	2	
Militia Staff Officers	4		
Detachment 4 Bn. R1. Artillery	1	5	24
41st Regt. of Foot	13	26	263
Royal Newfoundland Fencibles	4	8	41
Provincial Marine Department	5	9	119
Militia Force, 1st & 3rd Reg., York Militia	4	6	77
5th Lincoln 2nd York	3	3	59
1st Regt. York Militia	2	3	19
2nd Regt. Norfolk Militia	6	3	59
1st Middlesex (attached to Norfolk)	1		
Oxford Militia		2	11
1st Regt. Essex Militia	22	32	258
2nd Regt. Essex Militia	23	11	131
1st Regt. Kent Militia	9	8	46
Troop of Essex Militia Cavalry	1	1	4
Indian Department	5	11	
49th Regiment			1
Officers (Regiments not mentioned)	3		
Total	117	131	1112

GENERAL ORDER.

(Casselman's 1902 reprint, p. 59, of "Richardson's War of 1812," 1842.)

Head Quarters, Detroit, 16th August, 1812.

Major-General Brock has every reason to be satisfied with the conduct of the Troops he had the honor to lead this morning against the enemy. The state of discipline which they so eminently displayed, and the determination they evinced to undertake the most hazardous enterprize, decided the enemy, infinitely more numerous in men and artillery, to propose a capitulation, the terms of which are herewith inserted for the information of the Troops.

The Major-General requests Colonel Procter will accept his best thanks for the assistance he derived from his experience and intelligence.

The steadiness and discipline of the 41st Regiment, and the readiness of the Militia to follow so good an example were highly conspicuous.

The ability manifested by Captain Dixon of the Royal Engineers in the choice and construction of the batteries and the high state of the Royal Artillery under Lieut. Troughton,[1] afforded the Major-General much gratification, and reflect great credit on those officers.

The willing assistance given by Captain Hall and the Marine Department during the whole course of the service has been very conspicuous, and the manner the batteries were served this morning evinced a degree of steadiness highly commendable.

Lieut. Dewar, Dpt. Ass. Qr.-Master-General, afforded strong proof by the local knowledge he had acquired of the country, of an unremitting attention to his duty; and the care and regularity with which the troops were transported across the river, must in a like degree, be ascribed to his zeal for the service.

To Lieut.-Col. St. George, Majors Tallon and Chambers, who commanded brigades, every degree of praise is due for their unremitting zeal and attention to their respective commands. The detachment of the Royal Newfoundland Regiment, under the command of Major Mockler, is deserving every praise for their steadiness in the field, as well as when embarked in the King's vessels.

The Major-General cannot forego this opportunity of expressing his admiration at the conduct of the several companies of Militia who so handsomely volunteered to undergo the fatigues of a journey of several hundred miles to go to the rescue of an invaded district; and he requests Major Salmon, Captains Hatt,[2] Heward, Bostwick, and Robinson, will assure the officers and men under their respective command (s), that their services have been duly appreciated and will never be forgotten.

The Major-General is happy to acknowledge the able assistance he has derived from the zeal and local information of Lieut.-Col. Nichol, acting Quarter-Master-General to the Militia.[3]

---

[1] Felix Troughton, lieutenant in the Royal Artillery, was awarded a gold medal for his services at Detroit and granted the brevet rank of major, November 28, 1812. He was wounded at Frenchtown, January 22, 1813; and died on his way to England, June 26, 1815.

[2] Samuel Hatt, captain of a flank company of the 5th Lincoln, commanded a detachment of volunteers from the 2nd York and his own regiment organized in the vicinity of Burlington Heights.

[3] Robert Nichol was a native of Dumfriesshire, Scotland, who emigrated to Canada at an early age. He acquired considerable property in the vicinity of Port Dover where he owned a flour mill and warehouse. He was appointed lieutenant-colonel commanding the 2nd Regiment of Norfolk militia, February 12, 1812; and quartermaster-general for the

To his personal Staff the Major-General feels himself under much obligation; and he requests Lieut.-Colonel Macdonell, Majors Glegg and Givins, will be assured that their zealous exertions have made too deep an impression on his mind ever to be forgotten. The conduct of the Indians under Col. Elliott, Capt. McKee, and other officers of that department, joined to that of the gallant and brave Chiefs of their respective tribes, has since the commencement of the war been marked with acts of true heroism, and in nothing can they testify more strongly their love to the King, their Great Father, than in following the dictates of honor and humanity, by which they have been hitherto actuated. Two fortifications have already been captured from the enemy without a drop of blood being shed by the hands of the Indians; the instant the enemy submitted, his life became sacred.

By order of Major-General Brock.

J. B. GLEGG, Capt., A.D.C.

FROM CAPTAIN ROBERTS. (UNADDRESSED.)

(Canadian Archives, C 688A, p. 175.)

Michilimackinac, 16th August, 1812.

Dear Sir,

The Messenger I sent off to Colonel St George on the capture of this place returned on the 3^d instant without effecting the purpose of his mission, you are already acquainted of their having taken prisoner a Man of the (name) of Smith bound here with dispatches from General Hull who was permitted to escape but what is still worse a young Ottawa one of the Crew was the bearer of Wampum from a Chief called the Wing, in the River St Clair to the Ottawas here telling them they had done wrong in assisting their English Father that the Americans were as numerous as the Sand and would exterminate them.

The effect this had on the Indians in general was very perceptible but some of the principal Chiefs of the Ottawas who

---

militia of Upper Canada on June 27, immediately after the declaration of war became known to Brock. He was awarded a gold medal for his services at Detroit and was presented with a sword of honour by the Legislature of the province in recognition of his services during the war. He represented the county of Norfolk in the Legislative Assembly of Upper Canada from 1812 to 1824. His death was accidental, caused by driving over the cliff near Queenston on a dark night in May, 1824.

were here at the time held secret Councils, to which two Chippawas were invited.

I received information of their proceedings and it is most probable that the preparations they saw making led them to suspect their secret was discovered. They waited on me the following morning and requested leave to visit their Corn fields and their Families, it was not until after their departure that I was acquainted with the particulars that passed in their Council by one of the Chippawa Chiefs that was present and who openly avows it as his opinion that these people are both Traitors and Cowards, it seems they had determined to let go my hand to go down to Detroit and implore forgiveness on their knees from the Americans for what they had done and to demand of me the restoration of this Fort to that Government these are the inhabitants of a village called Abacroshe (L'Arbre Croche) fifteen leagues from hence who for the last thirty years have been the acknowledged favourites they parted from me with every *apparent* mark of satisfaction with promises to repair to me on the shortest notice they are now sent for and we shall see what measures they intend to pursue the weakness of my Garrison is a favourite topic of conversation amongst them and I must once more beg leave to repeat *that a strong and active force* is absolutely necessary here at this moment for the double purpose of defence against these treacherous Men and for encouraging them to come forward when called for which nothing but the shew of superiority on our part will I am confident effect.

Whilst we were yet celebrating the birth day of His Royal Highness the Prince Regent your Express arrived. The Indians were extremely anxious for the News I called them together the next morning when amongst other things they were made acquainted with the threatening Anathema of the American Commander about 200 Men were all we could collect at the moment all offered their services to go to Amherstburgh and some of the Chiefs and young men shewed great zeal. It would appear from your Letters that the General must have imagined that all the Indians brought here by Mr Dickson as well (as) those that had been collected for the expedition against this place were still here The dreadful consumption of Provisions caused by those people who flocked in from all Quarters with their Wives and Children obliged me to send them off as fast as possible and the distant Indians were no sooner served with presents that they were warned to return to their Country and nothing less than an immediate object of employment where great recompense was to be expected could I think have detained them.

Thirty Men of the Sioux Nation are all that remain of those that came with Mr D. I have urged him repeatedly to take them down but the necessity of their going to rouse their Countrymen and to afford relief to their starving Families is always pleaded in excuse they have this day received presents to an enormous amount and are to take leave tomorrow. The heavy responsibility I am incurring by sanctioning the enormous expenses which the Indian department *seems now to demand* gives me great uneasiness—

The Spark which gave life to every proceeding at the commencement of our operations seems to have nearly expired The Traders have most of them received their supplies and are departing for their Winter Grounds   private views and individual jealousies have overcome every other sentiment Without forcibly detaining *them* and offering a large bounty to their Engagees which I did not feel myself authorized to do I found it impossible to collect any number of Canadians. I had determined on seizing their goods and was issuing a Proclamation to this effect but it created such alarm in the minds of the Indians, fearing their families would be starved for want of the usual trading supplies an idea which these Gentlemen took care by every means to foment I thought it most prudent to abandon the measure, finding that nothing was to (be) expected from the exertions of individuals I determined on a different mode of acting and have applied to the representatives of the Northwest and Southwest Companies in their public capacity for such assistance as their influence can bring forward—Mr Pothier is gone to St Marys to consult on this Subject and thus stands the state of affairs and the cooperation so much desired by you and so eagerly embraced by me is for the present at a stand still, but preparations are making to expedite the transport of this party under the impression that we shall yet obtain a number of Men and Arms from St Marys—

An active intelligent Man well versed in the disposition of Indians is much wanted here, Mr Askin is indefatigable in his exertions but as Store keeper alone he has more to attend to than most Men would be capable of. In my last Letter by Amable Chevalier[1] I informed you of the materials of which

---

[1] An Ottawa chief, Pawquokoman, who was made an interpreter with rank of lieutenant in the Indian Department in 1813. See p. 234.

my Garrison was composed, the infamous conduct[1] of my own Men surpasses all precedent the punishments within my reach are resorted to in vain One of them is now in Irons for striking an Officer in the execution of his duty

GENERAL RETURN OF PRISONERS OF WAR SURRENDERED BY CAPITULATION AT DETROIT, AUG. 16, 1812.

(Canadian Archives, C 688 B, p. 6.)

Distribution.	Regulars Embarked	Regulars Rem^g. In Barr^{ks}.	Regulars Rem^g. Sick, &c.	Regulars Total	Ohio Volunteers Embarked	Ohio Volunteers Rem^g. In Barr^{ks}.	Ohio Volunteers Rem^g. Sick	Ohio Volunteers Total	Aggregate
Queen Charlotte	130								
General Hunter	80								
Nancy	146								
Helen	88								
Chippawa	21								
Mary					208				
Thames					223				
Salina					177				
Cayahoga					57				
Revenue Cutter					46				
McCalls Boat					50				
In Boats					283				
In Detroit Barracks		38				264	12		
In Amherstburg D.		52	27			179	25		
Waggoners, &c., in Q^r Mr Genl Dept					82				
	465	90	27	582	1126	443	37	1606	2188

NB. The Prisoners Surrendered at Michilimackinack & Captured in the Cayahoga are included in the above Return.

DETROIT, Augt 26, 1812.

ROBT. NICHOL, L^t. Col^o.
Q^r Mr Genl Militia.

---

[1] See despatch of Roberts to Glegg, July 29, p. 100.

RETURN OF ORDNANCE AND ORDNANCE STORES TAKEN AT DETROIT 16TH AUGUST, 1812..

(Canadian Archives, C 688 A, p. 179.)

Ordnance	Iron	24 prs.		9
		12 "		9
		9 "		4
		6 "		3
	Brass	6 "		3
		4 "		2
		3 "		1
		8 Inch Howitzer		1
		5½ " "		1
		2¾ " "		2
Carriages	Garrison	24 prs.		5
		12		5
		9		4
		6		3
	Travelling	24		2
		6		3
		4		2
		3		2
		8 Inch Howitzer		1
		5½ Do Do		1
		2¾ Do Do		1
Shot	24 pʳ	Round		1300
		Grape		20
		Case		12
	12 pʳ	Round		1650
		Grape		140
		Case		60
	9 pʳ	Round		900
		Grape		50
		Case		80
Shot	6 pʳ	Round		3138
		Grape		16
		Case		90
	4 pʳ	Round		210
		Grape		"
		Case		"
	3 pʳ	Round		3710
		Grape		"
		Case		33
Shells		10 Inch		272
		8 "		467
		5½ "		274
		2¾ "		3650
Powder		Barrels of 90 lbs		60
		Do 25 lbs		9

Cartridge paper, Reams	270
Musquets	2500
Bayonets	2500
Cartouches with Belts	2500
Rifles	500
Flints	39000
Musquet ball Cartridge	80000
Swords with belts	17
Lifting Jacks	6
Gyn and Tackle	1
Sheets of Copper	23
Brass Quadrant	1
Boarding Pikes	100

RETURN OF ORDNANCE AND ORDNANCE STORES TAKEN AT
DETROIT 16TH AUGUST, 1812—*Continued.*

	Tons	Cwts.	Q^{rs}.
Sets of Cartridge Formers from 3 p^n to 24 p^n			1
Musquet Ball	"	10	"
Buck Shot	1	"	"
Flags { English			1
{ American			2

One Small Laboratory Still and an assortment of Laboratory implements and Stores.

FELIX TROUGHTON Lieut
Commg Royal Artillery

BROCK'S PROCLAMATION FOLLOWING THE SURRENDER OF FORT DETROIT.

(Canadian Archives, Q 315, p. 172.)

PROCLAMATION.

Copy

By Isaac Brock, Esquire, Major General, Commanding His Britanic Majesty's Forces in the Province of Upper Canada &c., &c., &c.

WHEREAS the Territory of Michigan was this day by Capitulation ceded to the Arms of His Britannic Majesty without any other condition than the protection of private property—And wishing to give an early proof of the moderation and justice of the Government, I do hereby announce to all the Inhabitants of the said Territory, that the Laws heretofore in existence shall continue in force until His Majesty's pleasure be known, or so long as the peace and safety of the said Territory will admit thereof—And I do hereby also declare and make known to the said Inhabitants, that they shall be protected in the full exercise and enjoyment of their Religion, Of which all persons both Civil and Military will take notice, and govern themselves accordingly.

All persons having in their possession, or having any knowledge of any Public Property, shall forthwith deliver in the same or give notice thereof to the Officer Commanding, or Lieutenant Colonel Nichol, who are hereby duly Authorized to receive and give proper Receipts for the same.

Officers of Militia will be held responsible that all Arms in possession of Militia Men, be immediately delivered up, and all Individuals whatever, who have in their possession, Arms of any kind, will deliver them up without delay.

> Given under my hand, at Detroit, this sixteenth day of August, One thousand eight hundred and twelve, and in the Fifty Second Year of His Majesty's reign.
>
> (signed) ISAAC BROCK,
> Major General.

MAJOR-GENERAL BROCK TO SIR GEORGE PREVOST.

(Canadian Archives, C 677, p. 45.)

Copy/

Head Quarters Detroit

August 16th 1812.

Sir/

I hasten to apprize Your Excellency of the Capture of this very important Post: 2,500 troops have this day surrendered Prisoners of War, and about 25 Pieces of Ordnance have been taken, without the Sacrifice of a drop of British blood; I had not more than 700 troops including Militia, and about 400 Indians to accomplish this Service. When I detail my good fortune Your Excellency will be astonished. I have been admirably supported by Colonel Procter, the whole of my Staff and I may justly say every individual under my command.

MAJOR-GENERAL BROCK TO SIR GEORGE PREVOST.[1]

(Canadian Archives, Q 118, p. 228.)

Copy/

Head Quarters, Detroit August 17th 1812.

Sir,

I have had the honor of informing Your Excellency that the Enemy effected his passage across the Detroit River on the 12th Ultimo, without opposition, and that after establishing himself at Sandwich he had ravaged the Country as far as the Moravian Town. Some Skirmishes occurred between

---

[1] A rough draft of this despatch may be found in *Canadian Archives,* C 688 A, p. 183.

the Troops under Lieu^t Colonel St George and the Enemy upon the River Canard, which uniformly terminated in his being repulsed with loss.

The Occupation of Sandwich was evidently productive of considerable effect on the minds of a large portion of the Inhabitants. The disaffected became more audacious, and the wavering more intimidated. I judged it therefore proper to detach at every risk a force down the River Thames capable of acting in conjunction with the Garrison of Amherstburg offensively, but Capt Chambers, whom I had appointed to direct this detachment, experienced difficulties from the prevalent spirit of the moment, that frustrated my intentions.

The intelligence received from that Quarter admitting of no delay, Colonel Procter was directed to assume the Command, and his force was soon after encreased with sixty rank and file of the 41st Regiment.

In the mean time the most strenuous measures were adopted, to Counteract the Machinations of the evil disposed, and I soon experienced the gratification of receiving Voluntary Offers of service from that portion of the Embodied Militia the most easily collected.

In the attainment of this important point, Gentlemen of the first character and influence shewed an example highly creditable to them, and I cannot on this occasion avoid mentioning the essential assistance I derived from John McDonell Esquire, His Majesty's Attorney General, who from the beginning of the War has honored me with his services as my provincial Aid-de-Camp.

A sufficiency of boats being collected at Long Point for the conveyance of three hundred men,[1] the embarkation took place on the 8th instant, and in five days arrived in safety at Amherstburg.

I found that the judicious arrangements which had been adopted immediately upon the arrival of Colonel Procter had compelled the Enemy to retreat and take shelter under the Guns of his Fort.

That Officer commenced operations by sending strong detachments across the river with a view of cutting off the Enemy's communication with his resources, this produc'd two smart skirmishes on the 5th and 9th instant, in both of which the Enemy's loss was very considerable—whilst ours

---

[1] The draft of this despatch in *Canadian Archives, C 688 A, p. 183*, shews that these consisted of 250 militia and 50 of the 41st Regiment.

amounted to three killed and thirteen wounded—amongst the latter I have particularly to regret Captain Muir and Lieut Sutherland of the 41st Regiment; the former an Officer of great experience, and both ardent in His Majesty's Service.

Batteries had likewise been commenced opposite Fort Detroit, for one 18 pounder, two 12, and two 5½ inch Mortars, all of which opened on the Evening of the 15th (having previously summoned Brigr. General Hull to surrender) and although opposed by a well directed fire from seven 24 pounders, such was their construction, under the able direction of Captain Dixon of the Royal Engineers, that no injury was sustained from its effect.

The force at my disposal being collected in the course of the 15th in the neighbourhood of Sandwich, the embarkation took place a little after daylight on the following Morning, and by the able arrangements of Lieutenant Dewar, of the Quarter Master General's Dept. the whole was in a short time landed without the smallest confusion at Spring Well, a good position, three miles West of Detroit.—The Indians who had in the meantime effected their landing two miles below, moved forwards, and occupied the woods about a mile and a half on our left.

The force which I instantly directed to march against the Enemy, consisted of thirty Royal Artillery, two hundred and fifty 41st Regt., fifty Royal Newfoundland Regiment, four hundred Militia and about six hundred Indians, to which were attached three 6 pounders and two 3 pounders.

The services of Lieut. Troughton Commanding the Royal Artillery, an Active and intelligent Officer, being required in the field, the direction of the Batteries was entrusted to Captain Hall, and the Marine Department, and I cannot with-hold my entire approbation of their conduct on this occasion.

I crossed the river with an intention of waiting in a strong position the effect of our fire upon the Enemy's Camp, and in the hope of compelling him to meet us in the field. But receiving information upon landing that Colonel McArthur, an Officer of high reputation, had left the Garrison three days before with a detachment of five hundred men, and hearing soon afterwards that his Cavalry had been seen that morning three miles in our rear, I decided on an immediate attack.

Accordingly the Troops advanced to within one mile of the Fort, and having ascertained that the Enemy had taken little or no precaution towards the land side, I resolved on an

Assault, whilst the Indians penetrated his Camp. Brig^r. Genl. Hull however prevented this movement by proposing a cessation of hostilities, for the purpose of preparing terms of Capitulation, Lieu^t. Colonel John McDonell and Capt Glegg were accordingly deputed by me on this Mission, and returned within an hour with the Conditions, which I have the honor herewith to transmit.

Certain considerations induced me afterwards to agree to the two supplementary Articles

The force[1] thus surrendered to His Majesty's Arms, cannot be estimated at less than Two thousand five hundred Men: in this estimate Colonel McArthur's Detachment is included, as he surrendered agreeably to the terms of Capitulation in the Course of the Evening, with the exception of two hundred men, whom he left escorting a valuable Convoy at some little distance in his rear, but there can be no doubt the Officer Commanding will consider himself equally bound by the Capitulation.

The Enemy's aggregate force was divided into
Two Troops of Cavalry.
One Company of Artillery, regulars.
The 4th United States Regiment.
Detachments of the 1st and 3rd United States Regiment, Volunteers.
Three Regiments of the Ohio Militia.
One d° of Michigan territory.

Thirty three pieces of brass and iron Ordnance have already been secured.—

When this Contest Commenced many of the Indian Nations were engaged in Active Warfare with the United States, notwithstanding the constant endeavours of this Government to dissuade them from it. Some of the principal Chiefs happened to be at Amherstburg trying to procure a supply of Arms and Ammunition which for years had been with-held, agreeably to the Instructions received from Sir James Craig, and since repeated by Your Excellency.

From that moment they took a most active part, and appeared foremost on every occasion, they were led yesterday by Colonel Elliott and Capt. McKee, and nothing could exceed their order and steadiness—a few prisoners were taken by

---
[1] For Hull's estimate of his force see his despatch to the Secretary of War, August 26, p. 184; see also Cass to the Secretary of War, September 10, p. 218.

them during the advance whom they treated with every humanity, and it affords me much pleasure in assuring Your Excellency that such was their forbearance and attention to what was required of them, that the Enemy sustained no other loss in Men, than what was occasioned by the fire of our batteries.

The high sense I entertain of the abilities and judgment of Lieu^t. Colonel Myers induced me to appoint him to the important Command at Niagara.

It was with reluctance I deprived myself of his Assistance, but had no other expedient.

His duties as head of the Quarter Master General's department were performed to my satisfaction by L^t. Colonel Nicholls Quarter Master General of the Militia.

Captain Glegg my Aid de Camp will have the honor of delivering this Dispatch to Your Excellency.—

He is charged with the Colors taken at the Capture of Fort Detroit, and those of the 4th United States Regiment.

Captain Glegg is capable of giving Your Excellency every information respecting the state of the Province, and I shall esteem myself highly indebted to Your Excellency to afford him that protection to which his merit and length of Service give him a powerful Claim.

P.S. I have the honor to enclose a Copy of a Proclamation which I issued immediately on taking possession of this Country—

I should have mentioned in the body of my Dispatch, the Capture of the *Adams,* she is a fine Vessel and recently repaired, but without arms.

SIR GEORGE PREVOST TO EARL BATHURST.[1]

(Canadian Archives, Q 118, p. 177.)

N°. 3.

Montreal 17th Augt 1812.

My Lord,

I have the honor to inform Your Lordship that an Invasion of Upper Canada took place on the 12th of July last, the Enemy having on that day crossed the River Detroit with a Force composed of Regular Troops and Militia together with Forty

---

[1] The Earl of Bathurst, formerly Lord President of the Council, had succeeded the Earl of Liverpool as Secretary of State for the Department of War and the Colonies. The Earl of Liverpool had become First Lord of the Treasury and Prime Minister.

or Fifty Cavalry amounting in the whole to about 2,300 men under the Command of Brigadier General Hull & took post at Sandwich.

The Militia in the neighbourhood not being able to oppose any effectual resistance retreated upon their approach towards Fort Amherstburg about twelve miles distant. Part of the Enemy's Force having since advanced to within about six miles of that Fort, several skirmishes have taken place between them & the Troops of the Garrison which have constantly terminated in favor of the latter, with the loss of several men on the part of the Enemy, & of only one Soldier of the 41st killed & another wounded, and a similar loss on the part of the Indians—And I am happy to say that on these different occasions His Majesty's 41st Reg^{t} in a particular manner distinguished themselves.

The last Accounts from Amherstburg are to the 30th Ult^{o} at which time Col. Procter of the 41st Reg^{t} who commanded there did not conceive the Post to be in any immediate danger, tho' at the same time he strongly pressed for a reinforcement.

Immediately upon the Invasion of the Province and upon the issuing of the Proclamation by General Hull, which I have the honor of herewith transmitting, it was plainly perceived by Genl Brock that little reliance could be placed upon the Militia, and as little dependance upon the active exertions of any considerable proportion of the population of the Country, unless he was vested with full power to repress the disaffected Spirit which was daily beginning to shew itself, & to restrain & punish the disorders which threatened to dissolve the whole Militia Force he had assembled—He therefore called together the Provincial Legislature on the 27th Ult^{o} in the hope that they would adopt prompt & effectual measures for strengthening the hands of the Government at a period of such danger & difficulty, & which were so necessary effectually to repel the Invasion made upon one part of the Province, & to defend it from the attacks menaced upon others.

In these reasonable expectations I am sorry to say Genl Brock has been miserably disappointed, and a lukewarm & temporizing spirit, evidently dictated either by the apprehension or the wish that the Enemy might soon be in complete possession of the Country, having prevented the Assembly from adopting any of the Measures proposed to them, they were prorogued on the 5th $Inst$.

This step[1] Gen¹ Brock was induced to take by the advice of the Executive Council, a Copy of whose proceedings on that head I have the honor to inclose to Your Lordship, & to which I beg leave to refer you as containing the fullest information of the then state of the Province, and of the means to be employed for its defence—

I have also the honor of transmitting to Your Lordship Copies of two letters[2] which passed between Gen¹ Hull and Lᵗ Col Sᵗ George then Commanding at Amherstburg as indicative of the temper and disposition in which the Invasion of Upper Canada has been undertaken.—

Gen¹ Brock fully aware of the great Importance of the Post of Amherstburg had previous to the Invasion of the Province strengthened it in every way which the small means in his power would permit, & finding from the result of the meeting of the Legislature that he was left to his own resources arising almost wholly from the regular Troops under his Command, to resist the further approaches of the Enemy, he left York on the 5ᵗʰ Insᵗ for Fort George for the purpose of putting himself at the head of a detachment of picked Militia Volunteers whom he was assembling at Long Point on Lake Erie, & with whom together with a party of 60 men of the 41ˢᵗ Regᵗ & such Indians as he could collect it was his intention to proceed to the immediate relief of Amherstburg, as upon the safety of that Post until the arrival of such reinforcements as I might be enabled to afford him from this Province, would in a great measure depend the Fate of the Province.

From the moment I had heard of the Invasion of the Upper Province I had not been unmindful of the necessity of reinforcing Gen¹ Brock to such an extent as the Exigencies of the service of this Province would permit, and arrangements were made accordingly for that purpose,—

A part of the 49ᵗʰ Regᵗ has already proceeded from Montreal to Kingston where it has probably arrived by this time, and has been followed by the remainder of the Newfoundland Regiment of some picked Veterans; the other Companies of the 49ᵗʰ Regiment will proceed to the same destination as soon as a sufficient number of batteaux can be collected—

I have also deemed it necessary to give Major Gen¹ Sheaffe a temporary Employment upon the Staff as Major General in Upper Canada, & from his long residence in that Country &

---

[1] See despatch, Brock to Liverpool, August 29, with enclosures, p. 190.
[2] For these letters, see pp. 69-70.

his known abilities, I feel confident he will prove of material assistance to Genl Brock under whose command I have placed him—The great superiority of our Naval Force on the Lakes has contributed in no small degree to protract the fall of Amherstburg, & will I have no doubt enable the destined reinforcements to reach it in safety; whilst at the same time the fortunate surrender of Fort Michilimackinac, the detail of which I have had the honor of transmitting to Lord Liverpool, may, as I trust it will, occasion a diversion by the Indians in the rear and on the flanks of the Enemy, so as to enable Genl Brock to attack them with advantage & probably compel them to retire from the Province.

To the prompt persevering & energetic measures of that Officer in a season of uncommon difficulty & embarrassment must be ascribed the present safety of the Upper Province, & I confidently look forward to its ultimate preservation from a continuance of the same zeal, judgment & ability which he has hitherto manifested in its defence. In addition to the other difficulties of Genl Brock's situation I ought not to omit to mention to Your Lordship the want of money, which could not be obtained at any discount for Government Bills of Exchange; all that possibly could be spared from the Military Chest in this Province has been sent to him, & I deem it a singularly fortunate occurrence that at this critical Juncture, the issue of Army Bills which I have made under the sanction of the late Act of the Provincial Legislature of Lower Canada now enables me to relieve him from the increased Embarrassments in which he would have otherwise been involved from the want of money both for the payment of the Regular Troops & of the Militia. Upon the Frontier line extending from Fort Erie to the Head of the Lake Ontario no attack has hitherto been made by the Enemy, nor is it apprehended whilst Amherstburg holds out that any will be made which the Force in that quarter is not adequate to repel. From Kingston to Montreal the Frontier line appears at present equally secure & such measures have been adopted for its defence by the supply of Arms & Ammunition to the Militia in that Quarter who appear particularly well disposed & active, as well by mounting guns on commanding positions, that the communication by the River to the Lake will be fully protected & the Country secure from any attempts of the Enemy to molest it—The arrival of the First Battalion of the Royals from the West Indies with the exception of one Transport captured by the

United States Frigate *Essex* but afterwards ransomed & sent to Halifax has principally afforded me the means of furnishing Gen[l] Brock with the reinforcements I have sent to him. The 8th or Kings Regiment has arrived this M(ornin)[g] from Quebec to relieve the 49th Reg[t]—This fine & effective Reg[t] of the 8th together with a Chain of Troops established in the vicinity of this place consisting of regular & Militia Forces, the whole amounting to near Four thousand five hundred men, effectually serve to keep in check the Enemy in this Quarter where alone they are in any strength, & to prevent any Attempt to carry on a predatory Warfare against this flourishing portion of Lower Canada.

Having thus detailed to Your Lordship the measures I have found it necessary to adopt for the security of the Canadas allow me to request you will submit them to His Royal Highness The Prince Regent with the expression of my humble hope that they may meet His Royal Highness's Approbation.

GOVERNOR HARRISON TO THE SECRETARY OF WAR. (EXTRACT.)

(Historical Narrative of the Civil and Military Services of Major-General Wm. H. Harrison, by Moses Dawson; Cincinnati, 1824; p. 279.)

Louisville, Ky. 18th *August*, 1812.

Sir,

The regiment of Kentucky volunteers destined for Vincennes, rendezvoused at this place yesterday..........A gentleman immediately from Vincennes, informs me that citizens there are under great alarm, and that information received from every quarter corroborates the account of the intended attack. I have sent off one company from the Indiana regiment of militia adjacent to this place, and have agreed to dismiss them in a month, on condition of their furnishing themselves with horses. When the regiment now here reaches Vincennes, it will be amply sufficient for the defence of that settlement. But I fear that colonel Wilcox will not be able to leave Jeffersonville until the 20th inst............In my letter of the 10th inst. I observed that it had been determined in a consultation with the friends of the administration, that it would be better to suspend the marching of any more of the Kentucky quota, until your further instructions should be received, or some further indication of hostility on the part of the Indians should make it necessary. Upon my return to Frankfort, however, a further consultation with governor Scott took place, and upon a representation being made by one of the colonels in writing, stating that it would be utterly impossible to collect the troops time enough for any offensive operations this fall, unless the order for their assembly should be soon given, we both united in opinion that it would be necessary, even upon the uncertainty of their being wanted, that a distant day should be appointed for their rendezvous at three different points. The day fixed upon is the 1st of September, and the places designated are Frankfort, Louisville, and Henderson, (Red Bank,) the former for the cavalry and two regiments of infantry, and at each of the others, one regiment of infantry. If none, or a part only, of these troops, should be wanted, they can be disbanded, and the only consequence will be, some disappointment in the men; but if they had not been ordered to assemble, and should there be occasion for their service some time in September, it would have been found almost impossible to get them to any distant scene of action until the season for such operations would have been too far advanced. Should the hopes which have been formed of the favorable effects of the council at Piqua not be realized, the government, at the moment which shall ascertain its failure, will have at its disposal, a formidable force ready to take the field; and the points of rendezvous have been so fixed as to give as great a choice as was possible, to the direction in which it may be moved.

COLONEL PROCTER TO CHIEF JUSTICE WOODWARD,[1] DETROIT.

(Canadian Archives, C 688A, p. 196.)

Detroit Aug: 20th, 1812

Sir

I enclose a Copy of a Proclamation issued by Major General Brock on the 16th Ins^t announcing among other Things, that wishing to give an early Proof of the Moderation and Justice of the British Government, the Laws heretofore in Existence shall continue in Force untill His Majesty's Plea-

---

[1] Augustus B. Woodward, chief justice of the territory of Michigan, was appointed civil secretary by Colonel Procter, and acted in that capacity for several months after the surrender of Detroit.

sure be known, or so long as the Peace and Safety of the Territory will admit thereof.

Understanding that you are the only Officer of the late Government at present here, I should be happy for such Information as you might please to afford on the following Points.

1st What are the geographical Limits of the Territory by the American Laws?

2d What are the settled and unsettled Parts; and what is the population?

3d What was the civil Government, and what were the Expenses of it's Administration?—can the civil Government be reorganized without a new supreme civil Magistrate. Do the Laws require such Magistrate, or any other, and if any, what others, to reside here. What offices might the Change of Flag render necessary to be superseded, and which are susceptible of being continued, and would those who heretofore held those Offices be willing to continue in the Exercise of them, their Allegiance not being otherwise affected, for the Time being, than as relates to the Tranquility of the Country under existing Circumstances.

CHIEF JUSTICE WOODWARD TO COLONEL PROCTER.

(Canadian Archives, C 688A, p. 199.)

Michigan, August 20, 1812.

Sir,

I return you my thanks for the copy of the proclamation which you have been so polite as to send. The determination of General Brock to continue the American laws for the time being and the full protection given to the private property, and to the religion of the inhabitants, while it renders an honorable tribute to the elevated sentiments which actuate his mind, cannot fail at the same time to conciliate and obtain the good-will of those affected by the late change in the posture of affairs, as well as to smooth the path of future accommodation when the existing misunderstandings between Great Britain and the American States shall be adjusted.

I reply with great pleasure to your several enquiries.

The geographical limits of the Territory of Michigan are designated by an act of Congress.

The boundary commences at the southern extremity of Lake Michigan, and is drawn east from that point until it shall intersect Lake Erie. This line has never been actually run. It is therefore uncertain where it would intersect Lake Erie. I have a minute of an observation taken by a British gentleman which makes the latitude of the southern extremity of Lake Michigan a degree and a half south of Detroit. This would carry the line entirely south of Lake Erie. I am in possession of some maps which so represent the country. On the contrary I have seen other maps and have received many oral communications which represent the southern extremity of Lake Michigan as nearly west of Detroit. The American government have been taking measures to remove this ambiguity which however may have been impeded by the troubles which have recently pervaded those regions. During the uncertainty the mouth of the River Miami has been assumed as the line the justices of the peace on the north side of that river acting under commissions derived from the Territory of Michigan and those on the south side of it acting under the commissions derived from the State of Ohio.

The boundary was common to Great Britain and the United States on the East and to the North.

From the southern extremity of Lake Michigan a line was required to run through the middle of said Lake to its northern extremity. It is uncertain whether the northern extremity of Lake Michigan is in Green Bay or at an intermediate point between Green Bay and the Straits of Michillimackinac.

From the northern extremity of Lake Michigan a line due north to the northern boundary of the United States in Lake Superior completes the western demarcation and closes the geographical limits of the country. Its greatest length may be five hundred miles, its greatest breadth three hundred. It includes two peninsulas one very large, the other small.

From the mouth of the River Miami to the head of the River Sinclair at the *embouchûre* or outlet of Lake Huron, the country is settled, though in a very sparse manner, on a continued line, without any settlements in the rear, every house forming as it were a double frontier. There were formerly some families at the River St. Joseph's near the southern extremity of Lake Michigan and the island of Michillimackinac also had a few settlements.

The population of the Territory of Michigan is more completely elucidated by the official return rendered to the American Department of State, a copy of which I enclose, than by any observations I should be capable of making.

The civil government of the Territory of Michigan must be considered under three distinct aspects; first, as a colonial establishment distinct from the several states; secondly, as forming a part of the United States for certain general and national purposes; and, thirdly, as internally distributed and partitioned for the purposes of domestic regulation and police.

Under the first aspect as a colonial establishment distinct from the several States the government consisted of one governor three judges and one secretary. The salary of the governor was four hundred and fifty pounds sterling per annum. The salary of each of the three judges was two hundred and seventy pounds sterling. The salary of the secretary was two hundred and twenty five pounds sterling. Seventy eight pounds fifteen shillings were allowed for incidental and contingent charges. All these expences were defrayed by the General Government of the United States. All these officers were required to reside in the Territory. They were further required to be possessed of certain portions of land.

The civil government unquestionably cannot be reorganized without a civil governor. He must supply the several offices which are vacant. One judge may hold the courts in the absence of the others. The secretary is also necessary in the capacity of lieutenant-governor, and for the preservation and transmission of executive and legislative transactions. The legislative regulations were required to be adopted from those of the original American States by a majority of the Governor and Judges.

Under the second aspect as forming a part of the United States for certain general and national purposes the Territory of Michigan embraced ten or twelve different officers. The following is an enumeration of them.

1. The postmaster of Detroit.
2. The postmaster at the River Raisin.
3. The postmaster at the River Miami.
4. The register of the land-office.
5. The receiver of public monies obtained for lands.
6. A deputy of an extra-resident surveyor-general for the execution of surveys of land.
7. A collector of the customs at the Port of Detroit.
8. A collector of the customs at the port of Michillimackinac.
9. A collector of the customs at Port Miami.
10. Sundry Indian Interpreters.

Most of these officers were paid by fees of office and certain very small salaries. All the revenue officers will be indispensible if the American Revenue laws are intended to be enforced. The others you will perhaps Sir be disposed to consider as superseded in consequence of the change of the flag.

Under the third aspect the Territory of Michigan is regarded as it is internally distributed and partitioned for the purposes of domestic regulation and police.

The following may embrace the various descriptions of officers which it comprehended.

1. The clerk of the Supreme Court.
2. The marshall of the Territory.
3. The attorney-general.
4. The treasurer.
5. The adjutant-general of the Militia.
6. The quarter master general of the Militia.
7. The marshall of the district of Detroit.
8. The marshall of the district of Erie.
9. The marshall of the district of Huron.
10. The marshall of the district of Michillimackinac.
11. Five commissioners of civil police for the relief of the poor, the repair of roads, bridges, &c. &c. &c. in those four several districts.
12. Their several clerks, assessors, collectors, treasurers, overseers of the poor, supervisors of high-ways, &c. &c. &c. in the four several districts.
13. The register, constituting the recording and probate officer one in each of those four districts.
14. From twenty to thirty justices of the peace throughout the Territory.

These officers, where paid at all, derived their compensations from some species of local revenue particularly appropriated to the service.

All these officers are susceptible of being continued for the present time.

The enquiry whether those who have heretofore held offices under the American government would be willing to continue in the exercise of them their allegiance not being otherwise affected for the time being than as relates to the tranquility of the country under existing circumstances is attended with a difficulty principally as it relates to that description holding their offices immediately and directly under commissions from the general government of the United States.

The inhabitants of a conquered or ceded country may it is conceived after the conquest or cession hold and exercise offices under the acquiring power, and if the country be afterwards retroceded it is believed they do not incur the penalties of treason by so doing. Neither the law of nations nor the American laws appear to require the inhabitants to quit this country and the liberal footing on which you propose to place the former laws and the administration of them, and the qualified and implied temporary allegiance which seems to be alone contemplated at present is calculated to obviate embarrassment. With regard therefore to all subordinate officers I am humbly of opinion that they may perhaps without impropriety act. Their willingness to do so can only be ascertained by personal reference.

With respect to that class holding commissions directly under the government of the United States I beg leave to lay before you the following extract from their constitution.

"No person holding any office of profit or trust under the United States shall, without the consent of the Congress, accept of any present, emolument, office, or title, of any kind whatever, from any king, prince, or foreign state."

The intention of this provision was not applicable to a case like the present; but its letter may affect it. It might be proper to permit the American government to be consulted on this point; as the citizens would act with more cheerfulness if they were informed that their conduct would not be disapproved.

JOHN HAYS[1] TO GOVERNOR EDWARDS, OF ILLINOIS TERRITORY.

(The Edwards Papers, Chicago Historical Society's Collection, Vol. III, p. 81.)

Sir:—

I had the honor of just receiving your letter of 19th inst. by mail, and agreeable to your request I answer your queries:

Ahe route from Montreal to Michilimackanac by the Grand river is called nine hundred miles, the most difficult route, per-

---

[1] John Hays was sheriff of St. Clair county, Michigan, at this time. In early life he had been a fur trader at Mackinac, the Lake of the Woods, and the source of the Mississippi.

haps, in the world. There are thirty-six carrying places where all the goods are carried on men's backs over those portages, and in most of those places the bark canoes are likewise carried on men's shoulders. There are likewise thirty-six places where half-canoe loads are carried owing to the great rapids. What is meant by half-loads, the canoe starts half-loaded and deposits the half-load at a certain place, and then returns for the other half-load. No boats of any kind can ascend this river, only bark canoes, which carry about seven thousand weight, or seventy pieces weighing one hundred pounds each; every man carries two of these pieces over each carrying place. Those canoes are navigated by ten, sometimes eleven men, with paddles. By this route all the merchandize from Montreal is carried to the Grand portage, Nippegand, Arthabaska, and all the other wintering places in Lake Superior, and the peltries return by same route; but a few years past all the merchandize from Montreal to Mackanac was taken there by the same route. I have come myself from Montreal to Mackanac by this river. The Fort St. Josephs is about seventeen leagues from Mackanac; it is an island about three leagues in length, pretty high land, about two leagues from mainland, and twelve leagues from Sou St. Mary's, and about six hundred miles from Grand portage. There is generally about sixty or seventy men at St. Josephs; a captain commands these. Sometimes assembles at the Grand portage, about fifteen or sixteen hundred men, generally in the spring, the latter end of May or in June; in the fall they are mostly all gone to their wintering grounds. I have never known more than a full company to be stationed at Mackanac. Goods may be brought from St. Josephs along the mainland and by the Island of Mackanac within six miles. Those brought the last fall into the Mississippi by Mr. Dickson and others were brought that route. Mr. Chenier[1] nor no other person has yet arrived from Mackanac. Knowing the difficulty for troops reaching that country by any other route than by Detroit, I can not help but concur with your opinion that Mackanac is not taken........
....

20th Aug., 1812.

---

[1] Antoine Chenier was made an interpreter in the Indian Department, with the rank of lieutenant, in September 1812.

CAPTAIN WM. ELLIOTT, 1ST REGT. ESSEX MILITIA, TO COLONEL PROCTER.

(Canadian Archives, C 688A, p. 218.)

Amherstburgh 22^d Augt 1812

Sir,

I have the honor to inform you that agreeable to my orders rec^d from his Honor Major General Brock at Detroit on the 16th Ins^t I proceeded to the River Rouge, where I met Co^l McArthur's Detachment who surrendered himself & the Detachment agreeable to General Hull's letter; and I left them in charge of Major Dixon, as the Detachment under Captn Brush with the provisions had not joined Co^l McArthur, and was supposed to be on their march, Co^l McArthur wrote on the back of General Hull's letter an order to Captn Brush, to conform to the terms of surrender with which letter & the copy of the terms of capitulation I proceeded to the River Reizen which place I arrived at, at two oclock in the afternoon of Monday, when I was at the distance of about half a mile from the fort stop(p)ed by a guard of twelve men, commanded by a capt^n who disarmed me & the three men, blindfolded us then conducted us to the Fort, as soon as we were within the gate it was shut & nailed up, Brush, the commandant ordered all his men under arms to see me hung as he said, and told me the papers I brought were forged after detaining me about an hour in the sun I was put into one of the block houses w(h)ere I was kept untill dark, when Captn Brush and his officers told me in the morning the(y) would give me a final answer, as they had learned from some of their men who had arrived that the papers I had were genuine, about twelve at night I was awakened by the noise of the men & waggons leaving the Fort, and was shortly afterwards liberated by Co^l Anderson who command the Militia of that place, Co^l Anderson proposed to surrender his Reg^t provided I would on the part of the Commander, His Honor General Brock, promise them the same terms that had been granted to the 1st Reg^t of Michigan Militia, this I undertook to do, agreeably to this arrangement Co^l Anderson ordered the men composing his Reg^t to parade at two P.M. when they laid down their arms, and surrendered to me the Fort with all the stores a schedule of which I subjoin, on wednesday evening after imbarking the arms &^{c} sett out for this place, but was detained by head winds untill the next morning, when on being informed of Co^l Elliott's arrival I returned up the River, and remained untill the next morning when I took Co¹ Elliott into the boat & returned to this place

Schedule[1]

114 muskets, 80 Bayonet's, 63 Cartridge boxes—7 Riffle's, 10 Powder horns, 6 Horsemens swords, 12 Pistols, 1 . 2 ¾ inch brass hoit, (Howitzer), 19 shot, 46 barrel's of flour, 12 ditto pork, 3 waggons,—

The arms I have delivered to Mr Wood of the field train, and four barrels of the Pork to the commissary at this place, the Remaining articles were left by me at the River Reizen in charge of a Mr F. Lascelle—

LIEUT. EDWARD DEWAR, D.A.Q.M.G. TO COLONEL PROCTER.

(Canadian Archives, C 688A, p. 222.)

Copy/ , Amherstburg August 28th 1812
Sir,

Though it does not properly belong to my Department to recommend Purchases to be made by Government, I yet think it my duty to represent to you the necessity of retaining for this Post all ·Provisions which may be intended for sale[2] to-morrow at Detroit. Having to furnish you with a Table of Resources of the District, I have already taken informations in general which lead to the following results—The Crop of wheat will not average one half of its usual quantity owing to the want of hands to get it in at the proper time and to the subsequent heavy rains—2dly. The Crop of Indian Corn will not average One quarter of the usual quantity from the same cause, want of hands to hoe which if not done at a particular time the consequence is an entire failure—Potatoes come under, exactly, the same head, and for the same reason as the last, they are now selling at a Dollar a bushel which is four times the price which I paid for them at this Season last year—Cattle is becoming very scarce, indeed, in the Lake Settlement, and Hogs which afforded not only the principal means of Subsistance to the Inhabitants of every class during Winter, but also one of the Staple Articles of Trade, have almost entirely disappeared, partly from the excessive rigor of the preceding Winter and still more from the shameful depredations that have been, and still are committed by the Indians, those very people whose

---
[1] Compare with return on p. 176.
[2] See pp. 247-48.

families we shall have to support next Winter, in addition to a strong Garrison of Regulars and Militia.—

Being upon the subject of the Indians I cannot help observing that their conduct becomes outrageous in proportion to the impunity with which they offend they have at least eight Boats at present in their possession—yesterday being informed that one of the North West Boats had drifted to Hartleys Point I sent two Dock yard People to bring it up, they had proceeded as far as Col^l Elliotts when a party of Indians rushed upon them and took the Boat from them by force accompanied with ill treatment.—A poor Canadian of the name of Denault, whose horse and Cart we had pressed some time since to convey Ordnance Stores to Sandwich, found the horse yesterday in the Town mounted by two Indians, he seized it, and they struck him, but procuring assistance, and the Indians finding themselves compel'd to submit, they ran their swords thro' the Animals body—of course Government will have to pay the value of this horse, as well as perhaps forty or fifty others, that were pressed and have been stolen, what aggravates the evil is that liquor is again sold here to Soldiers, from whom the Indians procure it—The Wind has not permitted the *Nid* to return to Detroit as yet—I will send all the Batteaux that I can man with the Scow, but must observe that we are in great want of hands.—

COLONEL PROCTER TO MAJOR-GENERAL BROCK.

(Canadian Archives, C 688A, p. 225.)

Detroit August 24th 1812

Dear Sir

I beg Leave to acquaint you that immediately after your Departure hence a Difficulty was experienced respecting the Administration of the Laws of this Territory, as announced in your Proclamation of the 16th Ins^t and that to remove the same on mature Deliberation I conceived (it) requisite to take upon myself a Responsibility of which, before you left this, I most certainly had not the least Idea. In so doing I have, to the best of my judgement, acted in Obedience to your Proclamation, and with the Spirit of which, I humbly conceive the annexed Regulation of the 21st Ins^t strictly accords. I hope you will do me the Justice to believe, that I have not been actuated by interested Motives, and that it has been with the greatest

Reluctance, your Approbation not having been previously obtained, that I have taken upon myself a Responsibility, which, however, it was requisite, should be immediately assumed, to restore to the affrighted Inhabitants, Confidence, the immediate Object, as I conceive, of your Proclamation. I enclose a Letter which I conceived it expedient to write to Mr Justice Woodward, and also his Answer which I hope you will find satisfactory. I was doubtfull whether the American Revenue Laws ought, or ought not to be enforced. Formerly they were productive I understand to the Amount of six or eight Times the Expences; but of late they have been reduced. If those Laws are not enforced the Inhabitants of this Territory paying no Customs or Duties will be placed on a better Footing than those of your Province which was not intended by your Proclamation. I shall therefore make a provisional Appointment of Collectors. Little however will be done in this, or any other civil Matter untill I have the Opportunity of hearing from you. In the hope of being soon favored with a Letter from you,..........

MAJOR P. L. CHAMBERS TO COLONEL PROCTER.

(Canadian Archives, C 688A, p, 229.)

Detroit 24th August 1812

Sir

In conformity to your Orders I on the 19th Instant proceeded in a Batteau to the River au Raisins at which place I arrived on the following day   on my arrival I met with Captain Elliott of the Essex Militia, who had Collected and Embarked all the Arms, and secured such Stores as remained in the House of Mr Lascelles, I then Effectually destroyed the Two Block Houses, which were surrounded by a Strong Stoccade and capable of making a vigorous Resistance. this Part of my duty having been performed, I in Conformity with my Instructions assured the Inhabitants of the Effectual Protection of his Majestys Government. But it is with Extreme Mortification I feel myself Compelled to state, that notwithstanding every Effort on my Part, to Insure it to them so strong was the disposition on the Part of the Indians in Particular the Wyandotts, to Pillage, Ravage, and destroy, that I could not Succeed, scarcely a House in that Settlement having escaped Pillage   Indeed it was one Universal scene of desolation

You may Easily conceive Sir with what repugnance to my feelings, I was constrained to Witness Scenes so disgraceful to Humanity and which I do not Hesitate to say might have been in a great Measure prevented had the Proper officers Exerted the Necessary Controul, but I am Compelled by a Sense of duty to state that it was with the Utmost difficulty, I could prevail on any of them to interfere and when they did it was with so little Interest it was of no avail. I must however in Justice to Major M°Kee say that He exerted himself to put a Stop to scenes so shocking and disgusting

The Next Morning I proceeded to the Foot of the Rapids of the Miamis to accomplish the Object of my Mission I then saw the Block House destroyed and Embarked the Public Property found.

I am sorry to say the same Ravages took Place there as at the River au Raisins notwithstanding my utmost Efforts to prevent it it affords me great Pleasure to say that the Conduct of Tecumthe the Shawanoe Warrior, and Round Head[1] of the Wyandotts, was such as reflect on them the Highest Honor. I enclose a return of the Property found. I omitted to mention that the Indians murdered and Scalped one of the Canadians who belonged to the Gun Boat Commanded by Lt Bender, and fired three shots at another.

RETURN [2] OF ARMS AND STORES FOUND AT THE RIVER AU RAISIN, 20TH AUGUST.

(Canadian Archives C 688A, p. 208.)

	Nos		
Howitzers Brass	1		
do Shot	19		
Muskets & Bayt^s	114		
Pistols	12		
Rifles	7		
Swords	6		
Cartridge Boxes	64—		
Pork, Barrels of	9—		
Flour "		46 not Embarked.	
Whiskey "	1	do	do
Wagons—	2	do	do

PETER LATOUCHE CHAMBERS
Major & Capt 41st

---

[1] Roundhead, an influential war chief of the band of Wyandots, or Hurons living in Upper Canada near the Detroit river. He particularly

RETURN OF PROVISIONS FOUND AT THE FOOT OF THE MIAMIS RAPIDS.[1]

(Canadian Archives, C 688A, p. 211.)

Barrels of Pork	77
Barrels of Flour	18
Barrels of Salt	2
Barrels of Whiskey	7

PETER LATOUCHE CHAMBERS
Major & Capt 41st

21st August 1812

SIR GEORGE PREVOST TO EARL BATHURST.

(Canadian Archives, Q 118, p. 196.)

Montreal 24th August 1812.

N° 4.

My Lord,

Since my last Dispatch to Your Lordship of the 17th inst, respecting the surrender of Michilimackinac to His Majesty's Arms, & the three attempts of Brig^r Genl Hull to approach Fort Amherstburg, in all of which he was repulsed and his Army compelled to return to their position at Sandwich, no movement of importance against Upper Canada has taken place. It is now evident that Genl Hull remains inactive from the want of the reinforcements & supplies which he is daily expecting. Our forces at Amherstburg augmented by the Junction of several Indian Tribes & a small party of the 41st Reg^t have on the contrary been enabled to detach a considerable body across the Detroit River into the United States, thereby transferring in some degree the scene of War from Upper Canada into the American Territory—

This mode of operating upon the enemy's line of communication & supply, has been attended with considerable success—

A mail from Detroit was taken on the 5th inst tho' escorted by 200 picked Riflemen, and in this affair, as well as in one

---

distinguished himself in the action at the river Raisin, 1813, in which General Winchester became his prisoner, but died in August or September of that year. "The Indian cause and ours experienced a serious loss in the death of Roundhead."—*Procter to de Rottenburg*, October 23, 1813 *Canadian Archives, C 680, p. 273.*

[2] Compare with schedule on p. 173.
[1] See extract from the Askin Journal in this bulletin, p. 246

which afterwards took place for the purpose of intercepting another Mail & the supplies expected at Detroit, the Enemy have suffered a severe loss, and been obliged to retreat: We had three men killed, thirteen wounded & two missing of the 41st Reg^t—one killed & two wounded of the Militia, & two killed & six wounded of the Indians; Captain Muir & Lieu^t Sutherland of the 41st are amongst the wounded, the former slightly, the latter seriously—

Your Lordship will observe in Genl Hull's intercepted Letter to the American Secretary at War, herewith transmitted, how much that Officer's expectations of conquering Upper Canada are diminished, & how strong his apprehensions are of being reduced to the necessity of returning to Detroit.

As Genl Dearborn had not the power of including Genl Hull's Army in the arrangement made by him with Col. Baynes, which I had the honor of communicating to Your Lordship in my Dispatch of the 17th ins^t N° 2, I have not thought it necessary to restrain Major General Brock from adopting any measures he might judge fit for repelling the Invasion of the Upper Province & for compelling General Hull to retire from it—

I have therefore used every exertion to forward the supplies of Men, Money & Ordnance Stores requisite, for the accomplishment of these Objects.

I have reason to think Genl Brock reached Amherstburg on the 12th ins^t carrying with him a reinforcement of 260 picked Militia men & 40 of the 41st Reg^t—this accession to the Force at that Post together with a body of several hundred Men under Capt Chambers, consisting of 50 men of the 41st & of Militia & Indians, approaching the Enemy's flank, aided by the Indians expected from Lake Superior in consequence of an Express sent to them for that purpose by the Ottawa River, will I trust be amply sufficient to enable Genl Brock to compel Genl Hull to relinquish his plans of conquest upon the Province, & to punish him for his presumptuous endeavours to alienate the minds of His Majesty's Subjects.

Force in Upper Canada.
Roy^l Artill^y.. 90
10th R. V. Batt^n.. .. 180
41st Reg^t.. 970
49th " 720
R^l Newf^d Fencibles. 360
2320

Since the return of Col^l. Baynes I have not received any further communication from the United States upon the sub ject of his Mission,[1] am happy however to find that the advantages to result from the arrangement entered into by him with the Commander in Chief of the American Army, in the event of the Government of the United States persevering in their views of conquest in Upper Canada are becoming every day more apparent.

In the absence of Instructions from His Majesty's Government founded on their knowledge of an actual state of hostility with America, Your Lordship must be aware that I am necessarily obliged to confine myself to measures of defence, & to combine every movement with that object.

A suspension of hostilities therefore on a considerable portion of the extremely extensive line of Frontier which I have to defend has enabled me rapidly to strengthen the Flank attacked. The decided superiority I have obtained on the Lakes in consequence of the precautionary measures adopted during the last winter has permitted me to move without interruption, independently of the arrangement, both Troops & supplies of every description towards Amherstburg, whilst those for Genl Hull having several hundred miles of wilderness to pass before they can reach Detroit, are exposed, to be harassed and destroyed by the Indians. Another consequence of the Mission of Col^l. Baynes and of the arrangement resulting from it, has been the Discovery of the inability (of) the Government of the United States to overrun the Canadas & of their unprepared state for carrying on the war with vigour; this has become so manifest that His Majesty's Subjects in both Provinces are beginning to feel an increased confidence in the Government protecting them, and as the means & resources which have been displayed appear to have far exceeded their expectations, so has it effectually secured their best exertions for the defence of their Country against any tumultuary force—In the mean time from a partial suspension of hostilities I am enabled to improve & augment my resources against an Invasion, whilst the Enemy distracted by Party broils & intrigues are obliged to remain supine & to witness the daily diminution of the Force they had so much difficulty in collecting.

I cannot conclude this Dispatch without acquainting Your Lordship that the Army Bill expedient has answered the purpose for which it was intended beyond my most sanguine expectation, I have also the Satisfaction of informing Your Lordship that after having overcome some insubordination and

---

[1] See despatches on pp. 127 and 129.
17804—12½

many prejudices, I have succeeded in establishing four Battalions of select Militia at the expence of the Province amounting to Two Thousand three hundred men for the service of Lower Canada.

From this view of the present posture of our affairs particularly as it respects the War with the United States, Your Lordship will be enabled to judge of the Policy of the measures I have pursued, & which I hope will meet the approbation of His Royal Highness The Prince Regent as they may ultimately effect the object I have so much up at heart, the security & welfare of the important Provinces committed to my charge.

COLONEL PROCTER TO MAJOR-GENERAL BROCK.

(Canadian Archives, C 688B, p. 3.)

Detroit August 26th 1812

Dear Sir

It has been extremely difficult from the Defect of System in the Departments of the captured Army, and the confused State in which all the public Store taken from the Enemy have been found to procure as yet any correct Return. I send you a Return[1] of the Ordnance & Ordnance Stores captured and have the Pleasure to acquaint you that they are nearly all sent to Amherstburg. I also send a Return[2] of Prisoners taken on the 16th Inst. I have not been able to procure as yet a Return of the other Stores taken, the moment I can, I will send off an Express. The Vessels have not yet returned from Cleaveland. Annexed are the Reports of Major Chambers, and of Captain Elliot(t). I daily expect a trusty Person whom I had sent to Sandusky, and when he arrives I shall send sufficient Force, which is ready, to take & destroy that Fort. Chicago at the southern Extremity of Lake Michigan is yet in the possession of the Americans. In my next Letter I shall report what Arrangements have been made respecting the Militia. I annex a Return of Deserters from the British Service, who were found in the captured Army. My Wish was to have made an Example of them summarily, and would have done so, but that I recollected that Deserters, similarly circumstanced were sent Home, from the Isle of France I think, were tried & suffered. I take upon myself to permit Major Chambers to return to

---

[1] For this return see p. 154.
[2] For quartermaster-general's return of prisoners see p. 153.

Niagara, recollecting that active Officers of his Rank may be wanted there. I should have preferred waiting a few Days ere I wrote, but that I am aware of your Wish to hear often. I have sent Captain Dixon to Amherstburg to compleat the Fort agreeable to the approved Estimate.

SIR GEORGE PREVOST[1] TO EARL BATHURST.

(Canadian Archives, Q 118, p. 210.)

N° 5.

Montreal 26th August 1812.

My Lord,

I feel the greatest Satisfaction in transmitting to Your Lordship a Letter[2] which I have this day received by Express from Major General Brock, announcing to me the surrender of Fort Detroit, on the 16th Inst, by Brigadier General Hull with the Army under his Command exceeding 2,500 Men, together with 25 pieces of Ordnance.—

In my Dispatches N° 3 and 4 of the 17th and 24th Instant, I had the honor of detailing to Your Lordship the operations which had taken place in Upper Canada in consequence of the invasion of that Province by the Army of the United States, Brig^r. Genl Hull having crossed the Detroit River on the 12th of last month with 2,300 Men, consisting of Regulars, Cavalry and Infantry, and Militia, bringing with him several Field Pieces, and having driven in the Militia towards Amherstburg, first advanced to Sandwich and afterwards approached Amherstburg with a part of his Army to the River Canard, about five miles from the Fort, where he was foiled in three attempts to cross that River, and suffered a considerable loss.—

The Garrison of Amherstburg Consisted at that time of a Subaltern's Detachment of the Royal Artillery, commanded by Lieut Troughton, of a detachment of 300 Men of the 41st Reg^t under the Command of Captain Muir, and of about as many of the Militia, the whole under the command of L^t. Col. St George Inspecting Field Officer of Militia in the District—

The state of the Province at this period from the weakness of the Regular Force in it, as well as from the disposition of

---

[1] There is a despatch of the same date from Prevost to the Duke of York, who was field-marshal and commander-in-chief of British forces to be found in *Canadian Archives, C 1218, p. 372*. The text bears but slight variation from Prevost's despatch to Bathurst here given.

[2] For this letter, see p. 156.

many of its Inhabitants, was highly favorable in the views of the American Government in invading it—

The Militia men who had been previously embodied were with Difficulty restrained from deserting to their homes, and those who had been called out to repel the invaders, in many instances absolutely refused to march.

The Indians of the Six Nations, at the same time, upon whose Services the Government had the strongest claim from the support it constantly afforded them, in general drew back from the assistance required of them, affecting to preserve a Neutrality, more dangerous than even open hostility, as more productive of Alarm to the Country, and affording the Inhabitants a plausible pretext for remaining in guard of their property.

Under these circumstances of extreme difficulty and Embarrassment, General Brock found himself disappointed in the Call which he had made upon the Provincial Legislature for relief, either by obtaining additional Supplies to meet the increasing wants of the public Service, or the necessary power for checking and punishing the insubordination of the Militia, and the disaffected among the People.—

Relying however upon the strong assurances I had given him of a reinforcement as prompt and as effectual as the circumstances under which I was placed by this new War, would permit me to send, General Brock adopted the most vigorous measures for the safety of that part of the Frontier which had been attacked. In these measures he was most opportunely aided by the fortunate surrender of Fort Michilimackinac which giving spirit and confidence to the Indian Tribes in its Neighbourhood, part of whom had assisted in its Capture, determined them to advance upon the rear and flanks of the American Army as soon as they heard that it had entered the Province.

The certainty of the expected reinforcements and the weakness of the Enemy on the Niagara Frontier had in the mean time induced General Brock to detach from the Garrison of Fort George 50 men of the 41st Reg^t under Capt. Chambers, into the interior of the Country for the purpose of Collecting such of the Indians and Militia as might be ready and willing to join him, and of afterwards advancing upon the left Flank of the Enemy:—

60 men of the same Regiment were also detached from that Garrison to Amherstburg, and 40 to Long Point to collect the

Militia in that Quarter—Having made these dispositions and having previously sent forward Colonel Procter of the 41st Regiment to Amherstburg where he arrived and assumed the Command on the 26th of last Month,—General Brock proceeded himself from York on the 5th Instant for Fort George and Long Point on Lake Erie, which last place he left on the 8th following for Amherstburg with 40 Rank & file of the 41st Reg^t and 260 of the Militia forces.

Whilst General Brock was thus hastening his preparations for the relief of Amherstburg, the prospects of the American Army under General Hull were becoming every day more unfavorable and their situation more critical, the intelligence of the fall of Michilimackinac had reached them which they knew must expose them to an attack of the Indians on one quarter, at the same time that they were threatened on another by the Force approaching under Captn Chambers, an Indian Tribe of the Wyandots whom they had in vain attempted to bribe, aided by a Detachment of the 41st Reg^t from Amherstburg, had succeeded in cutting off their supplies on the opposite side of the River, and in intercepting their Dispatches which described in very strong terms their apprehensions and despondency.—

The losses they had sustained in their different Actions upon the Canard River, as well as those for protecting their supplies, together with the mode of Warfare pursued by the Indians had greatly discouraged and dispirited them, and had convinced General Hull how hopeless any attempt would be to storm Fort Amherstburg, without great Reinforcements and a battering Train. It was under these circumstances at this critical period, and when the Enemy were beginning to consult their security by intrenching themselves, that General Brock entered Amherstburg with a reinforcement which he was fortunately enabled to do, on the 12th Instant, without the smallest molestation, in consequence of our decided Naval superiority on the Lakes.

To his Active and intelligent mind the advantages which the Enemy's situation afforded him over them, even with his very inferior force, became immediately apparent, and that he has not failed most effectually to avail himself of those favorable circumstances, Your Lordship will I trust be satisfied from the letter which I have the honor of transmitting

Having thus brought to Your Lordship's view the different circumstances which have led to the successful termination of the Campaign on the Western frontier of Upper Canada, I cannot with-hold from Major General Brock the tribute of applause so justly due to him for his distinguished conduct on this occasion, or omit to recommend him through Your Lordship to the favourable consideration of His Royal Highness The Prince Regent, for the great ability and judgment with which he has planned and the promptitude, energy and fortitude with which he has effected the preservation of Upper Canada, with a force not apparently adequate to its defence, and with the sacrifice of so little British Blood in accomplishing so important a Service.

My Aid-de-Camp Captain Coore[1] will have the honor of delivering to Your Lordship this Dispatch, and as he is well qualified to give Your Lordship information respecting the Military resources of this Command, and also of the state of parties and politics in the United States, Captain Coore having recently been employed by me on a Mission to Washington, I shall beg leave to refer Your Lordship to him for further particulars.

BRIG.-GENERAL HULL TO THE SECRETARY OF WAR.

(History of the War between the United States and Great Britain, compiled by J. Russell, jr.; Hartford, 1815; p. 142.)

Fort George, August 26, 1812.

Sir—

Inclosed are the articles of capitulation, by which the Fort of Detroit has been surrendered to Major-General Brock, commanding his Britannic Majesty's forces in Upper Canada, and by which the troops have become prisoners of war. My situation at present forbids me from detailing the particular causes which have led to this unfortunate event. I will, however, generally observe, that after the surrender of Michilimackinac, almost every tribe and nation of Indians, excepting a part of the Miamis and Delawares, north from beyond Lake Superior, west from beyond the Mississippi, south from the Ohio and Wabash, and east from every port of Upper Canada, and from all the intermediate country, joined in open hostility under the British standard, against the army I commanded, contrary to

---

[1] Captain Foster Lech Coore of the 3rd West India Regiment, aide-de-camp to the governor-general, and afterwards lieutenant-colonel of the York Light Infantry.

the most solemn assurances of a large portion of them to remain neutral; even the Ottawa Chiefs from Arbecrotch, who formed the delegation to Washington the last summer, in whose friendship I know you had great confidence, are among the hostile tribes, and several of them distinguished leaders. Among the vast number of chiefs who led the hostile bands, Tecumseh, Marpot, Logan, Walk-in-the-water, Split-Log, &c. are considered the principals. This numerous assemblage of savages, under the entire influence and direction of the British commander, enabled him totally to obstruct the only communication which I had with my country. This communication had been opened from the settlements in the state of Ohio, two hundred miles through a wilderness, by the fatigues of the army, which I marched to the frontier on the river Detroit. The body of the Lake being commanded by the British armed ships, and the shores and rivers by gun-boats, the army was totally deprived of all communication by water. On this extensive road it depended for transportation of provisions, military stores, medicine, clothing, and every other supply, on pack-horses—all its operations were successful until its arrival at Detroit,—in a few days it passed into the enemy's country, and all opposition seemed to fall before it. One month it remained in possession of this country, and was fed from its resources. In different directions detachments penetrated sixty miles in the settled part of the province, and the inhabitants seemed satisfied with the change of situation, which appeared to be taking place—the militia from Amherstburg were daily deserting, and the whole country, then under the control of the army, was asking for protection. The Indians generally, in the first instance, appeared to be neutralized, and determined to take no part in the contest. The fort of Amherstburg was eighteen miles below my encampment. Not a single cannon or mortar was on wheels suitable to carry before that place. I consulted my officers, whether it was expedient to make an attempt on it with the bayonet alone, without cannon to make a breach in the first instance. The council I called was of the opinion it was not—The greatest industry was exerted in making preparation, and it was not until the 7th of August, that two 24-pounders and three howitzers were prepared. It was then my intention to have proceeded on the enterprise. While the operations of the army were delayed by these preparations, the clouds of adversity had been for some time and seemed still thickly to be gathering around me. The surrender of Michilimackinac opened the northern hive of Indians, and they were swarming down in every direction. Reinforcements from Niagara had arrived at Amherstburg under the command of Colonel Procter. The desertion o fthe militia ceased. Besides the reinforcements that came by water, I received information of a very considerable force under the command of Major Chambers on the river Le Trench with four field-pieces, and collecting the militia on his route, evidently destined for Amherstburg; and in addition to this combination, and increase of force, contrary to all my expectations, the Wyandots, Chippewas, Ottawas, Pottawatamies, Munsees, Delawares, &c. with whom I had the most friendly intercourse, at once passed over to Amherstburg, and accepted the tomahawk and scalping knife. There being now a vast number of Indians at the British post, they were sent to the river Huron, Brownstown, and Maguago to intercept my communication. To open this communication, I detached Maj. Vanhorne of the Ohio volunteers with two hundred men to proceed as far as the river Raisin, under an expectation he would meet Capt. Brush with one hundred and fifty men, volunteers from the state of Ohio, and a quantity of provision for the army. An ambuscade was formed at Brownstown, and Maj. Vanhorn's detachment (was) defeated and returned to camp without effecting the object of the expedition.

In my letter of the 7th inst.[1] you have the particulars of that transaction, with a return of the killed and wounded. Under this sudden and unexpected change of things, and having received an express from General Hall, commanding opposite the British shore on the Niagara river, by which it appeared that there was no prospect of any co-operation from that quarter, and the two senior officers of the artillery having stated to me an opinion that it would be extremely difficult, if not impossible, to pass the Turkey river and river Aux-Cannard, with the 24-pounders, and that they could not be transported by water, as the *Queen-Charlotte* which carried eighteen 24-pounders, lay in the river Detroit above the mouth of the river Aux-Cannard; and as it appeared indispensibly necessary to open the communication to the river Raisin and the Miami, I found myself compelled to suspend the operation against Amherstburg, and concentrate the main force of the army at Detroit. Fully intending, at that time, after the communication was open, to re-cross the river, and pursue the object at Amherstburg, and strongly desirous of continuing protection

---

[1] See p. 125.

to a very large number of the inhabitants of Upper Canada, who had voluntarily accepted it under my proclamation, I established a fortress on the banks of the river, a little below Detroit, calculated for a garrison of three hundred men. On the evening of the 7th, and morning of the 8th inst. the army, excepting the garrison of 250 infantry, and a corps of artillerists, all under the command of Major Denny of the Ohio volunteers, re-crossed the river, and encamped at Detroit. In pursuance of the object of opening the communication, on which I considered the existence of the army depending, a detachment of six hundred men, under the command of lieut. Colonel Miller was immediately ordered. For a particular account of the proceedings of this detachment, and the memorable battle which was fought at Maguago, which reflects the highest honor on the American arms, I refer you to my letter of the 13th of August,[1] a duplicate of which is enclosed, in this. Nothing however but honor was acquired by this victory; and it is a painful consideration, that the blood of seventy-five gallant men could only open the communication as far as the points of their bayonets extended. The necessary care of the sick and wounded, and a very severe storm of rain, rendered their return to camp indispensably necessary for their own comfort. Captain Brush, with his small detachment, and the provisions, being still at the river Raisin, and in a situation to be destroyed by the savages, on the 13th inst. in the evening, I permitted Colonels M'Arthur and Cass to select from their regiment four hundred of their most effective men, and proceed (by) an upper route through the woods, which I had sent an express to direct Capt. Brush to take, and had directed the militia of the river Raisin to accompany him as a reinforcement. The force of the enemy continually increasing, and the necessity of opening the communication, and acting on the defensive, becoming more apparent, I had, previous to detaching Colonels M'Arthur and Cass, on the 11th inst. evacuated and destroyed the fort on the opposite bank. On the 13th, in the evening, Gen. Brock arrived at Amherstburg about the hour Colonels M'Arthur and Cass marched, of which at that time I had received no information. On the 15th, I received a summons from him to surrender fort Detroit, of which I herewith enclose you a copy, together[2] with my answer. At this time I had received no information from Cols.

[1] See p. 139.
[2] See pp. 144-45

M'Arthur and Cass. An express was immediately sent, strongly escorted, with orders for them to return.

On the 15th, as soon as General Brock received my letter, his batteries opened on the town and fort, and continued until evening. In the evening all the British Ships of war came nearly as far up the river as Sandwich, three miles below Detroit. At daylight on the 16th, (at which time I had received no information from Cols. M'Arthur and Cass, my expresses sent the evening before, and in the night, having been prevented from passing by numerous bodies of Indians) the cannonade recommenced, and in a short time, I received information, that the British army and Indians, were landing below the Spring wells[1] under cover of their Ships of war. At this time the whole effective force[2] at my disposal at Detroit did not exceed eight hundred men. Being new troops and unaccustomed to a camp life; having performed a laborious march; having been in a number of battles and skirmishes, in which many had fallen, and more had received wounds, in addition to which a large number being sick, and unprovided with medicine, and the comforts necessary for their situation; are the general causes by which the strength of the army was thus reduced. The fort at this time was filled with women, children, and the old and decrepit people of the town and country; they were unsafe in the town, as it was entirely open and exposed to the enemy's batteries. Back of the fort, above or below it, there was no safety for them on account of the Indians. In the first instance, the enemy's fire was principally directed against our batteries; and towards the close it was directed against the fort alone, and almost every shot and shell had their effect.

It now became necessary either to fight the enemy in the field; collect the whole force in the fort; or propose terms of capitulation. I could not have carried into the field more than six hundred men, and left any adequate force in the fort. There were landed at that time of the enemy a regular force[3] of much more than that number, and twice that number of Indians. Considering this great inequality of force, I did not think it expedient to adopt the first measure. The second must

---
[1] Spring Wells (Belle Fontaine) was three miles below Detroit.
[2] See despatch of Brock to Prevost, July 20, p. 73; same to same August 17, p. 159; and Cass to the Secretary of War, September 10, p. 221.
[3] For strength of Brock's force see his despatches to Prevost, August 16 and 17, pp. 156 and 158.

have been attended with a great sacrifice of blood, and no possible advantage, because the contest could not have been sustained more than a day for the want of powder, and but a very few days for the want of provisions. In addition to this, Cols. M'Arthur and Cass would have been in a most hazardous situation. I feared nothing but the last alternative. I have dared to adopt it—I well know the high responsibility of the measure, and I take the whole of it on myself. It was dictated by a sense of duty, and a full conviction of its expediency. The bands of savages which had then joined the British force, were numerous beyond any former example. Their numbers have since increased, and the history of the barbarians of the north of Europe does not furnish examples of more greedy violence than these savages have exhibited. A large portion of the brave and gallant officers and men I commanded would cheerfully have contested until the last cartridge had been expended, and the bayonets worn to the sockets. I could not consent to the useless sacrifice of such brave men, when I knew it was impossible for me to sustain my situation. It was impossible in the nature of things that an army could have been furnished with the necessary supplies of provision, military stores, clothing, and comforts for the sick, on pack horses through a wilderness of two hundred miles, filled with hostile savages. It was impossible, sir, that this little army, worn down by fatigue, by sickness, by wounds and deaths, could have supported itself not only against the collected force of all the northern nations of Indians, but against the united strength of Upper Canada, whose population consists of more than twenty times the number contained in the territory of Michigan, aided by the principal part of the regular forces of the province, and the wealth and influence of the North-West, and other trading establishments among the Indians, which have in their employment, and under their entire control, more than two thousand white men.

Before I close this dispatch it is a duty I owe my respectable associates in command, Cols. M'Arthur, Findley, Cass, and Lieut. Col. Miller, to express my obligations to them for the prompt and judicious manner in which they have performed their respective duties. If aught has taken place during the campaign which is honorable to the army, these officers are entitled to a large share of it. If the last act should be disapproved, no part of the censure belongs to them. I have likewise to express my obligation to General Taylor, who has performed the duty of quarter-master-General, for his great exertions in procuring every thing in his department which it was possible to furnish for the convenience of the army; likewise to brigade-major Jessup for the correct and punctual manner in which he has discharged his duty; and to the army generally for their exertions, and the zeal they have manifested for the public interest. The death of Dr. Foster, soon after he arrived at Detroit, was a severe misfortune to the army; it was increased by the capture of the Chachaga packet, by which the medicine and hospital stores were lost. He was commencing the best arrangements in the department of which he was the principal, with the very small means which he possessed. I was likewise deprived of the necessary services of Capt. Partridge, by sickness, the only officer of the corps of engineers attached to the army. All the officers and men have gone to their respective homes, excepting the 4th United States' regiment, and a small part of the first, and Capt. Dyson's company of artillery. Capt. Dyson's company was left at Amherstburg, and the others are with me prisoners—they amount to about 340. I have only to solicit an investigation of my conduct, as early as my situation, and the state of things will admit; and to add the further request, that the government will not be unmindful of my associates in captivity, and of the families of those brave men who have fallen in the contest.

MAJOR-GENERAL BROCK TO THE EARL OF LIVERPOOL.

(Canadian Archives G 473, p. 58.)

N°. 7

York Upper Canada 29th August 1812

My Lord/

Since the commencement of the War, my time has been chiefly occupied with my military duties, in various parts of the province—I have not failed regularly reporting to His Excellency the Governor in chief what I considered essential, who I make no doubt has put Your Lordship in possession of every necessary information

The invasion of the Western District by General Hull, was productive of very unfavourable sensations among a large portion of the population, and so completely were their minds subdued that the Norfolk Militia, when ordered to March, peremptorily refused—The state of the country required prompt and vigorous measures—The majority of the House of Assembly was likewise seized with the same apprehensions, and may be justly accused of studying more to avoid, by their proceedings, incurring the indignation of the enemy than the honest fulfilment of their duty. I thought it my duty at this critical moment to lay before His Majesty's Executive Council the representation of which the enclosed is a copy[a]. As no one advantage could result from their remaining longer in Session the Legislature was immediately prorogued, upon their passing the money Bills, which leave at my disposal for the use of the Militia, about Ten thousand Pounds. My Speech at the opening and close of the Session together with the answer of both Houses, I have the honour to transmit herewith[bbbb].

I cannot hide from Your Lordship, that I considered my situation at that time extremely perilous; not only among the Militia was evinced a disposition to submit tamely, five hundred in the Western district having deserted their Ranks, but likewise the Indians of the six Nations, who are placed in the heart of the Country on the Grand River, positively refused, with the exception of a few individuals taking up arms—they audaciously announced their intention, after the return of some of their chiefs from General Hull, to remain neutral, as if they wished to impose upon the Government the belief that it was possible they could sit quietly in the midst of War—This unexpected conduct of the Indians deterred many good men from leaving their families and joining the Militia—they became more apprehensive of the internal than the external enemy, and would willingly have compromised with the one to secure themselves from the other

I shall think it my bounden duty at some future day to call your Lordships attention to the absolute necessity of removing this infatuated people from their present situation. The loud voice of self preservation, every consideration of Policy recommends the measure,—although they have changed their tone with the late success yet the necessity of guarding against the evil they may still commit, is not less imperious.

The Proclamation[c] which General Hull published upon his taking possession of Sandwich, tended in a great degree to create the disposition in the inhabitants already noticed, and his emissaries were numerous and active. I caused a Counter Proclamation[1] to be issued[d] which I had the satisfaction to

---

[1] For text of these proclamations, see pp. 56 and 81 respectively.

find produced immediate effect among the well disposed who from that day increased in their activity and Vigilance. Having declared my intention of proceeding to the Western District with such of the Militia as might Voluntarily offer to accompany me, in a few days five hundred, principally the sons of Veterans, whom His Majesty's munificence settled in this Country cheerfully tendered their service. The threatening attitude however of the enemy, on other parts of the frontier obliged me to content myself with half the number, with whom I arrived in safety late on the 13th ins^t at Amherstburg. In no instance have I witnessed greater cheerfulness and constancy than were displayed by these Troops under the fatigue of a long journey in Boats and during extremely bad Weather, and it is but justice to this little band to add that their conduct through(ou)t excited my admiration.

To my official dispatch[1] to His Excellency the Commander of the Forces I beg leave to refer your Lordship for my subsequent proceedings. (*(e)Dispatch of the 16 Aug^t: (e)Capitulation 16 Aug^t: (e)Proclamation at Detroit to the People of the Michigan Territory.*)

Among the Indians whom I found at Amherstburg, and who had arrived from distant parts of the Country, I found some extraordinary characters. He who attracted most my attention was a Shawnee chief, Tecumset, brother to the Prophet, who for the last two years has carried on (contrary to our remonstrances) an Active Warfare against the United States—a more sagacious or more a gallant Warrior does not I believe exist. He was the admiration of every one who conversed with him: from a life of dissipation he has not only become, in every respect, abstemious but has likewise prevailed on all his nation and many of the other Tribes to follow his example. They appear determined to continue the contest until they obtain the Ohio for a boundary. The United States Government is accused, and I believe justly, of having corrupted a few dissolute characters whom they pretended to consider as chiefs and with whom they contracted engagements and concluded Treaties, which they have attempted to impose on the whole Indian race—Their determined opposition to such fictitious and ruinous pretensions, which if admitted would soon oblige the Indians to remove beyond the Mississippi, is the true ground of their enmity against the Americans. The jealousy with which they view the British Merchants continue

---

[1] For this despatch, see p. 156.

their commercial intercourse with the Indians has likewise been attended with serious inconvenience. Under the difficulty the Merchant experienced few goods could be introduced into the interior, and their own measures, the operation of the non intercourse (act) precluded even their own people from furnishing the Indians with Clothing of the first necessity. The consequence has been fatal to many—Deprived of ammunition the poor Indian was unable to provide the necessary quantity of food or even cover his nakedness with the skins of animals. The Armistic[1] concluded between His Excellency, Lt Genl Sir George Prevost and General Dearborne, has suspended all active operations—However wise and politic the measure must be admitted to be, the Indians, who cannot enter into our views will naturally feel disheartened and suspicious of our intentions. Should hostilities recommence I much fear, the influence the British possess over them will be found diminished: no effort however of mine shall be wanting to keep them attached to our cause. If the condition of this people could be considered in any future negotiation for peace, it would attach them to us for ever. The reinforcements lately arrived from the Lower Province places this portion of the country beyond the likelihood of an attack. The enemy must encrease his present force considerably before he can hazard an Invasion with a view of keeping possession of the country

MINUTES OF COUNCIL, AUGUST 3^d.

(Enclosure [a] *in Despatch N° 7.)*

At a Council held at the Government House, York Upper Canada, Monday 3rd August 1812.

Present

Major General Brock
Honble The Chief Justice
Honble James Baby
" Alex^r Grant
" John McGill
" Mr Justice Powell
" Prideaux Selby

His Honor The President represented to the Board that the hopes he had entertained from the Call of the Legislature was likely to be disappointed.

---

[1] See despatches on pp. 127 and 129.

That the Lower House of Assembly instead of prompt exertion to strengthen his hands for the Government of the Militia, providing for Security from internal treason, by partial Suspension of the Habeas Corpus Act, authorizing a partial exercise of Martial Law, concurrently with the Ordinary Course of Justice, and placing at his disposal for the defence of the Province, the Funds not actually applied upon past appropriations, had consumed eight days, in Carrying a Single measure of party—the repeal of the School Bill, and passing an Act for the Public disclosure of treasonable practices, before the Magistrates should have power to commit without bail. That under such circumstances little could be expected from the prolonged Session of the Legislature. That the Enemy had invaded, and taken Post in the Western District—was multiplying daily his preparation to invade in others; that the Militia, in a perfect state of insubordination, had withdrawn from the Ranks in actual Service; had refused to march when legally commanded to reinforce a detachment of the Regular Force for the relief of Amherstburg—had insulted their Officers, and some, not immediately embodied, had manifested in many instances a treasonable Spirit of Neutrality or disaffection—That the Indians on the Grand River, tampered with (by) the disaffected whites, had withdrawn from their Volunteer Services, and declared for a neutrality, which in respect of them was equally inadmissible, as with the King's other subjects—That in the Western and London Districts, several Persons had negotiated with the Enemy's Commander, hailing his arrival and pledging support—That the Regular Force Consisted of One Regiment, the 41st nine hundred strong, and part of the Royal Newfoundland Regiment, two hundred, with a detachment of the Royal Artillery, and several Armed Vessels.

That the extent of coast exposed, and the great distance of the prominent points, had obliged him to divide that Force to Support and Countenance the Militia; that the Conduct of the Western Militia had exposed to imminent danger the regular Force at Amherstburg, and however inconvenient, he had made a large Detachment of the 41st with Militia from the Home and Niagara Districts, with the few Indians not Corrupted, to reinforce that Garrison, if time would admit.

That on the other hand, the Commandant at St Joseph, had, with his Garrison and Indians, taken the Island of Michilimackinac, the Garrison of which Capitulated without firing a Shot—That in all probability part of that Force might descend to Detroit and in such case a Cooperation with the Garrison in Fort Amherstburg, reinforced by the detachment now on its march to Long-point, might compel the Invader to retire or Surrender, but that no good result from any Military Expedition could be expected, unless more powerful restraint could be imposed on the Militia, than the Actual Law admits, and that he had power to restrain the General population from treasonable adherence either to the Enemy or neutrality, by summary proceeding and punishment, nor could the Colony be considered safe from the Indians in its very bosom, whilst liable to be tampered with by disaffected persons, exposed only to the Slow progress of Conviction by Criminal Law—That with this view of the Situation of the Colony, he submitted for the consideration of the Council how far it might be expedient to prorogue the general House of Assembly, and proclaim Martial Law, under the powers of the King's Commission in case of Invasion.

The Council adjourned for deliberation—

August 4th 1812.

In Council

Present the same Members as Yesterday—

The Council having deliberated upon His Honor's representation is unanimously of Opinion that under the circumstances of the Colony, it is expedient upon Prorogation of the General Assembly, to proclaim and exercise Martial Law, according to the powers of His Majesty's Commission to the Governor General.

SPEECH UPON OPENING THE LEGISLATURE.

(Enclosure$^{(b)}$ in Despatch N°. 7.)

Honorable Gentlemen of the Legislative Council And Gentlemen of the House of Assembly.

The urgency of the present Crisis is the only consideration which Could have induced me to call You together at a time when Public as well as private duties elsewhere demand Your care and attention.

But Gentlemen, when invaded by an Enemy whose avowed object is the entire Conquest of this Province, the voice of Loyalty as well as of interest calls aloud to every Person in the Sphere in which he is placed, to defend his Country.

Our Militia have heard that voice and have obeyed it, they have evinced by the promptitude and Loyalty of their Conduct, that they are worthy of the King whom they serve, and of the Constitution which they enjoy; and it affords me particular Satisfaction, that while I address You as Legislators, I speak to men who in the day of danger, will be ready to assist, not only with their Counsel, but with their Arms.

We look, Gentlemen, to our Militia as well as to the Regular Forces for our protection; but I should be wanting to that important trust committed to my care, if I attempted to conceal what experience (the great instructor of Mankind, and especially of Legislators) has discovered, that amendment is necessary in our Militia Laws to render them efficient.

It is for You to Consider what further improvements they still may require.

Honorable Gentlemen of the Legislative Council, And Gentlemen of the House of Assembly—

From the history and experience of our Mother Country, we learn, that in times of actual invasion or internal Commotion, the Ordinary Course of Criminal Law has been found inadequate to secure His Majesty's Government from private Treachery as well as from Open disaffection, and that at such times its Legislature has found it expedient to enact Laws restraining for a limited period, the liberty of Individuals in many cases where it would be dangerous to expose the particulars of the Charge; and altho' the actual invasion of the Province might justify me in the exercise of the full powers reposed in me on such an emergency, yet it will be more agreeable to me to receive the sanction of the two Houses.

A few Traitors have already joined the Enemy; have been suffered to come into the Country with impunity, and have been harboured and Concealed in the interior; Yet the General Spirit of Loyalty which appears to pervade the Inhabitants of this Province, is such as to authorize a just expectation that their efforts to mislead and deceive, will be unavailing. The disaffected I am convinced are few—to protect and defend the Loyal Inhabitants from their machinations is an object worthy of Your most serious deliberations.

Gentlemen of the House of Assembly.

I have directed the Public Accounts of the Province to be laid before You, in as Complete a State as the unusual period will admit; they will afford You the means of ascertaining to what extent You can aid in providing for the extraordinary demands occasioned by the employment of the Militia, and I doubt not but to that extent You will Cheerfully Contribute.

Honorable Gentlemen of the Legislative Council And Gentlemen of the House of Assembly.

We are engaged in awful and eventful Contest. By unanimity and despatch in our Councils, and by vigour in our Operations, we may teach the Enemy this lesson—that a Country defended by Free-men, enthusiastically devoted to the cause of their King and Constitution, can never be Conquered.

ADDRESS OF THE LEGISLATIVE COUNCIL IN ANSWER TO SPEECH UPON OPENING THE LEGISLATURE.

(Enclosure[b] in Despatch N°. 7.)

To His Honor Isaac Brock Esquire, President Administering the Government of the Province of Upper Canada, and Major General Commanding His Majesty's Forces in the said Province.

May it please Your Honor!

We His Majesty's dutiful and Loyal subjects the Legislative Council of Upper Canada in Parliament assembled, return our most grateful thanks for Your Honor's Speech at the Opening of this Session of the Legislature.

When invaded by an Enemy whose avowed object is the entire Conquest of this Province, We, laying aside all inferior Considerations, do most willingly obey Your Honor's Commands, by appearing in Our Legislative Capacity for the purpose, of using our utmost efforts for the protection and defence of every thing that is dear to us as Subjects and as Men.

We shall be happy indeed if by the promptitude, Loyalty, and vigour of our Conduct, we prove ourselves worthy of the King whom we serve, and of the Constitution which we enjoy.

The commendation which Your Honor has been pleased to bestow on our Militia, affords us the highest gratification, whilst the attention which You have paid to the Laws already enacted respecting that Body of Men, calls for our most grateful acknowledgements—it shall be our endeavour to Consider what improvements may still be wanting to render those Laws more efficient and Salutary.

We feel the Force of what Your Honor has been pleased to state respecting the Laws that have been enacted in times of danger in our parent Country, whereby a Nation the most free upon Earth, did voluntarily for a time, resign a portion of its liberty, that it might be enabled to transmit it entire to future generations.

Placed in similar circumstances, it shall be our most solemn duty to consider whether we ought not to follow that example.

Altho' a few Traitors may have joined the Enemy, and may have been harboured and concealed by Persons equally wicked with themselves; Yet we are happy to learn from Your Honor, that the disaffected are but few in number, and that a general spirit of Loyalty appears to pervade this Province.

We are fully sensible that we are engaged in an awful and an eventful Contest, and that it is only by unanimity and despatch in our Councils, and by vigour in our Operations, that we can hope to teach our Enemies that a Country defended by Free-men, enthusiastically devoted to the Cause of their King, can never be Conquered.

Permit us to add, that we repose the highest Confidence in Your Honor's unremitting attention to whatever may be necessary to the protection, Safety and prosperity of this Province.

Thos Scott
Speaker

Legislative Council Chamber
29th July 1812.

ADDRESS OF THE HOUSE OF ASSEMBLY IN ANSWER TO SPEECH UPON OPENING OF THE LEGISLATURE.

(Enclosure[b] *in Despatch N°. 7.)*

To His Honor Isaac Brock, Esquire, President Administering the Government of the Province of Upper Canada, and Major General Commanding His Majesty's Forces therein.

May it please Your Honor.

We His Majesty's most dutiful and Loyal Subjects, the Commons of Upper Canada, in Provincial Parliament assembled, beg leave to return You our unfeigned thanks for Your most Gracious Speech at the Opening of the present Session.

We are Convinced that the urgency of the present Crisis is the only Consideration that Could have induced Your Honour to call us together at a time when Public as well as private duties must elsewhere demand our Care and attention.

But when invaded by an Enemy whose avowed object is the entire Conquest of this Province, we feel that the voice of Loyalty, as well as of interest, calls aloud to every person in the Sphere in which he is placed, to defend his Country.

That our Militia have heard that voice and have obeyed it; that they have evinced by the promptitude & Loyalty of their Conduct that they are worthy of the King whom they serve and the Constitution which they enjoy, are to us the sources of the most pleasing Satisfaction—And we have the utmost Confidence that in Your Honor's anticipation of our readiness to assist in the day of danger, not only with our Counsels but with our Arms, You will not be disappointed.

We feel that we must look to our Militia as well as to the Regular Forces for our protection; and we are fully impressed with the important truth, which experience (the great instructor of Mankind as well as of Legislators) has discovered, that amendment is necessary to our Militia Laws to render them efficient—We will consider what further improvements may still be necessary, and will Cheerfully Concur in such Amendments as will render that part of our Force equal to the crisis in which they are called to act.

We agree with Your Honor, that from the history and experience of Our Mother Country, we learn that in time of Actual Invasion or internal Commotion, the ordinary course of Criminal Law has been found inadequate to secure His Majesty's Government from private treachery as well as from open disaffection, and that at such times its Legislature has found it expedient to enact Laws restraining the liberty of Individuals in many Cases where it would be dangerous to expose the particulars of the Charge—And we shall Cheerfully co-operate with the other Branches of the Legislature, in adopting such measures (Consistent with the liberty and safety of His Majesty's subjects) as the present Crisis and the Security of the Province require.

We feelingly lament that even a few traitors should have already joined the Enemy; that they should have been suffered to come into the Country with impunity, and have (been) harboured in the interior—Their number, however, is small; and we are happy to perceive that the General Spirit of Loyalty which appears to pervade the Inhabitants of this Province, is such as to authorize the just expectation that their efforts to mislead and deceive will be unavailing.

With Your Honor we are convinced that the **disaffected are few**, and that to protect and defend the **Loyal inhabitants** from their machinations is an object worthy of our most serious deliberations—We shall pay every attention to the Subject, and will on our part, adopt such Salutary regulations as will, we trust, fully answer the object in view.

When the Public Accounts are laid before us, we shall have the means of ascertaining to what extent we can aid in providing for the extraordinary demands occasioned by the employment of the Militia, and to that extent we will Cheerfully Contribute.

We feel that we are engaged in an awful and eventful Contest, and that by unanimity and dispatch in our Councils, and vigour in our operations, we may teach the Enemy this lesson—that a Country defended by freemen enthusiastically devoted to the cause of their King and Constitution, can never be Conquered.

To obtain that important end, we pledge our most zealous co-operation, and we trust that the exertions we shall make in defence of our liberties and possessions, will, aided by Your Honor's professional Talents and experience, be such as to do honor to the cause we have to defend, and to the Country of which we form a part.

(signed) ALLAN MACLEAN
Speaker

Commons House of Assembly
28th July 1812.

PRESIDENT'S SPEECH UPON CLOSING THE SESSION OF THE LEGISLATURE.

(Enclosure[b] *in Despatch N°. 7.)*

Honorable Gentlemen of the Legislative Council And Gentlemen of the House of Assembly.

Upon the eve of a necessary absence, I learned that You had got through such Bills as were thought expedient to submit to me for His Majesty's assent.

That You may not unnecessarily be detained from Your homes, I hastened at a moment's preparation to meet You, to declare His Majesty's assent to the Bills You might present, and Close the present Session of the General Assembly.

Gentlemen of the House of Assembly,

I thank you in His Majesty's name, for the liberal Grant of all the monies at Your disposal, and assure You that they shall be faithfully applied to the best of my Judgment, in the defence of the Province against its Enemies.

COLONEL PROCTER TO MAJOR-GENERAL BROCK.

(Canadian Archives, C 688B, p. 10.)

Detroit Augt 29th 1812

Dear Sir,

I received your Letters of the 24th & 25th Ins^t as also Colonel Baynes's of the 8th Ins^t to you. The Expeditions[1] intended will not be sent, and every Measure is & will be taken without acquainting the Indians of the Cause, to restrain them, Should however Hostilities recommence the Armistice I fear will be injurious to our cause here. It is confidently asserted that a General Wells with Three Thousand Kentucky Men are on the Route to this Place, I have sent (to) ascertain the Truth, and shall act accordingly. As General Hull acted independently of General Dearborn, so may General Wells, if coming, on the same Service. This I humbly conceive it requisite to ascertain without delay, and before I or any part of our Force Should leave this, I shall go to the Foot of the Rapids, on the pretence of seeing the Country between this Place and the Miamis, but also to be at Hand to receive any Communication that may be made or to act as may be requisite. I feel it an Object to know, at least to see, a Country that may be the scene of Action. I hope to return before the Vessels from Fort Erie. After this Country is placed as far as we can see in Safety, I request even if you should deem it requisite for me to be Stationed here, Your Permission to go to Fort George. I enclose you two Letters one I have received from Mr Dewar, as his report which I have required. The other from the Commissary, on both of which I shall act, on Mature deliberation as I shall conceive most to the benefit of His Majesty's Service & I hope to your Satisfaction. I have been waiting some Hours for a List of the public Stores captured, and am now obliged to send off my Letter without it, I understand that the Vessels are returned from Clieveland, but have not received any Report

---

[1] The expedition against Fort Wayne; see p. 248.

P.S. I have just seen an Officer who was on Board one of the Vessels which has returned from landing the Ohio Volunteers at Cleveland, he reports the entire satisfaction as to the conduct of the British towards them, & complete disgust of their Canada Expedition, He mentions that there were between two & three Hundred Men at Cleveland who were to be joined by eight Hundred more, & that there were at the Miamis Rapids to be completed to Three thousand, five Hundred Men, intended for this Place, No time shall be lost in sending of(f) the remainder of the Prisoners. The Ordnance is all at Amherstburg and shall be forwarded as Opportunities occur to Fort Erie. I shall write as soon as I can give you any certain information.

GOVERNOR HARRISON TO THE SECRETARY OF WAR.

(Dawson's Life of Harrison, p. 283.)

Cincinnati, 28th August, 1812.

Sir:—

Before this reaches you, a despatch from the Governor of Kentucky to yourself and another from the Honorable Mr. Clay to the Secretary of State will have arrived at Washington communicating the circumstances which occasions my having the honor to address you from this place. Being at Frankfort on the 24th inst. making arrangements for the eventual march of the residue of the Kentucky quota to Indiana and Michigan Territories, an express arrived at that place with despatches for Governor Scott containing information of Governor Hull being shut up in Detroit and the probability of his being obliged to surrender unless immediately relieved. Upon a consultation with Governor Scott it was thought advisable as he was the next day to go out of office, to wait the arrival of his successor, Colonel Shelby[1] and to request the advice and assistance of all the public characters in the State within reach and expresses were sent to solicit their attendance on the next day. The meeting accordingly took place consisting of Governor Shelby, the former governor, Greenup, the Speaker of the House of Representatives of the United States, several other members of Congress, the Judges of the United States and of

---

[1] Isaac Shelby (1750-1826) had served in the American Revolution as a colonel of militia, being particularly distinguished by courage and ability at the battle of King's Mountain in 1781. He was governor of Kentucky, 1792-96 and 1812-16.

the Supreme Court of the State, General Hopkins,[1] the Major General of the Kentucky quota, and it was unanimously recommended to Governor Scott to order another detachment of the State quota to follow the one which had marched under General Payne, to request me to take command of the whole, and for the purpose of removing all difficulty to give me a commission of Major General by brevet of Kentucky militia. I could not permit myself to hesitate when urged by an authority so highly respectable, especially when urged by the large concourse of the citizens from all parts of the State which had collected on account of the inauguration of the new governor, that it was the unanimous wish of the people of Kentucky that I should do so. Before I left Frankfort Governor Shelby urged the propriety of sending one regiment more to Newport than was at first intended and hearing of the fall of Detroit a few miles from that place I sent back and recommended still another. My command then consists of three regiments of Kentucky troops, Colonel Wells's detachment, and a troop of twelve months volunteers making an aggregate of about 2100 at this place and three regiments of infantry, five troops of dragoons, and five hundred mounted volunteer riflemen on their way to join me. Those that first arrive will not, however, be here before the 30th inst. and it will be impossible to get them from here for some days after.

Until this day I had some hope that the account of the fall of Detroit was not true but a letter received a few hours ago from Messrs. Worthington[2] and Meigs to Colonel Wells, leaves no longer room for doubt. Three persons of the quartermaster general's have returned to Piqua who were in Detroit when it was surrendered. The object of the letter from Messrs. Worthington and Meigs was to request Colonel Wells to hasten his march and to take the route to Dayton and Piqua rather than the direct one to Urbana for the purpose of relieving Fort Wayne which was said to be in danger of an immediate attack. By a gentleman who has this moment arrived from Piqua the taking of Chicago, and the massacre of the garrison is also put beyond doubt. Poor Wells has also perished in endeavoring to save Capt. Heald with his company.

---

[1] Major General Samuel Hopkins of the Kentucky militia, born 1750, died 1819. He was a representative in Congress from 1813 to 1815.
[2] Thomas Worthington (1768-1827) United States senator from Ohio, 1803-07 and 1811-14; governor of Ohio, 1814-18.

I shall march to-morrow morning with the troops that I have here taking the route for Dayton and Piqua. The relief of Fort Wayne will be my first object and my after operations will be governed by circumstances until I receive your directions.

Considering my command as merely provisional, I shall cheerfully conform to any other arrangements which the government may think proper to make. The troops which I have with me and those which are coming from Kentucky are perhaps the best material for forming an army that the world has produced. But no equal number of men was ever collected who know so little of military discipline nor have I any assistance that can give me the least aid if even there were time for it but Captain Adams of the Fourth Regiment who was left here sick and whom I have appointed Deputy Adjutant General until the pleasure of the President can be known. He is well qualified and I hope the appointment will be confirmed. You may rely, Sir, upon my utmost exertions but the confusion which exists in every department connected with the army is such as can only be expected from men who are perfectly new to the business they are engaged in. No arms for the cavalry have yet arrived at Newport and I shall be forced to put muskets in the hands of all the dragoons. I have written to the quartermaster at Pittsburg to ask him to forward all the supplies of arms, equipment, and quartermaster's stores as soon as possible. I have also requested him to send down a few pieces of artillery without waiting for your order and wait your instructions as to a further number. There is but one piece of artillery, an iron four pounder, anywhere that I can hear of in this country. If it is intended to retake the posts we have lost and reduce Malden this season the artillery must be sent on as soon as possible.

GOVERNOR HARRISON TO THE SECRETARY OF WAR.

(Dawson's Life of Harrison, p. 286.)

Cincinnati, 29th August, 1812.

Sir:—

I did myself the honor to write to you yesterday and despatched the letter by an express, thinking he would overtake the mail at Chillicothe. The troops marched this morning for

Piqua. I shall follow and overtake them to-morrow. Another letter was received from General Worthington last evening, covering one from Captain Rhea of Fort Wayne stating that a large body of Indians were near the fort and he expected to be attacked that night. I shall lose not a moment in marching to his relief and think it more than probable that we shall have to encounter all the Indians who assisted at the taking of Detroit, those t whom Chicago surrendered[1] and a very large number of others who will be induced by the fame of their exploits to join the hostile party.

Permit me to recommend that a considerable supply of tents, swords and pistols, camp kettles, cartridge boxes, rifle flints, and artificers' tools of every description be forwarded immediately as well as the artillery and every species of ordnance stores. Medicine, instruments, and hospital stores of every description will also be wanted for the large force which it will require to reinstate our affairs upon the northwestern frontier. It is important also that some disciplined troops should be sent here; a company or two of artillery and an experienced engineer will be indispensable.

I have caused a travelling forge to be prepared and ammunition waggons are now building. It appeared to me, Sir, that some one should undertake the general direction of affairs here and I have done it. The critical situation of affairs in this country in my opinion authorized a departure from the common line of procedure, (to wait for orders), and should it have been considered by government as improper, I shall hope to be pardoned for the purity of my intentions.

You may rely upon it, Sir, that the western country was never so agitated by alarm and mortification as at the present moment.

LIEUT.-COLONEL MYERS TO MAJOR-GENERAL BROCK.

(Canadian Archives, C 688B, p. 19.)

Fort George Augt 30, 1812

My Dear Sir,

The enclosed Despatches arrived here at two oClock, I took upon myself to open Col Procters, & from the Statements in his of the 24th judge it proper to send them forward to you,

---

[1] Fort Dearborn (Chicago) surrendered to the Indians, August 15th. See note on Captain Wells, p. 78, and a letter of Captain Heald to the Secretary of War, p. 225.

I have not read them with much attention, excepting the part relating to my own Department, I find by the Return enclosed by Lt Col Nichol that 465 Prisoners were embarked, (or are stated to have been Embarked) on board the Several vessels for Fort Erie, the Numbers that arrived here are as follows—

	Commiss^d Officers.	N C (O). & Rank & file	Total
in the Chippawa	3	17	20
in the other vessels	23	350	373
			393
Women & Children			50
			443
deficient			22
			465

Whether Women Children or officers are included in Lt Col Nichols Return I do not know, no other Return was sent with the Prisoners than a Disembarkation one by Capt Hall of the *Queen Charlotte,* and I can assure you it occasioned no small degree of trouble to me, as to their Numbers—on their Embarkation I counted their Files & I took a List by Name Rank & Corps of the Officers, the Returns are forwarded by Major Shakelton[1] to Quarter Mas^r Genl, and I have found (it) my Duty to write to the ass^t Quarter Mas^r Genl at Amherstburg, to explain to me for the information of Col Macdonnell his unpardonable neglect, for which there appears no excuse, as I embarked the Prisoners here in less than an Hour, & ascertained their Numbers, I had trouble it is true, but I never consider the discharge of my Duty in that light

I enclose a Letter from Col Talbot received yesterday, Mr Eakins who brought it awaits your arrival here—

I hope very soon to have the Satisfaction of seeing you back to us

(P.S.) The Vessels with the Prisoners Sailed Friday the 28th Ins^t.

---

[1] Charles D. Shekleton, major of brigade, Lower Canada.

MAJOR-GENERAL R. H. SHEAFFE TO CAPTAIN CHARLES ROBERTS.

(Canadian Archives, C 688B, p. 28.)

Copy/

York 1st Septr. 1812.

Dr Sir,

M. General Brock is so much engaged by urgent Business that he has directed me to write to you on the several points noticed in your Letter of 29th July addressed to Capt: Glegg— The capture of Detroit and of Genl Hull and his Army has removed the grounds of some of your difficulties and respecting other matters touched on by you, the present uncertain state of affairs precludes his sending you any Instructions now. he approves generally of what you have done and hopes you will accomplish your design of removing the Chippewas to the vicinity of M.M.[1] if it be likely to be attended by the good effects you purpose but it must be kept in mind, that M.M. may be restored to the Americans & that we ought not to run the risk of conferring a future permanent advantage on them, for a present temporary one to ourselves but this is left to your discretion as you possess the best means of deciding on the merits of the case. The navigation being now secure, a market is opened for the Furs from Chicago, if one be not offered where they are—

If you decide on sending them down it may be necessary to appoint an Agent at Montreal or otherwise to send them to Mr Clarke[2] there, through the Commissariat to be disposed of as may hereafter be directed.

Colonel Procter will forward to you extracts of Letters addressed to him, and such other Instructions & documents as he may deem useful   Accept my congratulations on your success on the opening of the campaign

(P.S.) The Deserters are to be sent down with every information regarding them in your power to afford   The General is to go down very soon to Kingston from whence he will probably send up to you Twenty or Thirty of Fifty picked Veterans lately arrived there

---

[1] Michilimackinac.
[2] Asst. Commissary-General Isaac W. Clarke.

MAJOR-GENERAL SHEAFFE TO COLONEL PROCTER.

(Canadian Archives, C 688B, p. 33.)

York 1st September 1812.

My dear Colonel,

M. General Brock being very busily employed in writing Dispatches for England, has transferred to me the task of acknowledging the receipt of your several Communications to the 24th Instant inclusive, which arrived last (night?) by express from Fort George, and he has instructed me to write to you as follows—he approves of the Measures you have adopted for the Administration of the Laws in the Michigan Territory, as well as those others reported by you, which existing circumstances have dictated; he wishes you to remain above 'till further orders, as he thinks that the present unsettled state of things does not admit of your being withdrawn: You may detain fifty of the hundred Men of the 41st Regiment, before ordered down, if you see sufficient reason to do so, and even the whole hundred, if circumstances unknown to the General shall have occurred to render it necessary—in deciding on which, you will allow due weight to the consideration, that if Hostilities be renewed We shall have to contend on the North East side of Lake Erie for the security of Amherstburgh—the *Hunter* is to be dispatched without delay to M. Mackinac with the Indian Presents Stores &c. and with such proportion of Provisions as after consulting the A D Commissary General may be deemed *amply* sufficient—enclosed herewith is a Copy of the Return[1] of Provisions taken at M. Mackinac, from which and from the A D Commissary General's knowledge of the probable remainder at St Joseph's a tolerably correct judgment may be formed of the specie and of the quantity of each which will be required; should the fifty six Barrels of Flour sent from hence to Lake Huron for St Joseph's not have reached its destination, Capt. Roberts may find it necessary to send the *Genl Hunter* for them, if no preferable mode present itself—You will please to have prepared correct Lists in duplicate of all those who aided in the capture of Detroit—the Names at full length—distinguishing how serving or what belonging to—41st—Indian Dept—Naval Do—Militia (—Regt Compy &c) &c &c &c—those of the Naval Department assisting in Vessels or Boats and those in the Batteries on our side

---

[1] For this return, see *Canadian Archives, C 688 A, p. 161.*

— — against Detroit, to be included but neither *Indians* nor the Militia from this vicinity are expected to be found in your List—Clothing is to be sent up for the Militia—The General expects that all prudent and proper means are adopted for the protection of the Inhabitants on both sides of the Streight from the depredations and lawless violence of the Indians which he trusts will be in a great measure checked by employing the influence of the Officers of the Indian Department and the authority of the Chiefs—He is particularly anxious too that the Garrison of Chicago should be rescued from their fury and is therefore desirous of obtaining its Surrender to us as the only means of effecting it—If Captain Roberts have it in his power to accomplish this object, he will perform a Service which will be highly appreciated—The Deserters from our forces which you have in Custody are to be sent down to Fort George the General sent up Instructions for having a certain quantity of the Stores &c brought down to Fort Erie and he desires that with each gun a proportion of Shot &c may be sent he wishes that when there is nothing more important to employ the *Queen Charlotte,* she may cruise in the Lake and near the Enemy's Shore.

In the actual posture of affairs it is of course uncertain for what duration or under what Title you will hold the Administration of the Government of the conquered Territory —but should circumstances prove such as to encourage you to desire it the *Queen Charlotte* shall be directed to convey to you Your family and Baggage—

J. WILLCOCKS [1] TO LIEUT.-COLONEL JOHN MACDONELL.

(Canadian Archives, C 688B, p. 30.)

Grand River Septr 1st 1812

Sir

In consequence of General Brock's commands communicated to me thro' you, relative to the Indians upon the Grand River,

---

[1] Joseph Willcocks was a son of Robert Willcocks of Palmerton in County Dublin, Ireland, a man of some property and influence. He sailed from Cork in the ship *Fortitude* bound for New York, December 1, 1799, and arrived at York, Upper Canada, March 20, 1800. William Willcocks, a distant relative who was also a first cousin of Hon. Peter Russell, the receiver-general of the province, welcomed him to his house and interested himself on his behalf, and on May 1st he was appointed a clerk in the receiver-general's office. In 1803 he was appointed sheriff

I made no delay in going among them, and upon seeing several of the Chiefs, attached to both parties, and communicating my business to them, it was agreed that a Council should be held that Evening at their Village, in order that all matters of dispute between the contending parties should be done away, and the necessary arrangement made for their departure to Amherstburgh. But before the Council could possibly meet, I was seized with a most violent bilious cholic which had nearly deprived me of existance, indeed it was with much difficulty I could be removed that Even^g from the village to Woodruff's Tavern, where I have been confined, seriously ill, for nearly four weeks. However on the third day of my illness an Indian

---

of the Home district, an office of considerable dignity and emolument. In this capacity he appears to have taken an active part in securing the election of Robert Thorpe, a justice of the Court of King's Bench, as a member of the House of Assembly to represent the counties of Durham, Simcoe, and the east riding of York in opposition to the candidate supported by the government. Lieutenant-Governor Gore promptly removed Willcocks from office, assigning as a reason "his general and notorious bad character . . . . as a turbulent Irishman." In the summer of 1807, Willcocks began the publication at Niagara of a weekly newspaper entitled 'The Upper Canada Guardian and Freeman's Journal' in which the acts of the government were fiercely criticised. This paper soon obtained a wide circulation, and in the autumn of the same year Willcocks was elected a member of the Assembly for the ridings of West York, 1st Lincoln and Haldimand to fill the vacancy caused by the death of Solomon Hill. He took his seat January 26, 1808, and four days later a member gave notice of motion for a committee to consider a paragraph which had been printed in the 'Guardian' of the 1st of October of the previous year, reflecting on the conduct of members of the House. Nothing further was done in the matter until February 18, when David Cowan, one of the members for Essex, accused Willcocks of making a verbal statement that the members were afraid to proceed against him as he could prove that they had been bribed by Lieut.-Governor Hunter. A resolution was then carried declaring this statement, which Willcocks admitted that he had made, to be "false, slanderous and highly derogatory to the dignity of the House." Two days later the speaker issued his warrant committing the offender "to the common gaol until discharged by the Commons House of Assembly." On the 16th of March, just before the prorogation of the Legislature, a motion was passed for his discharge. He was re-elected at the general election in January, 1808 as member for the 1st riding of Lincoln and Haldimand, and during the next four years was the acknowledged leader of the opposition which on many questions had a majority in the Assembly. He was again elected in the spring of 1812 to represent the 1st riding of Lincoln. About the same time he ceased to publish the 'Guardian' for want of support. For some time after the declaration of war he steadily affirmed his loyalty and seems to have borne arms at Queenston in the action of October 13, 1812. (General Order by the Adjutant-General, Montreal, October 12, 1812.) In September, 1812, he was indicted for sedition by the Grand Jury of the county of Norfolk. Sometime in June or July 1813, he joined the enemy at Niagara and was appointed with the rank of major to the command of a corps called the Canadian Volunteers which was to be formed of deserters and refugees. His services in this capacity were acknowledged by Brigadier-General Boyd in a letter to the Secretary of War, dated August 17, 1813. He was subsequently promoted to the rank of lieutenant-colonel, and was killed in a sortie from Fort Erie, September 4, 1814.

Chief called Abraham Hill, accompanied by one George Martin, another Indian, came to my lodging, and requested that I would permit them to bring there two Chiefs from each Nation on the River, in order that I might communicate to them that which I intended to have spoken at the proposed Council. To this I agreed; and on the following day the Chiefs attended; and altho' in a state of the greatest agony, I made them a Speech the substance of which was " that unanimity among the several Chiefs and tribes was at that time, indispensibly necessary for their own preservation and happiness. That they were bound by every tie of gratitude and interest to take up Arms during the present contest with the United States in defence of their King, their Country and their personal safety. That their personal exertions were immediately required at Amherstburgh. That Gen' Brock had already gone there, and expected that all the Chiefs and Warriors would follow him without a moments delay. These and many other circumstances of a similar nature I impressed upon their minds with all the force my bad state of health would permit, and as they led me to believe with no small portion of success. They thanked me for the trouble I had taken, and all parties pledged themselves in the most solemn manner strictly to attend to the several things which I had recommended. And indeed it appears they were not wholly forgetful of their promises, for on the day following sixty four of the Chiefs and Warriors started for Amherstberg. Karrihoga, (John Norton) for some cause unknown to me, did not attend the Council which was held in my room; and I have just learnt from some of the Indians that he has lately absented himself from the River, but where he is gone they know not. It is necessary to mention that since I began to recruit my health I have had much conversation with many of the influential Characters of the several tribes, from which I am led to believe that no difficulty or opposition will arise among their people, should their services be again called for. I regret much that I have not been able to have written you sooner, but I assure you that until a day or two back I have not been able to hold a pen, which I trust will be a sufficient appology not only to yourself, but also for not having written to the General, or Colonel Myres agreeably to your desire—If I can be of any service here I beg you will write me—It is at present my intention to return to Niagara so soon as my strength will permit

BRIG.-GENERAL WILLIAM HULL TO SIR GEORGE PREVOST.

(Canadian Archives, C 677, p. 73.)

Montreal 8th Sept' 1812.

Sir—

In my letter of the 15th of Aug[1] addressed to Major General Brock, I observed, " that the flag of truce, under the direction of Cap' Brown, proceeded contrary to the orders, and without the knowledge of Col°. Cass, who commanded the Troops, which attacked your picket guard, near the River Canard Bridge."

As this is not only a subject of national honor, but of delicacy to the Officers, who were concerned in the transaction, it is necessary that the whole case should be stated—

The object of the expedition, under Col°. Cass, was to reconnoitre the Country as far as the River Canard, and I had no expectation of his passing the River and making the attack.

Cap' Brown was sent by my orders, under the sanction of a flag of truce. As he proceeded down the River, he had an interview with Col° Cass, and the Col° informed him of his intention to pass the river and attack the picket guard, and desired Cap' Brown not to proceed to Amherstburg untill the event had taken place.

Cap' Brown informed me, it was his intention not to have proceeded in consequence of this information, untill he knew there was no active hostility on our part—

Being however unacquainted with the Shore of the Detroit River, he unexpectedly turned a point of land, which brought him with his flag in full view of the Fort at Amherstburg— He then considered, situated as he unexpectedly was, that there would be more propriety in proceeding than remaining in that situation; expecting that he should be able to return, before any active operations were commenced.

---

[1] For this letter, see p. 144.

A. W. COCHRAN [1] TO HIS MOTHER. (EXTRACT.)
(Canadian Archives, Cochran Papers, M 147, p. 222.)

Quebec 13th September, 1812.

Part of The American prisoners taken in Detroit[2] have arrived here the evening before last; I have seen all the officers but do not recognize any of my Boston military acquaintances as I expected I should; Both men and officers are a shabby looking set as ever you set eyes on, and reminded me of Falstaff's men very forcibly.—Some of the officers talked very big, and assured us that before long there would be *100,000* men in Canada and that they would soon have Quebec from us; —They do not speak very respectfully of their *General,* and he in his turn, (Mr Brenton writes me) is or pretends to be very much irritated against his Government who he says have sacrificed him by not complying with his repeated and urgent demands for reinforcements to save him from the fate which has now come on him.—Sir George has let him go home on his Parole (together with such of his officers as were married,) in order that he might further embarrass the Government by his complaints and throw his weight into the scale against Madison's party;—But I fear Sir George's hopes on that score will not be realized as Hull is a plausible fellow and little credit is to be given him for sincerity in the violence that he shews against Madison;—No harm however can arise from sending (him) home on his parole, unless he should be dishonourable enough to break it and take up arms again before he is exchanged, and even then his conduct as a General hitherto shews that there is not much to fear from his military prowess;—I should not be at all surprized to hear of his taking some command

---

[1] Andrew William Cochran, born at Windsor, Nova Scotia, son of the Reverend Dr. Cochran. He was appointed assistant civil secretary to the governor-general, with the rank of ensign in the Quebec militia, May 1, 1813. In November 1814, he was appointed to act as a deputy judge advocate. He became a member of the Legislative Council for Lower Canada. He died July 11, 1849. A considerable number of interesting private letters written by him to kinsfolk and friends are preserved in the *Canadian Archives* under the title of *Cochran Papers, M. 147.*

[2] General Hull, with 25 officers and 350 rank and file, was immediately sent to Quebec. He was released on parole, and in December was exchanged for 30 privates. His court-martial in 1814 lasted nearly three months; he was sentenced to be shot, but President Madison remitted the execution in consideration of his services in the Revolutionary War, his name being dropped from the Army List.

immediately on his return in spite of his parole, as I believe him to be both rogue and fool;—In one of the letters from him to General Brock when the latter summoned him to surrender, he says (as I suppose you will have seen in the papers before now) that a flag of truce that had been carried by a Captain Brown of his army had been unauthorized by him;—Captain Brown is among the Prisoners who arrived here the other evening and he told my friend Mr Mure that he could shew General Hull's own order and handwriting, authorizing him to go with the flag of truce;—This will give you some idea of General Hull's regard for his honour; His dwelling house is very near Detroit and also the house of Colonel Baby[1] of the Upper Canada militia, a man of great respectability in that Province; The two families were on the most intimate terms before the war but when the American troops came there Hull allowed them to pillage Colonel Baby's house in the most shameful manner and when Baby expostulated with him and reminded him of their former intimacy Hull answered that it was true enough but *circumstances were changed now;*—When Hull surrendered, Baby went over to see him in General Brock's tent,— " Well General, says he, *circumstances are changed now indeed."*

OBSERVATIONS BY TOUSSAINT POTHIER ON MICHILIMACKINAC.

(Canadian Archives, C 695A, p. 4.)

Observations by Toussaint Pothier at the request of His Excellency Sir George Prevost &c &c &c on the Capture and State of Michilimackinac when he left it.

On the third July last I arrived at Fort St Joseph, from Montreal in the Capacity of Agent for the South West Fur Company appointed by Messrs McTavish McGillivrays & Co & Forsyth Richardson & Co.

That Post was under the Command of Capt Charles Roberts of the Royal 10th Veteran Battalion with a detachment composed of three Subaltern Officers and between forty and forty five non commissioned officers and privates of said Battalion.

There were also arrived at that Post from the wintering grounds several of the Traders Equiped by said Company among whom was Mr Robert Dickson who brought in with him

---

[1] Colonel James Baby, see note p. 45.

from the Mississipi a Band of Indians, Scioux, Puants and Folles Avoines, Composing a body of one Hundred and thirty warriors, Commanded by the principal Chiefs of their tribes, who accompanied Mr Dickson in consequence as I understood of an understanding between him and General Brock and with the View of Supporting the British interest in that Country.

The number of Canadians at St Joseph at this time were but few, the Traders having chiefly left their men and returns at the Post of Michilimackinac.

On the 9th of the same month an Express arrived from General Brock announcing the declaration of War by the Americans against Great Britain, and on the 10th a requisition was made by Capt Roberts, that all the Boats, arms, an(d) ammunition in my possession should be immediately placed at his disposal, which was accordingly done.

The situation in which I was placed representing the Trade and Interest of the Company induced Capt Roberts to confer with me upon public measures necessary to be taken in the event of a descent on the Island of Michilimackinac, at which time he made me acquainted with the weak state of his Garrison as well as other means in his power which were of themselves very insufficient for the undertaking, having but Forty Guns in the Indian Store, and no Gun powder but what was required for the great Guns of the Garrison and Ball Cartridges for his own men only, not a flint, in short the Garrison was defficient of every necessary for such an undertaking without the assistance which fortunately happened to be within my power to afford him; with this assistance he determined upon an attack on Michilimackinac as soon as he should receive instructions to that effect and preparative measures were adopted accordingly.

In consequence of this determination an Express was sent to Mr Shaw and the other Agents of the North West Company at Fort William Soliciting such assistance as might be within their power to Contribute, a vessel of theirs being at that time at St Joseph was also put in requisition, and those Gentlemen with great alacrity came down with a strong party to Cooperate; bringing to St Maries Several Carriage (Guns) and other arms, and altho the distance between the St Joseph's and Fort William is about 500 Miles they arrived at Michilimackinac the ninth day from the date of the Express and found us in peaceable possession.

Between the ninth and the fifteenth on which day the Express arrived authorising the undertaking several Band of Indians came in among whom were the principal Outawas Chiefs. On the day of their arrival the Counsel Room was opened to them when the Commanding Officer acquainted them of the declaration of War and required of them that assistance which from their former professions he had every right to expect; they appeared very luke warm, and after a great deal of prevarication reluctantly agreed to Join the expedition; the other Indians were very unanimous, particularly the Western Indians whose animated example had great influence upon the Concurrence of the others. it may be proper to observe that Amable Chevalier a Courte Oreille, or Outawas Chief who has resided at the Lake of the two Mountains for several years past, returned to the upper Countries last fall, and this last Spring on hearing the probability of a War came to St Joseph and tendered his services to the Commanding Officer: this man's influence had been great amongst them heretofore, and altho he used every exertion in his power on this occasion to interest them in the British Cause, which he had heartily espoused, he never Could bring himself to have Confidence in their fidelity.

By this time most of the Indian Traders arrived at St Joseph with a number of their men, so that we were now enable(d) to form a force of about 230 Canadians and 320 Indians exclusive of the Garrison. With this Force we left St Joseph on the 16th at Eleven Oclock, A.M., landed at Michilim^k at three OClock the next morning, summoned the Garrison to Surrender at nine OClock, and marched in at Eleven.

Among the Indians that accompanied the expedition Were about thirty Outawas, Amable Chevalier having been despatched by the Commanding Officer to their Village in order to bring the others (between two and three Hundred Warriors in number) to form a Junction at a given point in which we were disappointed; two days elapsed after the Capitulation when we were informed that they were all encamped at a distance of fifteen miles from Michilim^k On this information a Canoe was dispatched from Michilim^k with Wampum and Tobacco to tell them the news and to invite them to come in and partake in concert with the other Indians of what was intended to be distributed generally, and they accordingly came in alledging their delay arose from the badness of the Weather; Soon after Amable Chevalier informed me privately their motives of delay was Occasioned by indecision on their part while the Conquest remained doubtfull and unknown to them and a predilection in favor of the americans Seemed to influence them.

They were in this state of indecision when advices of General Hull's landing at Sandwich arrived, with a force which they Considerably magnified and which tended greatly to damp the ardour of the other tribes, and the very men among them who Capt Roberts appointed to a village Guard, were those who held private Counsel, to which they invited the Saulteux for the purpose not only of abandonning the British Cause, but eventually to avail themselves of the first good opportunity of cutting off the Fort. this being rejected by the others, they Suddenly broke up their Camp and returned to their villages to the exception of a few young and old men of little or no importance.

A few days previous to my Coming away the principal Chiefs of this Tribe returned to Michilimac—at that time there were about two hundred Warriors of other tribes preparing to go to Amherstburg to Join the British, when at a Special Counsel they Declared their determination to remain Neutral and reproached the Commanding Officer with having taken them too abruptly at St Joseph, that their eyes were then shut, but now open, and that without them he Could never have got up there pointing to the Fort, and from the general conversation at that time gave to understand that the Future possession of the Fort depended upon them.

When I left Michilim^k on the Evening of the 25th July most of the Indian Traders and Men were gone off to their Wintering quarters, so that very soon after it would be left with no other protection than the Garrison; little or no Indian Goods remained, not much provision, and a great Scarcity of Gun Powder. Another evil which prevails there, is the Want of a good Interpreter an Object of the Greatest importance to His Majesty's interest in that Country.

Montreal 8th September 1812

T. C. POTHIER

COLONEL LEWIS CASS TO THE SECRETARY OF WAR.

(History of the War between United States and Great Britain, compiled by J. Russell, jr.; Hartford, 1815; p. 154.)

Washington, Sept. 10, 1812.

Sir—

Having been ordered on to this place by Col. M'Arthur, for the purpose of communicating to the government particulars respecting the expedition lately commanded by Brig. General Hull, and its disastrous result, as might enable them correctly to appreciate the conduct of the officers and men; and to develop the causes which produced so foul a stain upon the national character, I have the honor to submit for your consideration, the following statement.

When the forces landed in Canada, they landed with an ardent zeal and stimulated with the hope of conquest. No enemy appeared within view of us, and had an immediate and vigorous attack been made upon Malden, it would doubtless have fallen an easy victory. I know General Hull afterwards declared he regretted this attack had not been made, and he had every reason to believe success would have crowned his efforts. The reason given for delaying our operations was to mount our heavy cannon, and to afford to the Canadian militia time and opportunity to quit an obnoxious service. In the course of two weeks the number of their militia, who were embodied, had decreased by desertion from six hundred to one hundred men; and, in the course of three weeks, the cannon were mounted, the ammunition fixed, and every preparation made for an immediate investment of the fort. At a council, at which were present all the field officers, and which was held two days before our preparations were completed, it was unanimously agreed to make an immediate attempt, to accomplish the object of the expedition. If by waiting two days we could have the service of our heavy artillery, it was agreed to wait; if not, it was determined to go without it, and attempt the place by storm. This opinion appeared to correspond with the views of the General, and the day was appointed for commencing our march. He declared to me, that he considered himself pledged to lead the army to Malden. The ammunition was placed in the waggons; the cannon embarked on board the floating batteries, and every requisite article was prepared.

The spirit and zeal, the ardor and animation displayed by the officers and men, on learning the near accomplishment of their wishes, was a sure and sacred pledge, that in the hour of trial they would not be found wanting in their duty to their country and themselves. But a change of measures, in opposition to the wishes and opinions of all the officers, was adopted by the General. The plan of attacking Malden was abandoned, and instead of acting offensively, we broke up our camp, evacuated Canada, and recrossed the river, in the night, without even the shadow of an enemy to injure us. We left to the tender mercy of the enemy the miserable Canadians who had joined us, and the *protection* we afforded them was but a passport to vengeance. This fatal and unaccountable step dispirited the troops, and destroyed the little confidence which a series of timid, irresolute and indecisive measures had left in the commanding officer.

About the 10th of August, the enemy received a reinforcement of four hundred men. On the twelfth the commanding officers of three of the regiments, (the fourth was absent) were informed through a medium which admitted of no doubt, that the General had stated that a capitulation would be necessary. They on the same day addressed to Governor Meigs of Ohio, a letter,[1] of which the following is an extract.

'*Believe all the bearer will tell you. Believe it, however it may astonish you, as much as if told by one of us. Even a c..........n, is talked of by the.......... The bearer will fill the vacancy.*'

The doubtful fate of this letter rendered it necessary to use circumspection in its details, and therefore these blanks were left. The word 'capitulation' will fill the first, and 'commanding general,' the other. As no enemy was near us, and as the superiority of our force was manifest, we could see no necessity for capitulating, nor any propriety in alluding to it. We therefore determined in the last resort to incur the responsibility of divesting the General of his command. This plan was eventually prevented by two of the commanding officers of regiments being ordered upon detachments.

On the 13th the British took a position opposite to Detroit, and began to throw up works. During that and the two following days, they pursued their object without interruption and established a battery for two 18 pounders and an 8 inch howitzer. About sun-set on the evening of the 14th a detach-

---

[1] For this letter, see p. 137.

ment of 350 men from the regiments commanded by Col. M'Arthur, and myself, was ordered to march to the river Raisin, to escort the provisions, which had some time remained there protected by a party under the command of capt. Brush.

On Saturday, the 15th about 1 o'clock, a flag of truce arrived from Sandwich, bearing a summons from General Brock for the surrender of the town and fort of Detroit, stating he could no longer restrain the fury of the savages. To this an immediate and spirited refusal was returned. About four o'clock their batteries began to play upon the town. The fire was returned and continued without interruption and with little effect till dark. Their shells were thrown till eleven o'clock.

At day-light the firing on both sides recommenced; about the same time the enemy began to land troops at Spring wells, three miles below Detroit, protected by two of their armed vessels. Between 6 and 7 o'clock they had effected their landing, and immediately took up their line of march. They moved in close column of platoons, twelve in front, upon the bank of the river.

The fourth regiment was stationed in the fort; the Ohio volunteers and a part of the Michigan militia, behind some pickets, in a situation in which the whole flank of the enemy would have been exposed. The residue of the Michigan militia were in the upper part of the town to resist the incursions of the savages. Two 24-pounders, loaded with grape, were posted upon a commanding eminence, ready to sweep the advancing column. In this situation the superiority of our position was apparent, and our troops, in the eager expectation of victory, awaited the approach of the enemy. Not a discontent broke upon the ear; not a look of cowardice met the eye. Every man expected a proud day for his country, and each was anxious that his individual exertion should contribute to the general result.

When the head of their column arrived within about five hundred yards of our line, orders were received from Gen. Hull for the whole to retreat to the fort, and for the 24-pounders not to open upon the enemy. One universal burst of indignation was apparent upon the receipt of this order. Those, whose conviction was the deliberate result of a dispassionate examination of passing events, saw the folly and impropriety of crowding 1100 men into a little work, which 300 could fully man, and into which the shot and shells of the enemy were falling. The fort was in this manner filled; the men were directed to stack their arms, and scarcely was an opportunity afforded of moving. Shortly after a white flag was hung out upon the walls. A British officer rode up to inquire the cause. A communication passed between the commanding Generals, which ended in the capitulation submitted to you. In entering into this capitulation, the General took counsel from his own feelings only. Not an officer was consulted. Not one anticipated a surrender, till he saw the white flag displayed. Even the women were indignant at so shameful a degradation of the American character, and all felt as they should have felt, but he who held in his hands the reins of authority.

Our morning report had that morning made our effective men present, fit for duty 1060, without including the detachment before alluded to, and without including 300 of the Michigan militia on duty.

About dark on Saturday evening the detachment sent to escort the provisions, received orders from Gen. Hull to return with as much expedition as possible. About 10 o'clock the next day they arrived in sight of Detroit. Had a firing been heard, or any resistance visible, they would have immediately advanced and attacked the rear of the enemy. The situation in which this detachment was placed, although the result of an accident, was the best for annoying the enemy and cutting off his retreat that could have been selected. With his raw troops enclosed between two fires and no hopes of succor, it is hazarding little to say, that very few would have escaped.

I have been informed by Col. Findley, who saw the return of their quarter-master-general the day after the surrender, that their whole force of every description, white, red, and black, was 1030. They had twenty nine platoons, twelve in a platoon, of men dressed in uniform. Many of these were evidently Canadian militia. The rest of their militia increased their white force to about seven hundred men. The number of the Indians could not be ascertained with any degree of precision; not many were visible. And in the event of an attack upon the town and fort, it was a species of force which could have afforded no material advantage to the enemy.

In endeavoring to appreciate the motives and to investigate the causes, which led to an event so unexpected and dishonorable, it is impossible to find any solution in the relative strength of the contending parties, or in the measure of resistance in our power. That we were far superior to the enemy; that upon any ordinary principles of calculation we would have defeated them, the wounded and indignant feelings of every man there will testify.

A few days before the surrender, I was informed by Gen. Hull, we had 400 rounds of 24 pound shot fixed, and about 100,000 cartridges made. We surrendered with the fort, 40 barrels of powder, and 2500 stand of arms.

The state of our provision has not been generally understood. On the day of the surrender we had fifteen days' provisions of every kind on hand. Of meat there was plenty in the country, and arrangements had been made for purchasing grain and grinding it to flour. It was calculated that we could readily procure three months' provisions, independent of 150 barrels flour, and 1300 head of cattle, which had been forwarded from the state of Ohio, and which remained at the river Raisin, under Capt. Brush, within reach of the army.

But had we been totally destitute of provisions, our duty and our interest undoubtedly was to fight. The enemy invited us to meet him in the field.

By defeating him the whole country would have been open to us, and the object of our expedition gloriously and successfully obtained. If we had been defeated we had nothing to do but to retreat to the fort, and make the best defence which circumstances and our situation rendered practicable. But basely to surrender, without firing a gun—tamely to submit, without raising a bayonet—disgracefully to pass in review before an enemy, as inferior in the quality as in the number of his forces, were circumstances, which excited feelings of indignation more easily felt than described. To see the whole of our men flushed with the hope of victory eagerly awaiting the approaching contest, to see them afterwards dispirited, hopeless and desponding, at least 500 shedding tears, because they were not allowed to meet their country's foe and to fight their country's battles, excited sensations, which no American has ever before had cause to feel, and which, I trust in God, will never again be felt, while one man remains to defend the standard of the Union.

I am expressly authorised to state, that Colonel M'Arthur, Col. Findley, and Lieut. Col. Miller, viewed this transaction in the light which I do. They know and feel, that no circumstance in our situation, none in that of the enemy, can excuse a capitulation so dishonorable and unjustifiable. This too, is the universal sentiment among the troops; and I shall be surprised to learn that there is one man who thinks it was necessary to sheath his sword, or lay down his musket.

I was informed by Gen. Hull the morning after the capitulation, that the British forces consisted of 1800 regulars, and that he surrendered to prevent the effusion of human blood. That he magnified their regular force nearly five-fold, there can be no doubt. Whether the philanthropic reason assigned by him is a sufficient justification for surrendering a fortified town, an army and a territory, is for the government to determine. Confident I am, that had the courage and conduct of the General been equal to the spirit and zeal of the troops, the event would have been as brilliant and successful as it now is disastrous and dishonorable.

A. W. COCHRAN TO HIS FATHER. (EXTRACT.)

(Canadian Archives, Cochrane Papers, M 147, p. 274.)

Montreal, October 10, 1812.

The man who came in from the American Camp brought a Plattsburgh paper of the 3rd instant and an Albany paper of the 22nd ult^{o}. In the Plattsburgh paper was General Hull's official letter to his Gov^{t} in which he makes out a good story for himself, by underrating his own force at *600* effective men and overrating our's at *2000* of whom he says *800* were regulars so that what with one lie and another he makes it out as clear as noonday that Alexander the Great himself c^{d} have done no more than he did,—In one place he says that he is convinced that his officers & men w^{d} have fought until their last cartridge was expended and their bayonets worn to the sockets! The Americans I think bid fair to rival & surpass the French in gasconading as well as in every thing that is dishonourable base & contemptible;—But after hearing Hull *audi et alteram partem.* In the Albany paper was contained the official report of Colonel Cass to the Sec^{y} at War in which he delivers (he says) the opinions of all the Colonels, who were with Hull; And Cass denies positively and roundly every fact stated by Hull as a reason for the surrender; His letter gives the lie point blank to Hull's whom he calls a coward or traitor in every thing but the express terms for he says that the Surrender was the effect of the General's *personal feelings* alone,—now those feelings must have been such as will stamp (him) either for a coward or a traitor; Colonel Cass letter is so far good that the material facts are truly stated, but these Yankees can not tell a plain story like other folks;—they cannot help *immersing the wig in the ocean* as Sterne says of the Frenchman, and Colonel Cass's high prancing words fall very little short of General Hull's or Commodore Rodgers' gasconades in point of vanity and absurdity.—

THE DUKE OF YORK[1] TO SIR GEORGE PREVOST.

(Canadian Archives, C 677, p. 116.)

Duplicate!

Horse Guards 7th Octr 1812.

Sir,

I have the pleasure to acknowledge the receipt of your Dispatch of the 26th August with its enclosed Report from Major General Brock, announcing the Surrender of Fort Detroit by Brigadier General Hull with The Army under his Command: and also reporting the arrangements & Operations connected with this Event.

An occurrence which so gloriously terminates a Campaign, commenced under the declared Confidence of Success on the part of an arrogant Enemy, cannot fail of being most acceptable to The Prince Regent and gratifying to The Country in general; and in communicating upon the Subject with His Royal Highness, I have His Commands to assure you that he highly approves the judicious and prompt arrangements which you adopted throughout The Province generally, for repelling the Progress of Invasion: and Major General Brock's exertions in The Country which was the more immediate object of The Enemy's attack, as well as the Skill and promptitude with which that Officer availed Himself of the Embarassments in which The Invader found Himself unexpectedly involved, are highly appreciated & acknowledged by His Royal Highness.

I have The Prince Regent's commands therefore, to desire that you will be pleased to convey to Major General Brock and The Officers & Troops employed under His Command, in the operations against Brigadier General Hull, the full Thanks of

---

[1] The Duke of York was field-marshall and commander-in-chief of all British forces.

His Royal Highness for the Important Services He, and They have performed upon this Occasion.

I have the pleasure to acquaint you that The Prince Regent has been graciously pleased to approve of the bearer of your Dispatches, Captain Coore of the 3rd West India Regiment, being promoted to the Rank of Major in The Army;—and His Royal Highness has further been pleased to approve of Major General Brock's Aide de Camp, Captain Glegg of The 49th Regiment, being promoted to The same Rank.—

CAPTAIN HEALD TO THE SECRETARY OF WAR.

(Historical Register of the United States, 1812-13; 2 ed., Philadelphia, 1814; Vol. II., p. 60.)

Pittsburg, Oct. 23, 1812.

On the 9th of August last, I received orders from general Hull to evacuate the post[1] and proceed with my command to Detroit by land, leaving it at my discretion to dispose of the public property as I thought proper. The neighbouring Indians got the information as early as I did, and came in from all quarters in order to receive the goods in the factory store, which they understood were to be given them. On the 13th, captain Wells, of Fort Wayne, arrived with about 30 Miamies, for the purpose of escorting us in, by the request of general Hull. On the 14th I delivered all the goods in the factory store, and a considerable quantity of provisions which we could not take away with us. The surplus arms and ammunition I thought proper to destroy, fearing they would make bad use of it if put into their possession. I also destroyed all the liquor on hand soon after they began to collect. The collection was unusually large for that place, but they conducted (themselves) with the strictest propriety till after I left the fort. On the 15th, at nine in the morning we commenced our march; part of the Miamies were detached in front, and the remainder in our rear, as guards, under the direction of captain Wells. The situation of the country rendered it necessary for us to take the

---

[1] In an original journal of Charles Askin, 1812, in the *Canadian Archives* there is a graphic account of the retreat from Chicago, depicting the horrors of the Indian massacre and the bravery of Captain Wells. "Captain Wells was murdered, his body cut open & his heart taken out & eat with apparent avidity by the Indians in presence of their prisoners and friends."

beach, with the lake on our left, and a high sand bank on our right, at about 100 yards distance. We had proceeded about a mile and a half, when it was discovered the Indians were prepared to attack us from behind the bank. I immediately marched up with the company to the top of the bank, when the action commenced; after firing one round, we charged and the Indians gave way in front and joined those on our flanks. In about 15 minutes they got possession of all our horses, provisions, and baggage of every description, and finding the Miamies did not assist us, I drew off the few men I had left, and took possession of a small elevation in the open prairies, out of shot of the bank or any other cover. The Indians did not follow me, but assembled in a body on the top of the bank, and, after some consultation among themselves, made signs for me to approach them. I advanced towards them alone, and was met by one of the Potawatamie chiefs, called the Black Bird, with an interpreter. After shaking hands, he requested me to surrender, promising to spare the lives of all the prisoners. On a few moments' consideration I concluded it would be most prudent to comply with his request, although I did not put entire confidence in his promise. After delivering up our arms we were taken back to their encampment near the fort, and distributed among the different tribes. The next morning they set fire to the fort and left the place, taking the prisoners with them.—Their number of warriors was between four and five hundred, mostly of the Potawatamie nation, and their loss, from the best information I could get, was about 15. Our strength was 54 regulars and 12 militia, out of which 26 regulars and all the militia were killed in the action, with two women and twelve children. Ensign George Roman and Dr. Isaac D. Van Voorhis of my company, with captain Wells, of fort Wayne, are, to my great sorrow, numbered among the dead. Lieutenant Lina D. T. Helm, with 25 non-commissioned officers and privates, and 11 women and children, were prisoners when we separated. Mrs. Heald and myself were taken to the mouth of the river St. Joseph, and both being badly wounded, were permitted to reside with Mr. Burnett, an Indian trader. In a few days after our arrival there, the Indians all went off to take fort Wayne, and in their absence I engaged a Frenchman to take us to Michillimackinac by water, when I gave myself up as a prisoner of war, with one of my serjeants. The commanding officer, captain Roberts, offered me every assistance in his power to render our situation comfortable while we remained there, and to enable us to proceed on our journey. To him I gave my parole of honour, and came on to Detroit, and reported myself to colonel Procter, who gave us a passage to Buffaloe; from that place I came by way of Presque Isle and arrived here yesterday.

CAPTAIN GLEGG TO COLONEL BAYNES.
(Canadian Archives, C 256, p. 229.)

York 11th Nov^{br}. 1812

My Dear Sir,

At the request of Mr Robert Dickson the bearer of this letter who intends proceeding immediately to Montreal on his private affairs, I take the liberty of giving him an introduction to you, in order, that previous to his being presented to His Excellency, some interesting particulars may be made known through your obliging communication.

Mr Dickson is closely connected with the most respectable families in this Province, who have invariably shewn themselves sincere and zealous friends to His Majesty's Government.

The Gentleman in question, has resided for a number of years in the character of a mercantile Trader in the Western Territory, and owing to his influence and assistance with the powerful Tribes of Indians some important services have been performed f orthe British cause—His influential Interest with the Western Indians has been repeatedly acknowledged by this Government, and his efforts in having decided that much injured race of Aborigines, to abstain from hostilities with the United States, have been well known here and duly acknowledged—During the month of Feby 1812, existing circumstances made it highly necessary to ascertain the sentiments and intentions of the Western Indians—Promises of their continued forbearance had been constantly made thro' the Agents of the Indian Department, but it was much apprehended by my vigilant and ever to be lamented friend,[1] that the attack made by General Harrison's army upon the Shawnese Indians assembled under the Prophet on the Wabash on the 7th Novr. 1811[2] might possibly produce some spirit of retaliation—It now became an object of considerable

[1] General Brock.
[2] The Battle of the Tippecanoe, see p. 6.

importance to open a communication without loss of time, with the neighbouring Indians bordering on the Misisipi.

No doubt could be then entertained of the premeditated destruction of the Indians by the Americans, and that merely because they had *presumed* to continue to establish themselves in the peaceful occupations of their native woods and villages— The most prompt measures were immediately adopted by the head of this Government, in conformity with the repeated Instructions of His Excellency and those of His Predecessor Sir James Craig, to prevent, by every possible exertion, the threatening flame from reaching our Frontier.

Mr Dickson's influence with the Indians being well known, the advantage of immediately opening a communication with him became obvious, and the accompanying paper number 1 was despatched to him early in february last by two confidential Indians—Mr Dickson was then at the Portage called Ouisconsin which is about one hundred and eighty miles from the Misisipi and the same distance from La Baie, about 800 miles from Amherstburg—He was then employed in administering in his mercantile capacity, to the severe distresses of their women and children who were literally languishing for want of food & clothing, owing to our supplies having been *discontinued* and to the severity of the season.

Mr Dickson received the enclosed paper N° 1[1] early in May and immediately replied to it N° 2—Previous to this date Mr Dickson had observed an unusual degree of activity in the American Agents who were then residing amongst the Indians, and having ascertained that presents were daily distributed by these people, which by the bye was a novel circumstance, he made immediate inquiry, and was informed by some of the Principal Chiefs, that the American Agents, had been directed by their Government, to invite some of their leading warriors from each nation, to pay an early visit to Washington—A combination of various circumstances left no doubt in the mind of Mr Dickson, that all this was intended as a prelude to more important events—His first endeavour was to dissuade the Chiefs from listening to the invitation of the American Government, and to point out the imminent danger of the proposed alliance—Mr Dickson fully succeeded in every object, and he received the strongest assurances of friendship and support in the cause of their Father the British

[1] These papers would appear to be the ones given on pp. 17 and 31, but there seems to be a discrepancy regarding the dates.

Monarch, whenever circumstances should render their assistance necessary—Soon after this communication passed, intelligence, reached the Wabash Indians, that General Hull with an army of two thousand men was on his march to Detroit—The Shawanese and other nations voluntarily offered to attack him on his route, but were still induced to desist from it, by the repeated entreaties of the friends and Agents of the British Government. It is however a well known fact, that General Hull's movements were all closely watched by Tecumpthsey's confidential Scouts, who were considered and received by the American General, as friends attached to their Interest—At the capture of Michilimackinac, Mr Dickson took an active part, and his services on that occasion, have been honorably recorded by Captain Roberts—After the surrender of that Post, an Expedition was immediately formed (at the solicitation of Major General Brock) by the Gentlemen of the Northwest and Southwest companies then assembled at Michilimackinac, to cooperate with the Force then contemplated to be employed against Detroit—So imperious however, was the necessity for despatch, in carrying this operation into execution, that the expedition under Major General Brock reached its destination and succeeded in its object, before the Indians intended for assistance, could form a junction with our little army—The intelligence of their approach had however reached the Enemy, and I have particular reason for knowing, that this circumstance produced very considerable influence in the final negotiation.

In justice to the memory of our lamented friend Major General Brock, and in obedience to what I am confident, would have been his intentions. I have taken the liberty of troubling you with this confidential communication, which you will be pleased to make use of, as your superior Judgement and discretion may point out—I am not aware of Mr Dickson's immediate views in soliciting an interview with His Excellency, but I have a perfect knowledge that there is no Gentleman in this Province more capable than himself of giving accurate information respecting the Western Indians than himself, and I am authorized in saying, that had General Brock survived the last contest, he intended pointing out Mr Dickson to the notice of His Majesty's Government, as a Gentleman who by his zealous and faithful services had proved himself deserving of their special protection.

STATEMENT OF ROBERT DICKSON.

(Canadian Archives, C 257, p. 39.)

Having obtain'd a supply of Merchandize at Saint Josephs from the Montreal Merchants, I left that place in the latter end of August 1811, and notwithstanding the impediments thrown in my way by the American Government I was fortunate enough to reach the Country where I usually carried on my trade.

During the Winter I found the Agents of the American Government using every means in their power to influence the Indians in their behalf, by making them unusual presents of goods and inciting them in the most pressing manner to visit the President of the United States at Washington, where, it was held out to them, they would hear something of the utmost importance.

From these circumstances I was induced to believe that something hostile was meditated against Our Government, and being the only individual in that Country possess'd of the means of frustrating their intentions I took such steps as I trust will be approv'd of by His Excellency the Commander in Chief.

The Calamitous state of the Indian tribes at that time was peculiarly distressing, the crops of those who cultivate the Ground having fail'd, from the great drought of the preceding Summer; and owing to the same cause those who subsisted entirely by the Chace were deprived of provisions, the large Animals having gone Northward in quest of food.

I left the River Missisippie on my return to St Josephs with a number of Indians after having supplied their families with ammunition and provisions at a great expence; I was met at the Portage of the Ouisconsing by Two Courriers from Amherstburg with a communication from General Brock, in consequence of which I sent a party of *Indians* from LaBaye to Amherstburg where they remain'd during the Summer and were in every engagement with the Enemy

I forbear entering into any detail respecting the Indians who accompanied me, as I presume that their conduct has already been made known to His Excellency the Commander in Chief.

A Statement of Expences incurr'd for the above purposes is here subjoin'd.—

1812

July 20 To amount of Robert Dickson & C^{os} account of sundries furnished the Scioux, Follesavoine & Winibigo Indians p^r account herewith N° 1   20973"   0
To paid Fran^s Bouthellier for sundries at Prairie du Chênes for d° p acco^t N° 2 $995" 0.   5970"   0
To paid Pierre Grignon for Funds for d° p acco^t N° 3.   624"   0
To Cash p^d Louis Grignon for an Ox for d°.   300"   0
To Cash p^d D^l Mitchell for provisions for d°.   876"   0
To Cash p^d Paul Ducharme for an Ox for d°.   300"   0
To amot^t of Jacob Franks account of sundries for said Indians p account N° 4.   12130" 18
To Cash p^d Lewis Crawford for provisions for said Indians at St Joseph p voucher N° 5.   350"   0
To Robert Dickson & C° disbursements for Said Indians at Michilimackinac p account N° 6.   3483"   0

Livres   45,006" 18

Hx Cy: £1875" 5" 9

Montreal December 3^d 1812—
    R. Dickson.

RETURN OF PRIZES MADE BY HIS MAJESTYS VESSELS ON LAKE ERIE, &c.[a]

(Canadian Archives, C 695, p. 89.)

Nature	Remarks
1 Sloop *Commencement*, Captured by the Boats of His Majestys Ship *Queen Charlotte*, Captain Hall off Fort Erie 27 June 1812 Cargo 12 barrels of Salt.	This Vessel taken into His Majestys service last fall and now lies in Chippawa Creek.—The Salt was sold for 7 Dollars p^r Barrell and Captain Hall will acco^t for the Amo^t to the Captors
2 Three Bales of cloth taken on Board His Majestys Ship *Queen Charlotte*, Capt Hall. This Cloth belonged to an American Citizen of the United States, and was ship'd on Board the *Queen Charlotte* before the declaration of War by the U.S was known at Fort Erie.	This Cloth was put into the Kings Store at Amherstburgh by Capt Hall and by order of Col^n St George it was Valued by Militia officers & Merchants of this place, the Valuation of it by the Officers, &c. accompanies this report and is marked One, Great part of this Cloth has been issued by order of Different Comm^{dg} Officers, for Clothing the Seamen, Troops, & Militia, And Capt Hall particularly requests that he may be instructed how he is to account to the owners or Captors.
3 Twelve Boats and Batteaux taken the Day after the Battle of Monguaga by the Boats of His Majestys Ship *Queen Charlotte*, Captain Hall, and His Majestys Brig *General Hunter*, Lieu^t Rollette, in these Boats was retaken Two wounded Soldiers of the 41st Regm^t and a few stands of Arms which was appropriated for Ships use.	These Boats were taken into the Quartermaster Generals Department and most of them sent off with Prisoners of War to Ciauga after the surrender of Detroit, And it is the oppinion of the Undersigned Officers that the lowest value of which they could set is £8 p^r boat.
4 One Large Boat captured in the (lake) off Fort Erie by the Boats of His Majestys Schooner *Lady Prevost* Lieu^t Barwis, and H.M.S *Queen Charlotte* Capt Hall in sight.	The Cargo of this Boat is in the Hands of the Officers of the Commissariat at Fort George. The Boat lies on the Rocks at Fort Erie, a return of which accompanies this mark(ed) N° 2. Lieu^t Barwis has already sent the acco^t of this Vessell to Col^n Myers.
5 The *Cayauga Packet* captured by the Boats of His Majestys Brig *General Hunter* Lieu^t Rollette Comd^r on the Day Lieu^t Barwis of the Navy and a Detachment of the 41st Regm^t under Lieu^t Hailes and entitled to share in this Capture as they had embark'd on board the *Genl Hunter* for the purpose of assisting, as appears to me, before the surrender of that Vessell, but Lieu^t Rollette is certainly to be considered as the Commander who made the Capture.	Such information as Lieu^t Rollette has furnished me, of this Vessell & Cargo, accompanies this and is mark'd N° 3.
6 A large raft intended for a floating Battery picked up in the River Detroit by the Guard Boats of His Majestys Ship *Queen Charlotte*, on the 1st August 1812	This raft has been taken by Captain Dixon of the Royal Engineers, his receipt for the same accompanies this return.

GEO. B. HALL Com^r Prov^l N(av)^y.

MEMORIAL OF LIEUT. JOSEPH LAMBETH. (EXTRACT.)

(Canadian Archives, C 231, p. 75.)

To His Excellency Sir George Prevost Governor General and Commander in Chief of His Majestys Forces in British North America &^{c} &^{c} &^{c}

The Memorial of Lieu^t Joseph Lambeth 10th R^l V^n Batt^n Sheweth

That your Memorialest being stationed at the Island of St Josephs under the Command of Captn Charles Roberts of said Regiment on the 12th July 1812 when the Expedition was forming to come against this Place your Memorialest was appointed by that officer—to doo the duty of Garrison & Fort Adjutant and his zeal and Perseverance in Capturing the Fort is well known to Captn Roberts as likewise to all the Gentlemen who took part in the same

your Memorialest was Order'd out and Captured on the 20th & 21st same Month two Sloops on their way down from Chicago Loaded with pellteries &^{c} which Vessels were taken into Government Service

Fort Michilimackinac 2^d June 1814.

EXTRACT FROM A MEMORIAL FROM JOHN ASKIN LATELY STOREKEEPER, INTERPRETER & CLERK AT ST. JOSEPHS, DATED 15TH OCT., 1816 AND ADDRESSED TO SIR JOHN SHERBROOKE.

(Canadian Archives, C 260, p. 445.)

Your Petitioner had enfluence enough to keep all the Indian Tribes (under his superintendence) faithful to our cause, and when War was declared in 1812, your Memorialist collected at a short notice 230 Indian Warriors, which he commanded at the taking of Michilimackinac the 17th of July 1812 (as will appear by Captain Roberts certificate hereunto annexed) and after that Fortress had Capitulated, your Petitioner collected upwards of 400 additional Warriors part of them, he sent down to the aid of Amherstburg and as Michilimackinac was Garrisoned only by 40 Soldiers of the 10th Royal Veterans & three of their Officers, your Memorialist always kept a large Body of Indian Warriors constantly on duty for the defence of that place, untill the arrival of Lieu^t Colonel McDouall with a reinforcement on the 18th of May

1814, all which time from 1807 to 1814 your Petitioner was the sole person who had the management of the Indians & their affairs at St Josephs & Michilimackinac, except a few Interpreters who were employed to accompany Indians sent out on parties—

I certify that John Askin Junior Esquire was present at the Capture of Fort Michilimackinac on the 17th of July in the Year 1812 and had the Command of 230 Chippewa and Ottawa Indians and is intitled to his proportion of Prize Money

Given under my Hand this 9th Day of September 1813 Fort Michilimackinac

CHARLES ROBERTS
Captain Comm^g

EXTRACT FROM MEMORIAL OF PAWQUAWKOMAN, AN OTTAWA CHIEF TO LORD DALHOUSIE, 6th NOVEMBER, 1826.

(Canadian Archives, C 266, p. 268.)

Requête de Pawquawkoman, *alias,* Amable Chevalier, chef Outawa, ci-devant de l'Arbre-Croche, Lac Michigan, actuellement du Lac des deux Montagnes.
Ecoutes moi, Mon Père.

Dès le commencement que nous avons été appellés à votre Service par Sir William Johnson, nous nous sommes rendus à Sa parole, et depuis ce temps mes oreilles ont toujours été ouvertes pour écouter ses Successeurs. Je rappelle le temps que les Sauteux ont défait le Fort de l'ancien Michilimackinac. J'étois du nombre de ceux qui ont été au Secours de vos troupes à la Baie-Verte, et qui ont ramené à Montreal plusieurs Traiteurs Anglois qui avoient été faits prisonniers après la défaite de vos Troupes.

Mon père, Au commencement de la première guerre avec l'Amerique le Major Depoyster, qui commandoit alors a Michilimackinac, nous a invités à prendre les armes avec les Colliers de guerre de Sir John Johnson; et J'étois du nombre de ceux qui les portèrent aux Puants, Follesavoines, Scioux, Renards, Sacques, et Poutowatamies. Ensuite nous nous sommes rendus à Montreal en obéissance aux ordres de Sir John Johnson. J'étois le Chef du guerre de mon Parti. J'ai suivi le Général Bourgogne dans sa Campagne, et dans le combat où il fut defait Je reçus une blessure à la tête dont Je porte encore la Cicartrice. Je perdis en cette occasion la majeure partie de mes Jeunes-gens. Aussitôt que Je fus retabli Je reçus, par les mains du Général Bourgogne, une Commission de Capitaine que J'ai perdu par une incendie.

Mon père, Sitôt que Je fus informé de la rupture avec les Etats Unis de l'Amerique en 1812, Je quittai mon village et me transportai immediatement en l'Isle St Joseph où J'offris mes Services au Commandant de la Place qui les accepta.

Mon père, La femme a pris le *Chikaquois,* et s'est mise à chanter la guerre, et tous les autres Sauvages de Michilimackinac voyant la femme chanter la guerre, suivirent son exemple: et après cela le Barbue et L'Etourneau changèrent et se mirent de notre côté. Après ce Conceil les Americains sont venus pour reprendre le Fort de Michilimackinac et neuf cents hommes ont debarqué. Nous n'étions que cinquante hommes Sauvages; nous avons tué le Chef qui les Commandoit et plusieurs de Ses Soldats—cequi les obligea de rembarquer. Dans l'automne de la même année Je descendis à Montreal, et me rendis à la parole de Sir George Prévost qui m'avoit mandé. Il me charges de porter ses paroles aux Sauvages des Pays d'en haut, et de leur dire, dans la vue de les exciter à prendre les armes contre les Americains, que le Gouvernement alloueroit des pensions a ceux d'entr'eux qui servient blessés, et pouvoiroit pour les femmes et enfans de ceux qui servient tùes dans le combat. Je fus mis sur la liste des Officers de Departement Sauvage comme Lieutenant. Il me fit présent d'un sabre et d'une paire de pistolets en présence de plusieurs officiers de son Staff et de M^r McGillivray, et me promit que Je serois récompensé. Me fiant, comme J'ai toujours fait, sur la parole de Mon Pere, Je n'hesitai pas de porter par des Colliers ses paroles par toutes les Nations, et de combattre contre les Americains dans les differentes occasions qui se sont présentées.

EXTRACT FROM AN ORIGINAL JOURNAL OF CHARLES ASKIN,[1] IN THE CANADIAN ARCHIVES.

Left Warner Nelles's Friday afternoon the 24th (July, 1812.) met on my way up to the Mohawk Castle two or three

---

[1] Charles Askin, second son of Lieut.-Colonel John Askin, was born at Detroit in 1780. He was appointed captain of the Canboro and Haldimand company of militia in September 1812, and served in various capa-

Indians who appeared alarmed one of them told me that an Indian had just come from Amherstburgh that he said there were a great body of American troops on their way up the River Thames, horse & foot.—this Indian appeared from his dress &^{ca} as if he had left home to go and meet the Enemy with the party under Major Chambers; but had got alarmed and was going back again.—after going a little further I came to a Village where I saw two or three hundred Indians, I found from some of them who rode up with me to Mohawk Castle that they had, had a Council and it was there determination not to fight the Americans. I afterwards learnt that General Hull had wrote them a letter which was brought to them by the Indian who had as I before mentioned come from Amherstburgh, which was the cause of their holding the Council—I got in the Even^g to the Bridge, there got a fresh horse and rode to Yieigh's where I got about 9 O Clock, I found Major Chambers' with the party under his Command, also Mr Wm Crooks, and Hamilton Merrit(t) with some Light horse who had Ebenezer Allan and two other men prisoners, that were taken at Delaware for some treasonable behavior—

Saturday 25th in the morning Mr Merrit(t) went off with his prisoners to Niagara, Major Chambers, young St John & myself rode down to G(rand) R(iver) to the Mohawk Castle, We found Capt Norton, there who told us that few of the Indians, were ready yet to go with him, but would be in a day or two   We returned from the Castle to Woodruffs at the G(rand) R(iver) Bridge dined there, Capt N. with us, from this Major C. and myself with Lieu^t Garner a Militia Officer (who volunteered his Services to go with the Major on the Expedition) went to Mount pleasant press'd a few waggons then rode to Yeigh's, Mr Hamilton,[1] Wilkinson,[2] and some of the men had left it and gone with part of the baggage to Oxford—

Sunday 26th Morn^g Our party left Yeigh's in Waggons and went to Oxford where We found some of the Oxford Militia under Col. Bostwick I think ab^t Seventy five of them.—

---

cities throughout the war. He was commissioner of Customs from 1824 until 1826. The fragments of his diary and his letters to his kinsfolk, which have been preserved, contain much interesting information not to be found elsewhere. Many of these are in the *Canadian Archives.*

[1] Captain George Hamilton of the 1st Regiment of Lincoln militia.

[2] Alexander Wilkinson, who served as a gentleman volunteer with the 41st Regiment; appointed ensign in the Canadian Fencibles, April 18, 1813.

Monday 27th In the morning Col. Talbot, arrived at our Camp, from Long P^t with young Mr Rolph and some Other Officers of the Long P^t Militia who Said that their Militia had been on their march to join us had got as far as Masacres: but there mutinied and went back,

Tuesday 28th I was taken ill in the morn^g occasioned by being out a great deal in the Rain, (continued ill Wed. 29th, & 30 in the afternoon on Thursday I went with Mr Carl to stay at his house as it was more comfortable there than where I was staying, and I thought I should soon recover,—before I left our Camp (for I know not what else to call it) Col. Talbot, had gone either to L^g P^t or Port Talbot, Capt Norton had joined us with ab^t 12 or 14 Indians, Wm Crooks & Mr Racey had been with us and had gone off with Westbrook of Delaware to take him down a prisoner as he was supposed to have some concern with the Enemy and suspected to have aided in having General Hull's proclamation promulgated.

Friday 31st Doct^r Sumner paid me a visit and wished to give me an Emetic but I felt myself so much better that I declined taking any, he advised then to remain for a few days where I was.—the Doct^r left me and soon after Mr Wilkinson came and informed me that the men were to march for Delaware that evening, I got the few things packed up I had with me and left Mr Carl's where I had been treated with very great attention and politeness, he has a large family most of them Sons growing up, they all appear much attached to the British Government, which I believe is the case with very few in Oxford Delaware, or the Grand River,—On my Arrival at my old Quarters, I found that Major Chambers and Mr Hamilton had been on their way to Delaware but had returned in consequence of some Despatches brought to the Major by young Mr Secord, I also learnt that we had taken Michilimackinack without firing a shot, it was said to be taken by a party of Indians under Mr Robt Dickson—

Saturday Augt 1st The Detachment left Oxford with the Dragoons, & ab^t 70 Oxford Militia—I was unwell & had to stay behind,

Sunday 2^d Left Fuller's with Doct^r Sumner and went to Yeighs, the fatigue of riding put me in a fever, the Doct^r left me here and went to Join the Detachment which had march'd to L^g P^t in the morn^g.

Monday 3^d I was so unwell that I was confined to bed most all day.

Tuesday 4th Felt much better. We heard that a few Light horse from York and about 100 of the York Militia were on their way to Long P^t—saw 3 Canadians to-day who were just from Amherstburgh on their way to Montreal—they mentioned that the Indians had had some skirmishes with the Americans near River Canard & had driven them once or twice—Got a note in the Evening from Mr Hamilton from L^g P^t advising me to join immediately—had a horse pressd in the morn^g and rode to Long P^t through a most beautiful country and very good roads—arrived at Dover ab^t 3 O Clock in the afternoon found a great many men there. Norfolk Militia, York Militia, Oxford Militia Dragoons & the 41st also some Artillery with a 6 pounder which was sent up from Niagara —heard on my way up that the General was coming,

Wednesday 5th heard that the *Nancy* had been to Fort Erie & had taken up about 60 of the 41st Reg^t—Was so weak that I could not drill with the men.

Thursday 6th Was unwell to day—the Militia were drilled by Capt Chambers.

Friday 7th Nothing remarkable occurred to day, in the Evening General Brock arrived. Mr Wilkinson, Hamilton & myself left Mr Nichols where we had been staying and went to Mr Williams where Capt Heward & other Officers of the York Militia were, here we staid all night. Lieu^t Jarvis arrived in the middle of the night—he came with a small party of Indians—

Saturday 8th we all embarked in boats, for Amherstburgh except the Norfolk Militia under Major Salmon & ab^t 14 or 16 Oxford D^o, who embarked in the *Chippawa*—Some of the Oxf^d & Norfolk militia were left behind for want of boats— I embarked on board the Largest boat with the 41st Major Chambers was so unwell that he had to remain behind, our boat being much loaded having the 6 pounder on board & many other things, we did not get off so soon as the other boats—we attempted to get to the carrying place but could not find the small creek that led to it nor could we get on shore, therefore anchored among the Rushes and staid there all night.

Sunday 9th Early in the morning we got under way and soon saw the General's Boat and several other, we got in the Cieek and went up to the carrying place, we had to take out most all our loading and then with the assistance of the other boats crews had great difficulty to get our boat over,—We had to caulk our boat here and then load and were so long doing this that Most of the boats were seven or eight miles a head of us before we could (get) off but the wind was fair and we came up to them, the General put in at Kettle creek and all our brigade—

Monday 10th Left Kettle Creek early in the Morning, the wind fair and a good breeze—the wind increased so and there was such an appearance of a storm, that McCaul who sailed our boat thought it advisable to put in at Port Talbot, distance 7 Miles from Kettle Creek, this was a very bad port for our boat, for we could not get her into the Creek, and had to haul her up the beach—here we remained all day, during the day Col. Talbot and Major Chambers arrived, also ab^t 28 Dragoons but these I did not see—they were ordered to Delaware immediately, during the night it rained so hard, that Mr Lenn[1] and myself were forced to leave our camp & go up to Col. Talbots, where we slept on our blankets before the Kitchen fire very comfortably, We found a man there who had just arrived with an express for General Brock, To day our party was strengthened by a Company of Riflemen in two boats under Capt Robertson of York,—

Tuesday 11th Left Port Talbot—we sail'd some time, then the wind changed and we had to row, we were left behind by all the boats, at length the wind increased so much that we went a shore and anchored off—the General who had put on shore a mile further (on) came down & had our boat taken up nearly a mile above where his Boat lay—we staid here the remainder of the day, in the even^g we got orders to get under way at 12 O Clock but that the General's boat would have a light in it and no boat should pass it,

Wednesday 12th ab^t 4 O Clock in the Morn^g we saw a boat with a light passing & we got off as soon as possible but all the boats were a great way a head of us—the Wind was fair and we passed them all before we got to Point aux Pins—the General desired us to Make the best of our Way up, the Wind was fair and we got to Point a Pelé at night, here we went on shore to cook something for the men, as we understood a party of American Light horse had been there—we patroled all night, not myself for I had not been well since I left port Talbot.

---

[1] Lieut. Charles Lenn of the 41st Regiment.

Thursday 13th Left Point au Pelé before day and arrived at Amherstburgh ab^t 8 O Clock in the night, we were saluted by a Number of Indians encamped near Capt Elliotts, heard On our way up at a house we stopp'd at to day, that the Americans had left Sandwich and returned to Detroit— —

Saturday afternoon 15th Augt 1812 the American Garrison was summoned to surrender by General Brock but refused, as soon as their answer came down to Gen. B.—the artillery Officer went up to the battery opposite Detroit and soon heard a firing commence which continued for a couple of hours, the party of the 41st which came up with us were called out, and 9 more of the Reg^t joined us—we were then I think Just 50 men including Mr Hamilton Mr Wilkinson & myself, we were in two divisions the first commanded by Mr Lenn and the 2^d, to which we belonged by Sergeant Blaney—Some Militia joined us and Major Chambers form(ed) into open Column & then into Line several times, every one, and every thing allmost, was at this time in motion, people passing in every direction— we were ordered to be in readiness at 4 O Clock next morn^g for marching, as soon as we were dismissed the Officers of Militia and most of us were very busy in preparing every thing for action, pistols swords, &^{ca}

Long before day we were up on Sunday the 16th then fell in—Major Chambers commanded the 2^d Brigade   strong, composed of 50 of the 41st including 3 vol^s—Mr Hatt's company (of) Militia—the Norfolk & Oxford Militia—Major Tallon[1] commanded the 3^d Brigade in which there was nothing, but the 41st & the 1st Brigade commanded by Col. St George consisted of the Essex militia, & some the Newfoundland Corps—the 2^d Brigade was halted a short time at Sandwich then marched down near to Parks Mill, where we embarked, when marching down we saw the 3^d Brigade and the General, and his staff crossing the River just below the Springwell—I think it was the handsomest sight I ever saw, the Indians were allready over—they just crossed before us, when we landed we formed in open column in the rear of the 3^d Brigade, a company of Riflemen from York went over with us, we all got over without any opposition—but (they) did not belong to our Brigade—they were most all painted as Indians— we were some time halted here, then marched up the road, I was much pleased to observe how unconcerned most of the men

---

[1] Major Joseph Tallon of the 41st Regiment.

were both Militia and Regulars—the first house we passed we observed the Indians had broke into and were plundering, we found them also running after horses in every direction—we marched at Quick time but had frequently to halt, the Carr Brigade passed us on the Road—I think there was about five or six Guns—and more I believe in front—I saw a number of inhabitants many of whom knew me and seemed happy to see me, we got at last to Mr Henry's about a Mile and a half from Detroit and there halted, from this place sent a flag of truce to the Garrison desiring them a 2^d time to surrender—it was a long time before we had an answer therefore was kept a long time in suspense—many were wishing them not to capitulate —there were young Officers who were anxious to have an opp^y of distinguishing themselves; but most of us wished I believe they should (not)—to spare the effusion of blood and for the sake of the poor Women and children who we knew would not be spared by the Indians should an action once commence— fortunately for us as it will appear afterwards the Americans after some time capitulated and surrendered themselves prisoners of War—I forgot before to mention that while we were marching up a constant firing was kept up from Our Battery at Mr Babys and from the American Fort, the American Guns were 24 pounders, while we staid at Mr Henry's two prisoners were brought in, one by an Indian and another by one of the Rifle Company, during our stay here a good many of the Canadian Militia belonging to Col. St George's Brigade joined us, Mr Wm Forsyth was living near Mr Henry's—I never saw a person more happy than he was to see us—he was so overjoyed that he could hardly speak—We marched up to the Garrison the Carr Brigade in front—I believe there was 6 pounders & the Ammunition Carrs—We marched into the Town and from that up into Fort *Lernou;* but there were so many American Troops in it, that we could not all get in, I believe our marching in was improper, and that it was done by mistake, for we were but a few minutes there before we were ordered to march out, I really think while we were in the Garrison (there were) two Americans for one of us and they had still their Arms, we formed on the West side of the Fort in line, untill all the Americans had marched out, but I was so situated that I could not see them coming out, they did not march with the honors of War—though I am told they were allowed to do it by the Capitulation but the Officers of the Am(erican) Army were so mortified that they had to surrender without fighting that they were indifferent about it or anything else then, the American colours were flying nearly an hour after we first marched into the Garrison, After the Americans had all marched out, the Grenadiers & Light Infantry of the 41st Reg^t and the Volunteers in that Reg^t, that is M^r. Geo. Hamilton, Wilkinson myself and Jno Richardson, commanded by Mr Bullock[1] of the Grenadiers, marched into the Fort, with Drum & fife to the tune of the British Grenadiers—I must say that I never felt so proud, as I did just then, as soon as we were in the Fort, the American Colours were taken down and ours hoisted, three Cheers were given as they were hoisted by the Militia and others outside the Fort— & the Indians when the Salute was fired with the Cannon gave an Indian Yell every shot—we the Volunteers remained with our Guard until the Colours of the 4th A(merican) Reg^t were brought by a part of our Guard & after which we got leave to go where we wished, I and Mr Hamilton went to see Mr Brush, where we dined—Two prisoners were taken in the Woods to day while we were at Mr Henry's, one by an Indian & another by a Rifleman.

There were about 2300 prisoners surrendered besides the Militia of the Michigan Territory, who gave up their arms that day, with the others, these were 3 or 4 hund. strong— most of the American army were composed of Militia from the State of Ohio, who had volunteered their Services for a year, some were cavalry vizt one company, (a) great number Riflemen, and some infantry—there were of the Regular troops,   of Artillery   of the 1st Reg^t and about 3 hun^d of the 4th Reg^t—this last Reg^t are highly spoken of by the Americans, indeed from the manner they speak of them you would suppose them to be Invincibles—the whole of their army were ill dressed, and few of them appeared healthy or well, indeed they seemed to me the poorest looking sett of men I have seen for a long time, their situation and dress may probably have made them appear so ill to me—seven hundred Rifles were taken and a great many Muskets nearly 3000 stand, & 32 p^s Cannon of all descriptions, a great number of waggons, horses &^{c}—

Monday 17th Remained at Detroit but did no duty, saw the American prisoners embarking, many of whom were unwell

---

[1] Captain Richard Bullock of the 41st Regiment.

with fevers & some wounded—poor fellows I fear few of them will ever get home,—All the Vessels from Amherstburgh I believe & those taken at Detroit were taking in prisoners; but there were not a sufficient number to take them all, and those who were on board were very much crowded, by the Capitulation, as I understand the Regular Troops were to be kept as prisoners of War and the Militia Reg^{ts} were to be sent to Cleveland or Sandusky, from whence they were to return home & not serve against the English again this war.— of the Regulars I suppose there is not more than 400, these I suppose will be sent to Quebec—

Tuesday 18th I crossed the River, went up, to my Father's dined there and then went down to Amherstburgh to see Major Chambers with whom I had volunteered to go to the River Raizin & Foot of the Rapids, in the Even^g I saw General Brock and his Aidecamp Col. McDonnell At Amherstburg— Mr Hamilton was down there also; but as he had embarked and I could not conveniently get on board I did not see him, For want of boats or something else we could not get off this evening for River Raizin—I saw Major Salmon & young Mr Rolph—Mr R. had bought a horse for 5 doll^s—some were sold for two doll^s I understood from the Indians, who took about three hundred on the Day of the Surrender and the day following, on the American Side—they plundered Knaggs's house and a few other houses and took a great deal from them—

Wednesday 19th Amherstburgh Last night or early this morn^g, the *Chippawa,* a small Vessel sailed from this, in which was passengers the General and his two Aidecamps,—and Mr Hamilton & Mr Jarvis, in the afternoon we got off from Capt Elliotts for River Raizin, Major Chambers, Capt McKee[1] & his son Alex^r, Mr Bap^t Barthe[2] & myself with some others went over in the same boat and landed below Brownstown, Alex McKee had his (horse) cross'd and I had another taken over he had lent me, we waited some time here, for the Indians to join us, at length *Tecomesé* with a few others came to us—& Gun Boat commanded by Mr Bender[3] of the 41st Reg^t came over—we all that is we Gentlemen embarked in the Gun Boat and got under way—our horses were sent on by land, when we got near the Point au Roche it blew Rather

---
[1] Captain Thomas McKee of the Indian Department.
[2] Captain Jean Baptiste Barthe of the Essex militia.
[3] Lieutenant Benoit Bender of the 41st Regiment.

hard and it was thought dangerous to go round the Point, we therefore put into the River Huron but how long we staid here I do not know; for I believe I was a sleep when we left it.

Thursday Morn^g 20th Got early in the morn^g to Rocky River. Rained a good deal this morn^g & I believe it did last night but I was under cover during the night and not exposed to it—We got into some houses that were deserted we made fires in them, and got some breakfast, three other boats were with us here, all under Bender's command—Capt Elliott and his Son Alex joined us here, the(y) came on horseback with a number of Indians—we most all got horses and Rode to the River Raizin where we arrived about 10 or Eleven O Clock A.M. We went towards the Blockhouse but finding that the Blockhouse was open, and nothing in it, we returned to Mr Lasselle's where we got Breakfast—some Indians (arrived) while we were here, we were still at Breakfast when a message came to us from Mrs Anderson begging that we would go and prevent the Indians from plundering her house—Major Chambers rode off immediately & I followed him as quick as I could—we found the Indians had taken a number of things—and were taking every thing valuable they could get hold of. they paid no attention to us whatever when we tried to make them desist. The Hurons were the first to break in & plunder this house. and some of them were Mr Anderson's friends—from this house they went to several other houses and plundered them, old Mrs Knaggs house was among others plundered, some Indians remained about Anderson's most all day, taking and destroying things. they emptied some flour out in the yard, which they did not want, Col. Elliott was with us at the time we first went to Andersons to prevent the Indians from plundering, but did not go with us— thinking that he would have more influence than Major C— or myself I went and requested him to go once or twice, I think twice—at last he went, it's true he was unwell, (but I think he might have gone at first as well as at last)—Yet for all the good he did he might as well have staid where he was— Major C. was much enraged at the behaviour of the Indians, & tried to prevent them from plundering as much as he could. Capt McKee when he joined us did the same—*Técompsé* the Indian General as he is called, behaved I must say remarkably well, he assisted us very much in trying to prevent the Indians from pillaging; but the Hurons could not be prevented from taking what they wanted—some Soucks that had begun to plunder were stopp'd by Maj C—and they even retur^d some things they had taken, the Indians took a great number of horses on the river—horses they have taken every where, the day of the surrender and the day following I fancy they did not take less than 300 from the people on the Detroit side,— Capt Elliot(t)[1] who was sent here with a flag of truce on Sunday last was still here—he found Capt Brush here who commanded a company of Gentlemen from Ohio, and a number of others with him from some of the corps serving in Detroit, when he saw the letter which was from General Hull the contents of which I know (not), (but suppose it was an order for him to surrender) he said it was a forgery and Elliott was an impostor, he had Capt E— confined and threatened to hang him—some of the Gentlemen in his company interfered and told him they would shoot him if he did, whether he thought it a forgery or not he and all those with him excepting a few sick made off that night, not in any order but as fast as they could get off six or seven of them together—in this disorderly manner they left the place—many of them taking horses with them that they took from the Inhabitants,—who complained very much of them,—when we found this party were so far a head of us that it was no(t) probable we could ever overtake (them) and that even if we should they had nothing with them that was worth going after, it was thought advisable to send back the Indians from this place and not allow them to go to the Foot of the Rapids where we dreaded they would behave in the same shameful manner they had done to day, at that place—some were in consequence of this sent back, and they would have all retur^d had not a scoundrel of the name of Amable Bellair (I think was his name,) come and said that he was from the foot of the Rapids, and that when he left it, there were 180 Americans there, that had gone from that place about a mile, and returned, we hardly credited what he said as a Doct^r Fairfield a very decent looking man had come from that place with a flag of truce, and said that there were none there but a few sick, as I interpreted I told Bellair who was a frenchman that if he deceived us he would be hung—the Scoundrel still insisted on it, I believe it was then determined that what Indians remained should go there, I was not much with them then; and did not know well what was to be done, as Major Chambers had requested me to take

---

[1] Captain William Elliott of the 1st Essex militia. See p. 172.

charge of a boat that was loaded with arms and take it to Amherstburgh he wrote Col. Procter and I had the dispatches —this night I slept at M`r` Jérome's where w^ most all staid; some Americans slept their also, who were much afraid that the Indians would murder them—

Friday 21st In the morn^g Major Chambers told me that Capt Elliot(t) would take charge of the boat, and wished me to go with him with a flag of truce to the Foot of the Rapids—Doct^r Fairfield, & a Capt Hull left the River Raizin with us, a Capt Hull went in a boat with Mr Bender, and Fairfield remained with us at the River au Loutre—we took a Canadian as an Interpreter in case we wished to speak to the Indians—a party of whom were a head of us with Alex^r Elliot(t)—we got to Foot of the Rapids about one or two O Clock in the afternoon, the Indians had just begun to plunder or began as soon as we got there, but did not take much here, except horses, they took several of these, there were no Americans here but a few that were sick, which belonged to the Army, a party of Yankees had passed that place the day before with 200 head of Cattle— but it was thought they had got out of our reach,—The Block-house here Técompsé had set fire to and was burning when we came here, the Inhabitants complained of Brush's company some of whom had stolen their horses and some other things,— we found[1] 77 bbls. pork, 18 of flour & eight or ten of whiskey here, which had been left by the American Army, We found no arms—I suppose they were hid and some other things also, The scoundrel Bellair that had told such a falsehood respecting the American troops being at this place, we were going to take with us to Amherstburgh, I took his pistols from him and we considered him as a prisoner but had no one to Guard him, some Indians begged he might be liberated which was done, and the fellow got his pistols again without my knowledge & I could never see him after—In the afternoon Mr Bender arrived with the Gun Boat and two other boats—we had before this collected all the water craft we could on the River, we had two boats and some canoes which we began to load, but they were all so leaky except some canoes that we could not make use of them, the Canadians were sett to work and loaded the Gun Boat and two other boats they brought with them— after getting all we could in these, we put what we still had to bring with us in five or six canoes, about 11 or 12 O Clock at night we left Mr Baugran's and went down the River with an Intention of going to the Lake I believe; but after going

---

[1] For official return, see p. 177.

six or seven miles the men one after another fell asleep & I did the same, whether the boats went a shore or not I cannot say—

Saturday 22^d In the morning we were on our way down the River I think when we woke, a Canadian came down running to us & crying; he and another had been left at the Foot of the Rapids, and we had not missed them, till this one joined us, in passing an Indian camp his comrade was stopp'd he supposed him murdered by the Indians,—a Maunsy Indian was taken from an Indian Camp, into one of the boats, that had just been stabbed by some Indian of a diff^t nation, we put on shore at Presqu'ile where we got a very good boat in which we put what was in the Canoes, we breakfasted here and then left this place—this day and night we got beyond the River Raisin, nothing remarkable occurred to day—

Sunday 23^d In the morn^g we got to Point au Roch(e)— the boat I was in was a great way behind the other boats, I then advised Major Chambers to get in another which we did, we left P^t au Roch(e) & got to Amherstburgh about 11 O Clock A M—Breakfasted at Capt Elliotts, then went up to Town, found that Major Chambers mare had been stolen by the Indians during his absence and an Immense number of other horses—were taken by them on this side the River—Dined at Doct^r Richardson's then rode up with Maj C— he went over to Detroit and I went to my Father's, before he left Amherstburgh he had a very serious quarrel with Col. Elliott—

From the 23^d to this date the 15th of September I have kept no journal—after my return from the Foot of the Rapids, I found Colonel Procter was acting as Civil Governor at Detroit & Judge Woodward an American Judge acting as his Secretary—many things have occurred during this short period which I have forgot, we had news that Chicago was taken by the Indians and no one saved but the Command^g Officer and his Wife—The Detachment that came up when I did and to which I belonged left Amherstburgh a few days ago, also some Grenadiers under Lt Bullock to return to Niagara— Major Chambers returned also, some time since by Land, Col. Procter & Mr Nichol went out to the Foot of the Rapids & returned soon, they went probably to view the Country as they had no forces with them—Capt Muir has been commanding officer at Detroit for some time—both my Brothers were doing duty with the militia there—An auction has been (held) at Detroit where part of the Public property taken at the

Surrender was sold, Some Waggons of which there was ab^t 60 sold very low, they were from 23 to eighty odd Dollars—many other things went very low also—Indians besieging Fort Wayne have sent for assistance & for some days past preparations have been making to go to that place—Last night part of the Expedition left Amherstburgh in a small Vessel and in Boats, they are all under the Command of Capt Muir a very Galant Officer—Indians have been going for some days past, & a party of Indians ab^t 200 in Number who arrived here a few days ago from Mackinac under the Direction of Jno B. Askin, have gone this morn^g with Capt McKee—Young Jno A. is also with them—they went off in great style, had a salute from the Garrison which they returned—The Expedition consisted of ab^t 150 of the 41st Reg^t 100 of the Militia & a party of Artillery & ab^t eight hundred (Indians)—these it was supposed would be joined by a great number of Indians, allready on their way, and before the place—the whole expedition were off this morn^g, the Officers Gone are

Capt Muir
Mr Bernard } 41st
Mr Hales—
Lt Troughton—R. Ar^y
Mr Dickson R. Engineers—
Capt Jacobs—
Wm Sterling—
Jno Pike } Militia.
J^s. Little
Nich. Little
Capt Caldwell.

Alex Askin } Militia.
Wm Hands
Capt Elliot(t) Com^g
Col. Caldwell Dp^y. Q^r M^r G.
Col. Elliot(t) Ind. Dep^t
Cap^s M^{c}êee   Do.
Doct^r Richardson Sur^g
Jno Do   Volunteer.

The Salina took part of the Expedition to Miami.

INDEX

Allan, Major William. Commands detachment proceeding to Amherstburg, 104.

American Army. Hull compares British force in Upper Canada with that of Michigan, 1-2; Hull compares resources with those of British force, 19-20; plans of mobilization of, 23, 24; Hull estimates his force as superior to the British, 36; extract from return of Hull's Brigade, 39; an estimate of Hull's forces at Detroit, 48; Hull reports his force unequal to reduction of Amherstburg, 50; takes possession of Sandwich, 57, 61, 62; Hull boasts of his redoubtable forces, 59; their numbers estimated from captured correspondence, 73; ill conduct of Ohio milita in skirmish at Canard river, 76; Hull requests large reinforcements from Kentucky and Ohio, 103; estimate of forces of, 105; recross river to Detroit, 126-127,139; large force sent to escort detachment conveying provisions from Ohio, 127; plans for guarding convoys with provisions for, 133; Cass, with other officers, lays before Governor Meigs the critical situation of, 137-138; return of killed and wounded in action at Maguaga, 141; Brock's estimate of numbers at surrender of Detroit, 156, 159; Anderson's detachment surrenders at River Raisin, 172; *see also* pp. 175-176; McArthur's detachment surrenders at River Rouge, 172; Hull's estimate of his force at Detroit, 188; plans for large reinforcements of, 202-203; Harrison takes command of Northwestern troops, 202-204; position of troops at surrender of Detroit, 220; report of number of troops on day of surrender of Detroit, 221; their indignation at capitulation of Detroit, 220, 221; Hull's estimate of, after capitulation, 223.

Amherstburg, Fort Malden. Brock advises necessity of maintaining strong position at, 16; Hull insists on danger to whole western country from, 21-23; report to Liverpool on state of fort and garrison, 26; report *re* work on

Amherstburg, Fort Malden—*Con.* fort, 47, 48; *see also* pp. 110, 181; Hull prepares for siege of Malden, 53; British force at Sandwich falls back on, 57, 61, 62; Hull reports making preparations for siege of Malden, 80-81; strength of St. George's force at, 109-110; Hull reports inadvisability of storming the fort without artillery, 116; Hull's reasons for not attacking fort, 126-127; opinion of American officers on ability of American forces to reduce Malden, 137-138; Harrison still hopes to retake fort, 204; Hull abandons plans of attack on, 218-219.

Anderson, Lieut.-Colonel John. His detachment of militia surrenders at River Raisin, 172; *see also* pp. 175-176.

Armistice. Dearborn to Secy. of War and to Hull on conditions of, 127-129; *see also* note, p. 127, pp. 178, 179; injurious to British cause if hostilities recommence, 193, 201.

Armstrong, Major-General John. Biographical note on, 3; his suggestions to the Secretary of War in event of hostilities, 3.

Army Bills. *See* under 'Currency.'

Askin, Captain Charles. Extract from journal of, 24 July-15 Sept., 1812, expedition against Detroit, its surrender, and after events, 235-248.

Askin, John. Commands Ottawa and Chippawa Indians at taking of Michilimackinac, note 2, p. 17; 67, *see also* pp. 233-234; commands Ottawa and Chippawas at Michilimackinac, 67; *see also* p. 152; represents his services to British cause, 233-234.

Aux Canards river. *See* 'Canard river.'

Baby, Captain François. Appointed Asst. Quartermaster-General, 51.

Baby, Colonel Jacques. Biographical note on, 45.

Barwis, Lieut. Thomas. Note *re*, 13; in command of the *Lady Prevost*, 232.

Bathurst, Earl of. Succeeds Liverpool as Secy. of State for Dept. of War and the Colonies, note, p. 160.

Baynes, Colonel Edward. Note *re*, 37; acts as British emissary *re* an armistice, 127; *see also* p. 179.

Blockhouses. Line of, erected to preserve western communication, 36, 38-39.

Bostwick, Captain John. Biographical note on, 99.

Bostwick, Lieut.-Colonel Henry. Biographical note on, 85.

British Army. Hull compares Michigan and Upper Canada forces, 1-2; Brock calls attention to inadequacy of forces available for defence, 16; assistants in commands at taking of Michilimackinac, note 2, p. 17; 54, 67; inquiry *re* support from western country, 18; Hull's estimate (March, 1812) of force to be met, 20; Brock reports loyalty of Upper Canada militia, 27-29; force raised under Supplementary Militia Act, 27; report on support expected from western country, 31-32; report that Brock takes troops to Malden, 36; Col. St. George's difficulties in collecting and organizing forces, 45-47; statement *re* collected force at Amherstburg, 49; establish post oppostie Detroit, 50; militia display lack of spirit, 51-52; Hull reports desertions of Indians and militia from, 53; the force at Sandwich falls back on Amherstburg, 57, 61, 62; desertion of militia and Indians from, 60, 61, 62-63, 90; statement of regulars, militia and Indians at reduction of Michilimackinac, 69; *see* p. 233; Brock reports ill conduct of the militia, 74-75; Capt. Chambers leads detachment to prevent inroads up Thames river, 90, 93, 96, 99, 114-115, 116; *see* pp. 157, 190-191; difficulties *re* discipline among the militia, 91; efforts to rally the Norfolk militia, 93-94, 98-99; *see* pp. 96, 157, 190; Talbot to Brock on the difficulties of securing and controlling militia and Indians, 93-94; *see also* pp. 96, 99, 157, 190-191; estimated number of Indians and militia at

British Army—*Con*.
Amherstburg, 96; Brock to Prevost *re* his critical situation owing to indifference of militia and influential officials, 99-100; *see* p. 161, 182, 191-194; militia at York freely volunteer services, 104; Brock highly commends York militia, 105; American estimate of forces of, 105-106; Brock's remarks on indifference of miltia officers, 107; difficulty *re* number of militia officers being out of proportion to their corps, 108; Brock commends regulars, militia and Indians, 112; Brock's situation made difficult by unsettled conduct of the militia, 119-120; *see also* p. 194; motion in Assembly that militia be at liberty to disband if not regularly paid, 121;. *see* pp. 142, 182, 191, 194; distinguished services of 41st Regt., 112, 124; *see* p. 90; transportation difficulties of reinforcement for Amherstburg, 130; numbers of the reinforcement for Amherstburg, 131; Procter reports that the militia and Indians are rallying, 136; *see also* p. 157; estimate of numbers in action, and of killed and wounded at Maguaga, 141; Brock organizes his forces attack on Detroit, 142-143, 145; Brock's commendation of regulars, militia and Indians at surrender of Detroit, 148-150; *see also* pp. 156-160, 192, 196; strength of, at surrender of Detroit, 158; Prevost details to Bathurst operations of force in Upper Canada, 160-164; transport with reinforcements captured by *Essex* is ransomed, 163-164; strength of force on Montreal frontier, 164; numerical strength of regiments in Upper Canada, 178; number of militia in western district who deserted, 191; *see* p. 218; reinforcements from Lower Canada place Detroit frontier beyond attack, 193; Hull's estimate of, after capitulation, 223, 223.

Brock, Major-General Isaac. Biographical note on, 4; his memo. on plans for defence, 12-14; to Prevost, on the means and necessity of gaining the Indian support, 16-17; calls attention to inadequacy of military forces, 16; to Liverpool, reports loyalty of militia and inhabitants of Upper Canada, 27-29; reported to have taken troops to Malden, 36; to Prevost, on the serious

Brock, Major-General Isaac—*Con.* situation in Upper Canada, 73-75; his proclamation to inhabitants of Upper Canada, 81-83; to Prevost, on the difficulties of the situation in Upper Canada, 91-93; his plans fustrated by refusal of Six Nations Indians to assist, 91; desires equal authority over military and militia, 92; to Prevost, stating his critical situation owing to the indifference of the militia, the magistrates and the House of Assembly, 99-100; *see* pp. 161, 182, 191-194; to Baynes, on the difficulties of his situation resulting from inaction of Legislature and indifference of all classes, 107, 118-120; *see* p. 194; to Prevost, on exercise of martial law, and payment of militia, 120-121; *see* pp. 182, 192; organizes his forces for attack on, 142-143; to Hull, demanding surrender of Detroit, 144; commends his force for conduct at surrender of Detroit, 148-150; his proclamation following surrender of Detroit, 155-156; to Prevost, despatches relating to operations in the surrender of Detroit, 156-160; to Liverpool, detailing legislative and military difficulties, with measures taken in Upper Canada, 190-201; represents to Executive Council his critical situation, indifference of the Assembly, and the insubordination of militia, requesting martial law be proclaimed, 193-195; leaves Amherstburg on the *Chippawa*, 243.

Brownstown. Grand council to effect Indian neutrality held at, 60, 78; *see* p. 36; British troops secure support of Wyandots at, 116; account of Indian ambuscade of Vanhorne's detachment at, 125-126; account of skirmish at, 135-136; *see* also p. 178.

Brush, Captain. His detachment evacuates the fort at River Raisin, 172; *see also* pp. 175-176, 186.

Brush, Colonel Elijah. Note *re*, 138.

Bruyères, Lieut.-Colonel Ralph H. Note *re*, 48.

Cadot, Lieutenant Jean B. Note *re*, 131.

Caldwell, Captain William. Note *re*, 51.

Cameron, Captain Duncan. Note *re*, 130.

Canadian Voyageurs. Corps raised by Northwest Company, note, p. 10.

Canard river. Skirmishes on, 71-72, 76, 89-90, 95-96, 119, 123-124, 157.

Cartwright, Lieutenant Edward. Note *re*, 120.

Cass, Colonel Lewis. Biographical note on, 41; (with other officers) to Governor Meigs on the critical situation of the American forces, 137-138; Hull commends conduct of, 189; to Secy. of War, critical report of causes and operations leading to surrender of Detroit, 218-223.

Chambers, Major Peter L. Biographical note on, 84; leads detachment to prevent American inroads up the Thames, 90, 93, 96, 99, 114-115, 116; *see* pp. 157, 190-191; commands Second Brigade before Detroit, 143; secures American stores and arms at River Raisin and Miami Rapids, 175-176.

Chevalier, Amable. Note *re*, 152; memorial of, shewing services to British cause, 234-235; *see also* p. 216.

Chicago, Fort Dearborn. Indian depredations at, and possible evacuation of, 55; Harrison advises chain of posts (to guard northwestern frontier) from the Mississippi to, 133-134; date of surrender, note, p. 205; account of massacre of garrison retreating from, 225-227.

Claus, Colonel William. Biographical note on, 5.

Cochran, Andrew W. Biographical note on, 213.

Coore, Captain Foster L. Carries to Bathurst despatch detailing surrender of Detroit, 184; promoted to majority, 225.

Couche, Dy. Commissary-General Edward. Difficulties of his department from lack of specie, 92.

Courts Martial. Brock desires authority over the military as well as the militia *re*, 92, 119; Brock requests information on his authority in, and the standing of militia officers in, 119, 121. *See also* under 'Martial Law.'

Crawford, Major Lewis. Assists at taking of Michilimackinac, note 2, p. 17; 54, 67.

Currency. Difficulties in carrying on public service for lack of specie, 92; paper money to be used in Lower Canada in lieu of specie, 97; embarrassments to public service, particularly the militia, from total want of specie, 111-112; Brock advises paper medium to satisfy demands of militia, 121; motion in Assembly that militia be at liberty to disband if not regularly paid, 121; *see* pp. 142, 182, 191, 194; the issue of Army Bills relieves situation in Upper Canada *re* payment of military and militia. 163; *see also* pp. 92, 110, 179, 191.

Declaration of War. News of, sent to Hull, 35 (*see* note); news first received in Canada through North West Company, 37; note *re* date of, 114.

Dearborn, Major-General Henry. Biographical note on, 40; to Secy. of War and to Hull on conditions of armistice, 127-129; *see also* pp. 178, 179.

Detroit. Artillery and naval equipment at, 4-5; Americans collect quantities of ordnance (January, 1812) at, 15; measures are taken (Feby., 1812) for defence of, 16, 19; Brock's opinion (Feby., 1812) that the fort is too strong to carry by assault, 16; importance of strong army at, advised by Hull, 22; American army re-cross river to, 126, 139; importance of keeping communication with Ohio open, 21, 36, 38, 50, 52, 116-117, 138; *see* p. 185; general orders to troops before attack on, 142-143, 145; demand and refusal to surrender, 144-145; articles and supplemental articles of capitulation of, 146-147; *see* p. 172; prize pay list at surrender of, 148; return of prisoners at surrender of, 153; return of ordnance, stores, &c., taken at, 154-155; Brock's proclamation following surrender of, 155-156; Brock's despatches on surrender of, 156-160; Prevost to Bathurst, detailing measures and operations terminating in surrender of, 160-164, 177-180, 181-184; frontier placed beyond attack by reinforcements from Lower Canada, 193; supply of stores, arms and provisions shortly before surrender of, 222; Cass to Secy. of War, report of causes and operations leading to sur-

Detroit—*Con.* render of, 218-223; Capt. Askin's *re* expedition against and surrender of, with after events, 233-248.

Dewar, Lieutenant Edward. Note *re*, 44; *see also* p. 149.

Dickson, Robert. Biographical note on, 17; takes leading part in capture of Michilimackinac, note 2, p. 17; 54, 67; reports on British support expected from the western country, 31-32; account of his services to British cause, 227-229; *see also* pp. 230-231.

Dixon, Captain Matthew C. Biographical note on, 44; *see* pp. 148, 232.

Earle, Captain Hugh. Note *re*, 14; *see* p. 232.

Edwards, Governor Ninian. Note *re*, 49.

Elkswatawa. Biographical note on, 7; American efforts to gain support of, 77; *see* p. 79; Harrison's suggestions for expedition against, 134.

Elliott, Colonel Matthew. Biographical note on, 5; *see* p. 63; two American detachments surrender acc'd'g to articles of capitulation to, 172; *see also* pp. 175-176.

Erskine, David Montague. Recalled from United States for exceeding instructions regarding peace, note, p. 128.

Eustis, Hon. William. Biographical not on, 1. *See also* under 'Secretary of War—American.'

Evans, Brigade Major Thomas. Note *re*, 113.

Executive Council. Brock represents critical situation of Province to, 120-121, 193-195; advise prorogation of Assembly and proclamation of Martial Law, 195.

Findlay, Colonel James. Note *re*, 39; *see* p. 221; (with other officers) to Govr. Meigs on critical situation of American forces, 137-138; Hull exonerates him from possible disapproval, 189.

Fitzgibbon, Lieutenant James. Note *re*, 107.

Flag of truce. Hull's explanation of incident *re*, 145, 212; Captain Brown's version of the incident *re*, 214.

SURRENDER OF DETROIT 253

Fort Dearborn. *See* under ' Chicago, Fort Dearborn.'

Fort Findley. Location of, 39.

Fort Malden. *See* under 'Amherstburg, Fort Malden.'

Fort St. Josephs. Suggestion to remove garrison of, to St. Mary's, 9-10, 14; report to Liverpool on, 26; commandant considers it indefensible, 65; *see* pp. 37, 54.

Fort Wayne. Harrison suggests that an army be collected at, 133; Harrison marches to relief of, 204, 205; expedition under Capt. Muir against, 248.

Foster, Augustus J. Note *re*, 127.

General Orders. American, 117; British, 84. 104, 112, 23, 125, 137, 138, 141, 145, 148.

Gilkinson, Captain William. Note on, 13.

Givins, Major James. Appointed Provincial A.D.C., 143 (*see* note).

Glegg, Captain John Bachevoyle. Biographical note on, 17; *see* p. 225.

Grant, Commodore Alexander. Biographical note on, 13.

Gray, Captain Andrew. Biographical note on, 8.

Habeas Corpus. *See* under ' Martial Law and Courts Martial.'

Hall, Captain George Benson. Biographical note on, 12; *see* pp. 149, 232.

Harrison, Major-General William Henry. Biographical note on, 6; to Secy. of War, on uncertain attitude of western Indian tribes, 42-43; *see* pp. 123, 164-165; his command to extend to Indiana and Illinois, 49-50; to Secy. of War advising offensive measures against Indians, 131-135; advises chain of posts from the Mississippi to Chicago to guard northwestern frontier, 133-134; to Secy. of War, on the situation, and measures taken on northwestern frontier 202-204.

Hatt, Captain Samuel. Note *re*, 149.

Hays, John. Note *re*, 170.

Heald, Capt. Nathan. To Secy. of War, account of massacre of garrison retreating from Chicago, 225-227; *see* pp. 54-55.

Heward, Captain Stephen. Note *re*, 105.

Hopkins, Major-General Samuel. Note *re*, 203.

Hull. Captain A. F. Note *re*, 60.

Hull, Captain D. Note *re*, 117.

Hull. Brigadier-General William. Biographical note on, 1; compares American with British resources, 1-2, 19-20; remarks to Secy. of War in view of hostitities, 1811, 1-3; to Secy. of War, on conditions and measures of defence advisable, 19-23; emphasizes importance of keeping open communication for supply of provisions, 21, 36, 38, 50, 52, 116-117, 138; *see* p. 185; Secy. of War sends news of declaration of war to, 35; *see* pp. 38, 43; confident of superiority of American force, 36; authorized to commence offensive operations, 37; to Secy. of War, *re* protection of northwestern frontier by line of blockhouses, 38; to St. George, with reply, *re* disposition of captured private papers and property, 40-41; 69-70; objects to his limited latitude, 44; important correspondence of, found on captured schooner, 44, 69-70; *see also* note, p. 19; pp. 43, 73, 90, 110, 113; to Secy. of War *re* prospects of success, 50; *see* pp. 53, 60; reports desertions of Indians and militia from British force, 53, 60; his proclamation to the inhabitants of Canada, 58-60; boasts of his redoubtable force, 59; threatens instant destruction to whites fighting with Indians, 59; his proclamation to the Six Nations Indians, 72; reports he has effected neutrality or support among the chief Indian tribes, 78; requests large reinforcements from Kentucky and Ohio, 103; to Secy. of War, is less confident of success, 115-117; to Secy. of War, reporting engagement at Brownstown, 125-126; to Secy. of War, giving reasons for not attacking Malden, 126; *see* pp. 116, 218-219; to Secy. of War, reporting action at Maguaga, 139-141; to Brock, refusing to surrender Detroit, 144-145; his explanation of the flag of truce incident, 145, 212; *see* p. 214; his intercepted letter to Secy. of War shews his attitude less confident, 178; to Secy. of War, detailing adverse circumstances leading to his surrender, 184-190; his estimate of his force at Detroit, 188; exonerates his associates in command, 189; soli-

Hull, Brigadier General—*Con.*
cits investigation *re* his surrender of Detroit, 190; sent to Quebec, released on parole, and exchanged, note 2, p. 213; court martial sentence of, remitted, note 2, p. 213; account of Col. Cass on his conduct during siege of Detroit, 218-223; his estimate of American and of British troops after capitulation of Detroit, 223.

Indians. Hull fears their becoming British allies, 2-3; number killed at the Tippecanoe, 8; of Michilimackinac country well affected towards the British, 15; Brock to Prevost, on the means and necessity of gaining support of, 16-17; officers in command of, at surrender of Michilimakinac, note 2, p. 17; 54, 67; American officers instructed to refuse their services and advise their neutrality, 20; *see* pp. 53, 78, 182; note on American campaign against tribes of western country, 21; British intercourse with, carefully conducted, 28; large numbers at Amherstburg and Brownstown supplied by British with provisions, 36; Hull reports many as friendly to American cause, 38; Governor Harrison reports uncertainty of support from, 42; grand council (British) held at Amherstburg, 46-47; number at Amherstburg attached to British cause, 49; Hull reports that British have control of, 50; Hull reports many desertions from the British force, and his influence for neutrality over others, 53; grand council (American) held at Brownstown to effect neutrality of all nations, 53, 60, 78; Dickson's remarks to Brock on state of western nations, 56; the part taken by, in reduction of Michilimackinac, 54, 66, 67-69; *see also* pp. 150-153, 214-217; Hull reports increased American influence over, 60; kept faithful to British by Tecumseh, 63; estimate of numbers taking part in reduction of Michilimackinac, 69; *see also* pp. 103, 233-234; Hull's proclamation to the Six Nations, 72; support of the far west tribes depends on fate of Michilimackinac, 73; Americans have skirmishes at River Canard with, 76; Americans arrange for grand council at Piqua, 77, 78; American newspaper reports *re* British tactics to gain

Indians—*Con.*
support of, 77; Hull reports neutrality or support among chief tribes, 78; Six Nations refuse to assist British, announcing a policy of neutrality, 90-91; *see also* pp. 94, 96, 191; report of Willcock's efforts to gain support of Six Nations for British, 209-211; unsatisfactory conduct of Ottawas and other tribes at Michilimackinac, 101-102, 150-151, 215-217; *see* p. 207; Hull's remarks on support British may command from, 116; Brock censures conduct of, 120; Governor Harrison's remarks on offensive measures against, 131-132; combination said to exist among western tribes, 131, 134-135; Harrison's plans for bringing them to decisive action, 134; Wyandots decide to join British cause, 135-136; *see* p. 126; fight under Tecumseh with great obstinacy at Maguaga, 140; Brock warns Hull he may lose control of, when contest commences, 144; Brock commends conduct of, at surrender of Detroit, 150, 159-160; outrageous conduct of, at Amherstburg, River Raisin and the Miami Rapids, 174, 175-176; Hull attributes his surrender to fear of atrocities by, 184-189; Brock warns Liverpool of danger from the Six Nations, 191; Brock remarks on treatment of, by Americans, 192; Brock directs that protective measures against their depredations on Detroit frontier be taken, 209; attitude of western nations influenced by Robt. Dickson, who opens British communication with, 227-229; *see* pp. 230-231; Jno. Askin's services in securing and retaining for British, support of, 233-234; those besieging Fort Wayne send to British for aid, 248. *See also* under Chevalier, Amable; Elkswatawa; Roundhead; Tecumseh.

Jarvis, Lieutenant Samuel Peters. Note *re*, 105.

Jessup, Major Thomas S. Biographical note on, 39; *see* p. 190.

Kingsbury, Colonel Jacob. To collect large force at Cincinnati to be sent to Detroit, 24.

Kingston, U.C. Is reinforced by men and stores to aid in preserving communication between Upper and Lower Canada, 98; *see* pp. 21, 120.

SURRENDER OF DETROIT 255

Lamont, Thomas. Note *re*, 107.

Land Grants. For families of deceased soldiers and marines, 28-29.

Lambeth, Adjutant Joseph. Represents his services to British cause, 233.

Legislative Assembly. Brock's opinion of, 99; Brock fears their refusal to amend Militia Act, 104; *see also* pp. 99-100; refuse to suspend the statute *re* Habeas Corpus, 104; motion that the militia should be at liberty to return home if not regularly paid lost by two votes, 121; Brock's hopes of effective measures by, not realized, 119, 161, 182, 191, 194, 195; Brock represents critical state of Province to, 195-197; President's speech to, and reply from, on opening the Legislature, 195-197, 199-200.

Legislative Council. President's speech to, and reply from, on opening Legislature, 195-199.

Lethbridge, Colonel Robert. Sent to Upper Canada for service, 97.

Liverpool, Earl of. Note *re* official position, 26.

Long Point. Brock collects a force for relief of Amherstburg at, 104, 119; *see also* pp. 122, 157.

Macdonell, Lieut.-Colonel John. Biographical note on, 85.

Maguaga. British troops secure support of Wyandots at, 116; account of action at, with return of killed and wounded, 139-141.

Marine Affairs. *See* under 'Naval affairs.'

Martial Law. If proclaimed, Brock fears dispersal of militia, 99-100; *see* pp. 194, 195; Brock deplores inaction of Legislature in suspension of statute *re* Habeas Corpus and, 104; *see also* pp. 119, 161, 182, 194; Prevost to Brock, remarks on authority to declare, 113-114; Brock requests information on the carrying into effect of, 119, 121; Executive Council advise proclamation of, 195; *see* pp. 193-194. *See also* under 'Courts Martial.'

McArthur, Colonel Duncan. Biographical note on, 31; (with other officers) to Govr. Meigs on critical situation of American forces, 137-138; his detachment at River Rouge surrenders acc'd'g to Hull's capitulation, 172; Hull exonerates him from possible disapproval, 189.

McDouall, Captain Robert. Note *re*, 124.

McKee, Major Thomas. Biographical note on, 142.

Meigs, Governor Return Jonathan. Biographical note on, 23; Cass and other officers lay critical situation of American army before him, 137-138.

Merritt, Lieutenant William Hamilton. Biographical note on, 85.

Miami Rapids. Return of provisions found at, 177; *see also* pp. 176, 246.

Michigan Territory. Hull compares its population and military strength with that of Upper Canada, 1-2, 19-20; Chief Justice Woodward to Procter, data on the civil government and geographical limits of, 166-170; question of operation of American revenue laws in, 175; Procter is temporary administrator of, 209; *see* pp. 165-166.

Michilimackinac. Memo. on numbers and loyalty of inhabitants of country of, 15; officers in command at surrender of, note 2, p. 17; preparations for attack on, 53-54; articles and supplement to articles of capitulation of, 63-64; despatches *re* the taking of, 65-69; *see also* pp. 72-73, 214-217. 223-235; sources of returns of ordnance, provisions and garrison on reduction of, note 3, p. 65; Roberts reports unsettled condition of affaires since its surrender, and desires reinforcements, 100-103; Roberts' difficulties with Indians, and with the garrison at, 150-153; *see* p. 207; observations on capture of state of, 214-217.

Michilimackinac Company. *See* under 'South West Company.'

Militia. *See* under 'American Army,' 'British Army'; regarding payment of militia, *see* under 'Currency.'

Militia Act, The Supplementary. Force raised under, 27.

Miller, Lieut.-Colonel James. Biographical note on, p. 72; leads force to meet detachment with provisions from Ohio, 127; leads American forces at Maguaga, 139-140.

Mills, Captain William. Note *re*, 14.

Mockler, Captain Robert. Note *re*, 47.

Money and Money Bills. *See* under 'Currency.'

Montreal Frontier. Strength of British force on, 164.

Moraviantown. British detachment sent to, to prevent American inroads up the Thames river, 90; *see also* under 'Thames River.'

Moy. *See* under 'Sandwich.'

Muir, Captain Adam. Biographical note on, 45; leads detachment in action at Brownstown, 136; commands expedition against Fort Wayne, 248.

Myers, Lieut.-Colonel Christopher. Note *re*, 91.

Naval Affairs. Hull advises (1811) strong force on Lake Erie, 3; Armstrong advises superior force on Lake Erie, 3; list of American armed vessels and British merchant vessels in western part of province, 5; vessels of the North West Co. offered for service, 11; Brock's memo. on plans for defence, 12-14; *Caledonia* assists in attack on Michilimackinac, note 2, p. 17; 54; capture of American schooner with important correspondence, note, p. 19; 43, 44, 49, 69, 73, 90, 113; with launching of *Adams* Hull hopes to command upper lakes, 53, 60; crews of the *Erie* and *Freegoodwill* included in capitulation of Michilimackinac, 64; *see also* p. 144; correspondence *re* disposition of private papers and property on captured vessel, 69-70; *see* pp. 40-41; loss of British transport with supplies of arms, 97; *Lady Prevost* and *Nancy* to convey reinforcements to Detroit frontier, 108; Brock comments on part taken by Marine Dept. at surrender of Detroit, 149; return shewing number of prisoners on vessels at surrender of Detroit, 153; *Adams* taken at surrender of Detroit, 160; British transport with re-

Naval Affairs—*Con.*

inforcements captured by *Essex*; is ransomed, 163-164; British superiority on the Lakes ensures Brock's safe entry to Amherstburg, 183; *see* p. 163; British ships reinforce Brock at Detroit, 188; return of prizes made by British vessels on Lake Erie, 232; capture of fur-laden sloops from Chicago, 233.

Niagara Frontier. Brock's opinion that enemy will not make early attack on, 75; *see also* p. 91; active operations not thought necessary by Brock on, 91; Hull complains of tardy operations of American army on, 115, 116; while Amherstburg holds out no American attack expected on, 163.

Nichol, Lieut.-Colonel Robert. Biographical note on, 149.

North West Company. Plans for their rendering services in event of hostilities, 9-11; *see* p. 38; bounds of their trading grounds, 10; raise the corps of Canadian Voyageurs, note, p. 10; memo. on strength and equipment of, 11; *see* p. 5; the *Caledonia* takes part in taking of Michilimackinac, note 2, p. 17; news of declaration of war first received through, 37; 70 men embodied, and their cargoes utilized by Col. St. George, 46; disposition of their vessel and boats causes concern, 47-48; promise men and provisions from Fort William, 54; numbers and loyalty of, at Fort William, 72-73; Roberts asks for the assistance of their influence at Milichimackinac, 152.

Norton, John. Assists in securing Indian support for British, 94 (*see* note).

Ohio. Importance of keeping open communication with Detroit, 21, 36, 38, 50, 52, 116-117, 138; Hull attributes his defeat in part to obstruction of communication with, 185.

Pawquokoman. *See* under 'Chevalier, Amable.'

Piqua. Americans arrange for grand council wih Indians at, 77, 78.

Pothier, Major Toussaint. Note *re*, 15; his memo. on loyalty and numbers of inhabitants of Michi-

Pothier, Major Toussaint.—*Con.* limackinac country, 15; assists in taking of Michilimackinac, note 2, p. 17; 53-54; his observations on capture and state of Michilimackinac, 214-217.

Powell, Grant. Note *re*, 107.

Prevost, Sir George. Biographical note on, 9; to Liverpool, extract of report on military position of North American provinces, 26; to Brock, *re* reinforcements, stores, arms, and lack of specie, 97-98; to Liverpool, on operations on Detroit frontier, 109-110; to Liverpool, on embarrassed financial position of provinces, 110-111; to Brock, remarks on authority to declare Martial Law, 113; to Bathurst, detailing state of affairs in Upper Canada, and measures adopted, 160-164, 177-180; *see also* pp. 143-144; confines himself to measures of defence in absence of instructions from Home Government, 179; to Bathurst, reviews operations terminating in surrender of Detroit, 181-184.

Prisoners of War. Return of, at Detroit, 153; numbers embarked for Fort Erie, 206; number of, sent to Quebec, note 2, p. 213; disposition of, at Detroit, 243.

Private Property. Correspondence *re* disposition of, papers, &c., 40-41, 69-70; *see also* p. 76.

Proclamations. Of Hull to inhabitants of Canada, 58-60; of Hull to the Six Nations Indians, 72; of Brock to inhabitants of Upper Canada, 81-83; of Brock following surrender of Detroit, 155-156.

Procter, Majer-General Henry. Biographical note on, 74; to Brock, reporting his arrival at Amherstburg, and state of the forces there, 89-90; to Brock, on matters concerning the militia, 108; to Brock, reports Wyandots have joined British cause, 135-136; to Woodward, requesting information *re* civil government, population and geographical limits of Michigan, 165-166; directions to, as temporary administration of western territory, 208-209.

Prophet (The). *See* under 'Elkswatawa.'

Raisin river. Measures for safe conveyance of provisions to Detroit from, 117, 127, 139; Colonel Anderson reports serious situation at, 117-118; *see* p. 125;

17804—17

Raisin River—*Con.* Brush's detachment evacuate the fort at, 172; *see also* p. 176; Anderson's detachment of militia surrender fort at, 172; *see also* p. 244; schedule of arms and provisions taken at, 173, 176.

Revenue Laws. Question of operation of, in Michigan, 175.

Roberts, Captain Charles. Note *re*, 37; despatches from, reporting capture of Michilmackinac, 65; 66; *see also* pp. 150-153; reports unsettled condition of affairs at Michilimackinac since capture, desiring reinforcements, 100-103; difficulties of his situation at Michilimackinac, particularly with the Indians, 150-153; *see* p. 207.

Robinson, Captain Peter. Biographical note on, 130.

Robinson, Commissary General William H. Represents embarassments to public service, particularly the militia, from total want of specie, 111-112; *see* note 1, p. 97.

Robinson, Sir John Beverly. Biographical note on, 105.

Rolette, Lieutenant Charles Frederick. Biographical note on, 13; commands vessel which captures the *Cayauga*, 232.

Rolph, Dr. John. Note *re*, 131.

Rouge river. McArthur's detachment surrenders at, 172.

Roundhead. Gallant conduct of, 176 and note.

Ryerson, Lieut.-Colonel Joseph. Note *re*, 98.

Salmon, Major George C. Note on, 84.

Sandwich. American force takes possession of, 57, 61, 62, 109; *see also* p. 157.

Scott, Governor Charles. Note *re*, 49.

Secretary of War—American. To Hull, announcing the declaration of war, 35; to Hull, authorizing him to commence offensive operations, 37; to Dearborn, instructing him to prepare the eastern wing of the army for service, 40; to Harrison, instructions *re* protection of northwestern frontier, 49-50; his correspondence with Hull found on captured schooner, 44, 69-70; *see also* note, p. 19; 43, 73, 90, 110, 113.

Secretary of War—British. *See* under 'Bathurst, Earl of,' Liverpool, Earl of.'

Shaw, Major Angus. Note *re*, 73.

Sheaffe, Major-General Roger H. Placed on Brock's staff, 113.

Shelby, Governor Isaac. Note *re*, 202.

Snelling, Major Joseph. Note *re*, 139.

South West Company. Also called Michilimackinac Co., 9; location of their trading grounds, 10; to act with N. W. Co. in measures of defence, 9; memo. from company's agent on support expected from country wherein they trade, 15; assist with stores, &c., 54; Roberts asks for the assistance of their influence at Michilimackinac, 152.

Specie. *See* 'Currency.'

Spring Wells. Location of, note, p. 188.

Springer, Captain Daniel. Biographical note on, 85; *see also* pp. 85-89.

Stanton, William. Note *re*, 124.

Steele, Commodore John. Note *re*, 14.

St. George, Lieut.-Colonel Thomas Bligh. Biographical note on, 24; to Hull *re* disposition of papers and prviate property on captured schooner, 41, 70; his difficulties in collecting and organizing forces at Amherstburg, 45-47; *see* pp. 51-52; strength of his command at Amherstburg, 109; commands First Brigade before Detroit, 142.

Talbot, Colonel Thomas. Biographical note on, 84; to Brock, on difficulties of securing and controlling militia and Indians, 93-94; directs efforts to rally Norfolk militia, 98-99.

Tallon, Captain Joseph. Commands Third Brigade before Detroit, 143, and note.

Taylor, General James. Note *re*, 138; *see* p. 189.

Tecumseh. Biographical note on, 33; his speech for the Wabash River Indians expressing loyalty to British, 34-35; keeps Indians faithful to British, 63; leads Indians and is wounded in action at Maguaga, 140-141; Brock's high opinion of, 192; *see* p. 229.

Thames river. British detachment sent to prevent American inroads along, 90; refusal of Norfolk militia to join Chambers' force on, 93, 96, 99; *see also* pp. 157, 190-191; Chambers' detachment on, moves to Delaware, 115, 116.

Tippecanoe. Account of battle of, 6-8.

Tousley, Major Sykes. Note *re*, 115.

Troughton, Lieutenant Felix. Has charge of Royal Artillery at Detroit, 149.

United Empire List. Families of deceased soldiers and marines to be placed on, 28-29.

Upper Canada. Hull's estimate of population and military strength of, 1811, 1-2; *see also* p. 20; communication with Lower Canada to be preserved by reinforcements at Kingston, 98, 114; *see* p. 120; Brock's remarks on apathy and disloyalty of the inhabitants, 91, 119-120, 193-195.

Van Horne, Major Thomas B. Note *re*, 117; commands in action at Brownstown, 125-126, 186; *see also* p. 140.

Watson, Simon Z. Biographical note on 86; seditious actions of, 92.

Wells, Captain William. Biographical note on, 78; gallant conduct of, at massacre of garrison of Chicago, 225-226; note, p. 225.

Wells, Colonel Samuel. Leads detachment for Hull's relief, 132.

Westbrook, Andrew. Biographical note on, 86; *see also* pp. 88, 89, 94-95.

Willcocks, Joseph. Biographical note on, 209; reports his efforts to gain support of Grand River Indians for British, 209-211.

Woodward, Chief Justice Augustus B. Acts as civil secretary to Colonel Procter, note, p. 165; to Procter, on the civil government, geographical limits and population of Michigan territory, 166-170.

Worthington, Governor Thomas. Note *re*, 203.

York, Duke of. To Prevost, after surrender of Detroit, 224-225.